E. Sandra Byers
Lucia F. O'Sullivan
Editors

Sexual Coercion
in Dating Relationships

*Pre-publication
REVIEWS,
COMMENTARIES,
EVALUATIONS . . .*

More pre-publication
REVIEWS, COMMENTARIES, EVALUATIONS . . .

"The stated goal of *Sexual Coercion in Dating Relationships* is to 'challenge current beliefs and to spur researchers forward onto new ground.' In nine chapters that cover a variety of theoretical, methodological, and empirical perspectives, the authors accomplish their goals. I found the book to be well-balanced in its presentation of gender-related issues pertinent to sexual coercion, professionally written, thought provoking, and possessing a good ratio of empirically-based and theoretical chapters.

Students and professionals interested in the area of sexual coercion will all benefit from the information presented in this volume. Because issues of sexual violence are so important in our culture today, it would make an excellent supplementary text for any course in human sexuality. I found the theory building aspects of the chapters most interesting. Not only were the empirical studies theoretically grounded, but theories not previously applied to the area of sexual coercion were presented."

Peter B. Anderson, PhD
Associate Professor
Department of Human Performance
and Health Promotion
University of New Orleans

"This book makes a significant contribution to our understanding of sexual coercion within dating relationships. Collectively, the nine papers challenge long-held assumptions while suggesting new approaches to research in this important field.

The authors address topics of particular importance to educators. These include the impact of traditional roles and scripts on male-female sexual expression, the dynamics of dating disagreements about levels of sexual intimacy, and the identification, by men, of the best ways for women to deflect unwanted sexual advances. Concrete information of this type will be useful to those developing teaching strategies about sexual coercion *and* about healthy sexual relationships."

Ann Barrett, BSc
Sexual Health Educator
Board Member
Sex Information and Education
Council of Canada (SIECCAN)

"**T**his collection of articles is on the cutting edge of research and theory on sexual coercion in dating relationships. A number of the articles take on the difficult task of validating the existence of coercion by women in heterosexual relationships while recognizing the gendered nature of most violence in dating relationships. Moreover, several of the articles emphasize that coercion should be seen as only one piece of women's sexual lives, with the more frequent situation being one where most conflict is resolved successfully. Some of the articles are more successful in these tasks than others, but all are well thought out and advance our knowledge in the field.

The collection is extremely valuable for researchers like myself who see contradictions in the field and variations in the competence of research on sexual coercion. It brings together many of the leading researchers, with some lesser known authors, to provide strong empirical findings interpreted within well articulated theoretical frameworks. It also creates an opening for research on positive resolution of sexual conflict to be integrated into the field.

I recommend this book to students who are beginning their reading in the field and want to learn how to critically evaluate research on sexual coercion, to researchers who have become disillusioned with the lack of theory in the field and need an energy boost, to educators who are interested in developing or changing their date rape prevention programs, and to anyone else who wants to understand and prevent sexual coercion in dating relationships."

Charlene Y. Senn, PhD
Assistant Professor
Department of Psychology
University of Windsor

The Haworth Press, Inc.

Sexual Coercion
in Dating Relationships

Sexual Coercion in Dating Relationships

E. Sandra Byers, PhD
Lucia F. O'Sullivan, PhD
Editors

The Haworth Press, Inc.
New York · London

Sexual Coercion in Dating Relationships has also been published as *Journal of Psychology & Human Sexuality*, Volume 8, Numbers 1/2 1996.

The development, preparation, and publication of this work has been undertaken with great care. However, the publisher, employees, editors, and agents of The Haworth Press and all imprints of The Haworth Press, Inc., including The Haworth Medical Press and Pharmaceutical Products Press, are not responsible for any errors contained herein or for consequences that may ensue from use of materials or information contained in this work. Opinions expressed by the author(s) are not necessarily those of The Haworth Press, Inc.

The Haworth Press, Inc., 10 Alice Street, Binghamton, NY 13904-1580 USA

Library of Congress Cataloging-in-Publication Data

Sexual coercion in dating relationships / E. Sandra Byers, Lucia F. O'Sullivan, editors.
    p. cm.
    "Also . . . published as Journal of psychology & human sexuality, volume 8, numbers 1/2, 1996"–T.p. verso.
    Includes bibliographical references and index.
    ISBN 1-56024-815-7 (thp : alk. paper).–ISBN 1-56024-844-0 (pbk. : alk. paper)
    1. Acquaintance rape. 2. Acquaintance rape–Psychological aspects. I. Byers, E. Sandra. II. O'Sullivan, Lucia F.
HV6558.S493 1996
362.88'3–dc20
                                        96-7979
                                         CIP

INDEXING & ABSTRACTING

Contributions to this publication are selectively indexed or abstracted in print, electronic, online, or CD-ROM version(s) of the reference tools and information services listed below. This list is current as of the copyright date of this publication. See the end of this section for additional notes.

- *Bibliography of Reproduction,* Reproduction of Research Info Service, 141 Newmarket Road, Cambridge CB5 8HA, England

- *Biology Digest,* Plexus Publishing Company, 143 Old Marlton Pike, Medford, NJ 08055

- *Cambridge Scientific Abstracts, Risk Abstracts,* Environmental Routenet (accessed via INTERNET), 7200 Wisconsin Avenue #601, Bethesda, MD 20814

- *CNPIEC Reference Guide: Chinese National Directory of Foreign Periodicals,* P.O. Box 88, Beijing, People's Republic of China

- *Digest of Neurology and Psychiatry,* The Institute of Living, 400 Washington Street, Hartford, CT 06106

- *Educational Administration Abstracts (EAA),* Sage Publications, Inc., 2455 Teller Road, Newbury Park, CA 91320

- *Family Life Educator "Abstracts Section",* ETR Associates, P.O. Box 1830, Santa Cruz, CA 95061-1830

- *Family Studies Database (online and CD/ROM),* Peters Technology Transfer, 306 East Baltimore Pike, 2nd Floor, Media, PA 19063

- *Family Violence & Sexual Assault Bulletin,* Family Violence & Sexual Assault Institute, 1310 Clinic Drive, Tyler, TX 75701

- *Higher Education Abstracts,* The Claremont Graduate School, 231 East Tenth Street, Claremont, CA 91711

(continued)

- *IBZ International Bibliography of Periodical Literature,* Zeller Verlag GmbH & Co., P.O.B. 1949, D-49009 Osnabruck, Germany

- *Index to Periodical Articles Related to Law,* University of Texas, 727 East 26th Street, Austin, TX 78705

- *INTERNET ACCESS (& additional networks) Bulletin Board for Libraries ("BUBL"), coverage of information resources on INTERNET, JANET, and other networks.*
  - JANET X.29: UK.AC.BATH.BUBL or 00006012101300
  - TELNET: BUBL.BATH.AC.UK or 138.38.32.45 login 'bubl'
  - Gopher: BUBL.BATH.AC.UK (138.32.32.45). Port 7070
  - World Wide Web: http: / / www.bubl.bath.ac.uk./BUBL/ home.html
  - NISSWAIS: telnetniss.ac.uk (for the NISS gateway)
  The Andersonian Library, Curran Building, 101 St. James Road, Glasgow G4 ONS, Scotland

- *Mental Health Abstracts (online through DIALOG),* IFI/Plenum Data Company, 3202 Kirkwood Highway, Wilmington, DE 19808

- *Periodica Islamica,* Berita Publishing, 22 Jalan Liku, 59100 Kuala Lumpur, Malaysia

- *Psychological Abstracts (PsycINFO),* American Psychological Association, P.O. Box 91600, Washington, DC 20090-1600

- *Referativnyi Zhurnal (Abstracts Journal of the Institute of Scientific Information of the Republic of Russia),* The Institute of Scientific Information, Baltijskaja ul., 14, Moscow A-219, Republic of Russia

- *Sage Family Studies Abstracts (SFSA),* Sage Publications, Inc., 2455 Teller Road, Newbury Park, CA 91320

- *Sage Urban Studies Abstracts (SUSA),* Sage Publications, Inc., 2455 Teller Road, Newbury Park, CA 91320

- *Social Planning/Policy & Development Abstracts (SOPODA),* Sociological Abstracts, Inc., P.O. Box 22206, San Diego, CA 92192-0206

(continued)

- *Social Work Abstracts,* National Association of Social Workers, 750 First Street NW, 8th Floor, Washington, DC 20002

- *Sociological Abstracts (SA),* Sociological Abstracts, Inc., P.O. Box 22206, San Diego, CA 92192-0206

- *Studies on Women Abstracts,* Carfax Publishing Company, P.O. Box 25, Abingdon, Oxfordshire OX14 3UE, United Kingdom

- *Violence and Abuse Abstracts: A Review of Current Literature on Interpersonal Violence (VAA),* Sage Publications, Inc., 2455 Teller Road, Newbury Park, CA 91320

SPECIAL BIBLIOGRAPHIC NOTES

related to special journal issues (separates) and indexing/abstracting

☐ indexing/abstracting services in this list will also cover material in any "separate" that is co-published simultaneously with Haworth's special thematic journal issue or DocuSerial. Indexing/abstracting usually covers material at the article/chapter level.

☐ monographic co-editions are intended for either non-subscribers or libraries which intend to purchase a second copy for their circulating collections.

☐ monographic co-editions are reported to all jobbers/wholesalers/approval plans. The source journal is listed as the "series" to assist the prevention of duplicate purchasing in the same manner utilized for books-in-series.

☐ to facilitate user/access services all indexing/abstracting services are encouraged to utilize the co-indexing entry note indicated at the bottom of the first page of each article/chapter/contribution.

☐ this is intended to assist a library user of any reference tool (whether print, electronic, online, or CD-ROM) to locate the monographic version if the library has purchased this version but not a subscription to the source journal.

☐ individual articles/chapters in any Haworth publication are also available through the Haworth Document Delivery Services (HDDS).

ABOUT THE EDITORS

E. Sandra Byers, PhD, is Professor of Psychology at the University of New Brunswick in Fredericton and a Clinical Psychologist in private practice. The author or co-author of nearly 40 journal articles, Dr. Byers has served as consulting editor for the *Canadian Journal of Human Sexuality,* the *Journal of Sex Research*, and the *Journal of Psychology & Human Sexuality*. In the past, she has been the Director of the Muriel McQueen Fergusson Centre for Family Violence Research at the University of New Brunswick and President of the Canadian Sex Research Forum. A current fellow in the Society for the Scientific Study of Sexuality and member of the Advisory Board for the Sex Information and Education Council, Dr. Byers recently led a sexology delegation to Russia and Estonia.

Lucia F. O'Sullivan, PhD, is a Social Psychologist and Postdoctorate Research Fellow at the HIV Center for Clinical and Behavioral Studies in the Department of Psychiatry at Columbia University. The author and co-author of numerous articles and chapters on the topics of sexual coercion and influence, communication, and gender roles in relationships, Dr. O'Sullivan was awarded the Society for the Scientific Study of Sexuality (SSSS) Authorship of Best Student Research. A board member of Planned Parenthood and a reviewer for *The Journal of Sex Research* and other scientific journals, she has served as reviewer, chair, and presenter of papers at SSSS and American Psychological Association (APA) meetings. Dr. O'Sullivan has also participated in nationally-syndicated radio series on sexual decision-making within intimate relationships.

Sexual Coercion in Dating Relationships

CONTENTS

Foreword

Good sexuality research should be subversive. It should challenge the way we conceptualize experience and as Michelle Fine (1992) suggests, unearth "secrets . . . disrupt[ing] prevailing notions of what is inevitable and natural" (pp. 21-22). To do our job well, we must recognize that science, especially sexual science, is inherently political. Instead of hiding behind an academic wall of pseudo-objectivity and tasteless, scentless fascination with scholarly minutiae, we must be activists. Let us make our science courageous, investigating the big issues and not the safe ones. Let us use science to liberate, applying our studies to the twin goals of increasing human pleasure, however unfashionable this seems in a period of self-righteous denial, while chipping away at the oppressions that some reactionary groups would like to keep silent. But, in fighting the good fight, let us not forget that we are scientists first and instruments of social change second. As good scientists, we need to improve our theories, develop superior methodologies, and put our ideas to the test. Rhetoric is insufficient. Activism in the absence of solid theory and empirical data is misguided. Important issues deserve and require both serious study and a healthy dose of skepticism about our work.

Sexual coercion is one of the most important issues studied by sexuality researchers. This volume answers my challenge to sexologists by tackling a big issue, sexual aggression and intimidation in intimate relationships, with the best tools presently available to social and health scientists. Coercive intimate relationships have always existed but until the final quarter of this century, victims were expected to suffer in silence. Sexual aggression and intimidation, so the myth went, was a rare and criminal event involving strangers—others, outsiders, those lacking education and social privilege. It was not something that involved people we knew; it was not something that could hurt us. It was not something that happened between

[Haworth co-indexing entry note]: "Foreword." McCormick, Naomi B. Co-published simultaneously in *Journal of Psychology & Human Sexuality* (The Haworth Press, Inc.) Vol. 8, No. 1/2, 1996, pp. xiii-xv; and: *Sexual Coercion in Dating Relationships* (ed: E. Sandra Byers, and Lucia F. O'Sullivan) The Haworth Press, Inc., 1996, pp. xi-xiii. Single or multiple copies of this article are available from The Haworth Document Delivery Service [1-800-342-9678, 9:00 a.m. - 5:00 p.m. (EST)].

people who cared about each other, people who knew each other, people who lived together, people who had relationships. Today we know better, thanks to the excellent research of the contributing authors of this collection and their colleagues across the globe.

As Edward Laumann, John Gagnon, Robert Michael, and Stuart Michaels (1994) document in their comprehensive U.S. survey, nearly 22% of American women report having been forced to have sex by a man. In contrast, only 2% of the men reported being forced to have sex by a man, slightly more than 1% of the men said that a woman forced herself sexually on them, and only a handful of women (0.3%) indicated that a woman pushed them into having sex (pp. 335-338). Consistent with a growing body of serious studies, Laumann and his colleagues found that an astonishing 96% of all forced sex experiences are with perpetrators who the victim knows: 19% are acquaintances; 22% are persons the respondent knew well; 46% were individuals with whom the respondent was in love; 9% were spouses. We have met the enemy and it is us!

Sexual coercion in dating relationships is not a feminist myth. Nor is it a tool of unscrupulous "liberal" researchers seeking funding for frivolous work. Sexual coercion is a serious social, psychological, and medical problem, affecting almost one in four North American women. Sexual coercion robs women of their sexual autonomy and in many cases causes long-term damage to their health, ability to experience pleasure, self-confidence, and sense of well-being. Yet, as I write, recurrent efforts are underfoot to silence the voices of those who have experienced sexual coercion again. Serious scientific studies, like those reported in this volume, are needed to keep this from happening!

I celebrate the courage of the authors and editors of this collection, all renowned researchers and clinicians, for pulling their mutual talents together to create this excellent publication describing the latest research on sexual coercion in dating relationships! I celebrate, too, the theoretical and methodological richness of these articles. Here, sexual scientists tackle, not just the problem of coercion, but problems with coercion research. All good skeptical inquirers question how the framing of our studies may influence and even distort our results, how men imagine they would experience female sexual coercion, the extent to which script theory explains (and doesn't explain) sexual predation and victimization, women's cognitive strategies for coping (or self-blame) after coercive experience, the dynamics of dating disagreements and the dilemma of turning down a partner's sexual advances when the relationship is highly valued, and the type of attitudes which best predict men's sexually aggressive behavior. Perhaps the most remarkable thing about these excellent articles is the thread of optimism that remains despite the depressing topic. Each author applies empirical data and theoretical insight constructively to chip away at oppression, acknowledging the strength of women who have experienced sexual coercion while struggling to eliminate sexist assumptions that deny women sexual autonomy and pleasure.

Naomi B. McCormick, PhD
Department of Psychology
State University of New York at Plattsburgh
Plattsburgh, NY

REFERENCES

Fine, M. (1992). *Disruptive voices: The possibilities of feminist research.* Ann Arbor: The University of Michigan Press.

Laumann, E. O., Gagnon, J. H., Michael, R. T., & Michaels, S. (1994). *The social organization of sexuality: Sexual practices in the United States.* Chicago: The University of Chicago Press.

Introduction

E. Sandra Byers, PhD
Lucia F. O'Sullivan, PhD

Most social scientists consider Eugene Kanin's 1957 publication of the article "Male aggression in dating-courtship relations" to be the first scientific investigation of sexual coercion in dating relationships. Perhaps the world was not ready to hear about sexual coercion at that time, because other researchers only began to attend to this issue in the late 1970s and early 1980s. Increased research attention was undoubtedly related to the consistent finding of high prevalence rates and damaging sequelae related to sexual coercion. And yet, in many ways the world is *still* not ready to hear about sexual coercion.

Outside of research and feminist communities, sexual coercion is frequently minimized and too often stereotyped. The words "sexual coercion" (synonymous at times with "sexual aggression" and "sexual assault") tend to conjure up a particular image for members of the general public. This image is of a deranged man attacking a woman he does not know in a dark, secluded public setting where she had the poor judgment to be wandering alone; or, similarly, of a man's brutal rape of a woman after breaking into her locked apartment or home. The woman struggles to get free, but the man uses his physical strength to overpower the woman and force her to engage in sexual intercourse. This is the type of sexual coercion that is most frequently depicted in media portrayals. In fact, the general public often does not acknowledge other forms of sexual coercion which are missing these essential ingredients. Even within the criminal justice system, other sexual coercion scenarios are often dismissed as women's craving for attention, attempts to gain revenge on an unfaithful boyfriend, or plausible coverup for an active sexual life. As has been

[Haworth co-indexing entry note]: "Introduction." Byers, E. Sandra, and Lucia F. O'Sullivan. Co-published simultaneously in *Journal of Psychology & Human Sexuality* (The Haworth Press, Inc.) Vol. 8, No. 1/2, 1996, pp. 1-5; and: *Sexual Coercion in Dating Relationships* (ed: E. Sandra Byers, and Lucia F. O'Sullivan) The Haworth Press, Inc., 1996, pp. 1-5. Single or multiple copies of this article are available from The Haworth Document Delivery Service [1-800-342-9678, 9:00 a.m. - 5:00 p.m. (EST)].

demonstrated repeatedly in social psychological studies, the general public is reluctant to place blame firmly on the shoulders of the perpetrator and is willing to attribute at least some responsibility to the victim in situations that do not conform to the stereotypic image of sexual coercion.

Researchers first challenged the extent to which this stereotype represents real life experiences of sexual coercion when they chose to assess unreported sexual assaults amongst undergraduate college women. In so doing, they uncovered a number of myths surrounding our understanding of sexual coercion. Most notably, researchers discovered that sexual coercion is not a particularly rare event. Current estimates suggest that anywhere between 22% and 83% of women will experience sexual coercion in their lifetime. In addition, the stereotype reinforces an image of sexual coercion as a crime that is perpetrated by a small group of deranged or "perverted" men. However, research failed to support this belief in the psychopathology of perpetrators. Furthermore, although the most prevalent form of sexual coercion by far is perpetrated by men against women, we now know that some men coerce other men and some women coerce men and other women. Finally, contrary to the stereotype, the perpetrator is rarely a stranger, but is usually an acquaintance of the victim, often someone with whom the victim has an established romantic relationship. Sexual coercion by someone known to the victim has equally, perhaps greater, detrimental consequences for the victim as does sexual coercion by a stranger.

This media-endorsed stereotype of sexual coercion can be considered a reflection of societal values about the types of sexual assaults to be considered most important. Equating sexual coercion with forced intercourse stems from the myth that forced intercourse is the most "serious" form of sexual coercion. Even the use of the term "date rape" connotes this value. In fact, many acts of sexual coercion do not involve penile-vaginal intercourse, and may involve a range of coercive tactics including verbal threats, pressure, deception, and harassment. As with other forms of abuse, the trauma and long-term detrimental consequences for the victim may come more from the sense of powerlessness, stigmatization, and violation of trust than from the actual nature of the forced activity.

Clearly, most researchers and theorists are well aware of the discrepancies between the public image of sexual coercion and the reality of coercive experiences. However, researchers need to challenge some assumptions that continue to guide or influence investigations of sexual coercion. This volume is designed to help researchers challenge some of these assumptions, and to serve as a catalyst for future research and critical thinking in this area. We use the term "sexual coercion" in its broadest sense. Sexual coercion is any form of force or pressure used in an attempt to make a nonconsenting other engage in some type of sexual activity. Our focus is on dating relationships because it is a form of close, intimate relationship that is particularly prone to sexual coercion. Our use of the term "dating relationship" includes all intimate relationships with a romantic or sexual basis, from the early, newly acquainted first date to the highly committed, well-established premarital forms.

ARTICLES WITHIN THIS VOLUME

The nine articles in this volume address theoretical and empirical issues regarding the nature, causes, and consequences of sexual coercion in dating relationships. Each article contributes to the objectives guiding this publication: to challenge current beliefs and to spur researchers forward onto new ground.

Most sexual coercion research has been conducted atheoretically. When research has been theory-driven, the traditional sexual script is the most prevalent theory guiding such research. This is a theory that describes how the differential socialization of men and women cues sexual coercion. The validity of this theory has often been accepted on logical rather than empirical grounds. Sandra Byers reviews aspects of the traditional sexual script that have been theorized to cause sexual coercion and presents a program of research designed to test empirically some of the assumptions inherent in the theory.

Research on attitudes toward sexual coercion has also not generally been informed by theory. In particular, social psychological theory has established that attitudes consist of affective, behavioral, and cognitive components. However, this tripartite model has not been adopted by researchers studying sexual coercion. To rectify this, Jacquelyn White, Patricia Donat, and John Humphrey analyzed the attitude-toward-rape literature within this social psychological framework. They also assessed the usefulness in discriminating between affectively-based attitudes and cognitively-based attitudes, and the predictive ability of both. A more complex view of attitudes may enhance our ability to develop successful rape preventive efforts.

Lucia O'Sullivan and Sandra Byers argue that sexual coercion should be examined in the broader framework of the use of influence because sexual coercion represents an extreme means of influencing a partner to engage in undesired sexual activity. They examined discrepancies in desired level of sexual intimacy between dating partners—the basic situation in which influence in general and sexual coercion in particular are likely to occur–to determine the types of coercive and noncoercive influence used by men and women. Moreover, they tested a number of traditional assumptions about behavior in such situations, such as men's higher likelihood of employing coercive tactics compared to women, and the accompanying negative emotional and relational consequences associated with disagreements about desired sexual intimacy.

Recent research has established that some women use sexual coercion against their male dating partners. Matthew Hogben, Donn Byrne, and Merle Hamburger challenge the view that sexual coercion is equally a problem for women and men. Past studies examining the prevalence of both men's and women's experiences and use of sexual coercion produce inconsistent findings. These researchers set out to clarify these inconsistencies and, in doing so, they note a number of methodological issues that demand attention in research of this nature. They also address some political pitfalls that surround such investigations.

Although some similarities between men's and women's sexual experiences are apparent, men's and women's experiences of and reactions to sexual coercion are different and should continue to be examined separately. The findings of two studies highlight these differences. Catalina Arata and Barry Burkhart examined symptoms of posttraumatic stress disorder in a sample of college women who reported sexually coercive experiences. Although a number of other detrimental psychological consequences of sexual coercion have been documented in the past, this is the first study designed to assess such an extreme form of consequence amongst a college sample.

David Struckman-Johnson and Cindy Struckman-Johnson expanded upon recent research suggesting that, in marked contrast to most women's experiences, many men may report neutral or even favorable reactions to coercive interactions. They conducted a vignette study designed to investigate how level of force, attractiveness of the coercive woman, and type of romantic relationship contributed to men's reactions. This study clearly challenges many of the assumptions we have made about the inherently detrimental nature of sexually coercive experiences.

Mary Krueger argues succinctly that current conceptions of women's sexuality are inadequate. She addresses the harmful consequences associated with an exclusive focus on sexual coercion when considering women's sexuality and of traditional approaches to prevention which may suppress women's erotic expression. She makes clear the urgent need to restructure these culturally-endorsed attitudes.

One means of empowering women at risk of sexual coercion is to increase their sense of efficacy in terms of successful resistance. Acknowledging that sexual coercion is never the fault of the victim, Paula Nurius and Jeanette Norris present an ecological model which they believe may be usefully employed to predict women's resistance to sexual coercion. This model incorporates background, environmental and intrapersonal variables related to experiences of sexual coercion. They draw upon existing empirical research to support each component of the model.

Charlene Muehlenhard, Sandra Andrews, and Ginna Beal challenge the promotion of the hackneyed expression "Just Say No" in sexual coercion preventive measures. Aggressive refusal of an unwanted sexual advance from a dating partner may not be consistent with a woman's goal of maintaining a relationship with her partner. In one study, these researchers assessed how a woman's open communication of her sexual limits influenced a man's response. In a second study, they obtained responses that men rated most effective in terms of stopping their persistent sexual advances, and determined the effect each response might have on a dating relationship. In short, these findings constitute a repertoire of practical preventive measures women can employ in coercive sexual dating situations.

In summary, we hope this publication will remedy in some small degree the lethargy and ennui that is apparent in sexual coercion research. Most of the studies in this area still are designed to assess the prevalence of sexual coercion and predict likely perpetrators and victims. Although invaluable, it is high time to shake out the cobwebs and adopt new research goals. We also need to question some of the assumptions that guided us in the past. The new ideas and findings in this volume may serve as a necessary impetus to more productive research in this culturally, socially, politically, and individually important area of work. Further, they may contribute to our understanding of the complex nature of sexual coercion, as well as the causes and consequences related to this phenomenon.

How Well Does the Traditional Sexual Script Explain Sexual Coercion? Review of a Program of Research

E. Sandra Byers, PhD

SUMMARY. Male use of sexual coercion against an unwilling female partner is all too prevalent in North American society. Several theorists, most notably feminist theorists, have hypothesized that socialization practices with respect to traditional gender roles, and corresponding cultural attitudes, cause sexual coercion. Although not always labeled in this way, these theorists posit that the "traditional sexual script" supports and condones male sexual coercion against women and that this sexual script remains the normative dating script in our society. In this article, I first review the aspects of the traditional sexual script that have been theorized to promote and maintain sexual coercion. Then I review the results of a program of research I conducted in conjunction with colleagues and former graduate students, which tested the validity of this theory for understanding coercive sexual interactions between dating partners. I con-

E. Sandra Byers is affiliated with the University of New Brunswick, Department of Psychology and Muriel McQueen Fergusson Centre for Family Violence Research, Fredericton, New Brunswick, Canada E3B 6E4.

Address correspondence to E. Sandra Byers, Department of Psychology, University of New Brunswick, Fredericton, NB, Canada E3B 6E4.

The author would like to offer a sincere thank-you to all her graduate students and colleagues who, over the years, have collaborated with her on this program of research. She is particularly indebted to Lucia O'Sullivan for her helpful comments on an earlier version of this article and for her collaboration on a number of studies.

[Haworth co-indexing entry note]: "How Well Does the Traditional Sexual Script Explain Sexual Coercion? Review of a Program of Research." Byers, E. Sandra. Co-published simultaneously in *Journal of Psychology & Human Sexuality* (The Haworth Press, Inc.) Vol. 8, No. 1/2, 1996, pp. 7-25; and: *Sexual Coercion in Dating Relationships* (ed: E. Sandra Byers, and Lucia F. O'Sullivan) The Haworth Press, Inc., 1996, pp. 7-25. Single or multiple copies of this article are available from The Haworth Document Delivery Service [1-800-342-9678, 9:00 a.m. - 5:00 p.m. (EST)].

7

clude that the traditional sexual script has proven useful as a frame-work for understanding sexual coercion in heterosexual dating relationships. However, our research calls some aspects of this theory into question. Some modification to this theory is needed. *[Article copies available from The Haworth Document Delivery Service: 1-800-342-9678.]*

Male use of sexual coercion against an unwilling female partner is all too prevalent in North American society. Although most research on sexual coercion has been conducted with college students, even among this relatively advantaged population, researchers have consistently found that between 22% and 83% (depending on the wording of the items) of the women surveyed report having been coerced into engaging in some form of unwanted sexual activity at some time in the past (see Craig, 1990, for a review of prevalence studies). A smaller, but substantial, percentage of men (between 20% and 42%) acknowledge having engaged in sexual activity by using sexual coercion (Craig, 1990). Most of these incidents occurred within the context of dating or other non-stranger peer relationships.

Several theorists, most notably feminist theorists, have hypothesized that socialization practices with respect to traditional gender roles, and corresponding cultural attitudes, cause sexual coercion (Brownmiller, 1975; Burt, 1980; Clark & Lewis, 1977). Although not always labeled in this way, these theorists posit that the "traditional sexual script" supports and condones male sexual coercion against women and that this sexual script remains the normative dating script in North American society. These theories stand in contrast to theories that place the causes of sexual coercion in specific characteristics of offenders that are not seen to be normative, such as offenders' psychopathology, coercive dispositions, or hypererotic orientation (Craig, 1990; Kanin, 1985).

In this article, I first review the aspects of the traditional sexual script that have been theorized to promote and maintain sexual coercion. Then I present the results of a program of research I conducted in conjunction with colleagues and former graduate students that is designed to test the validity of this theory for understanding coercive sexual interactions between dating partners.

THE TRADITIONAL SEXUAL SCRIPT

Scripts are cognitive frameworks for how people are expected to behave in social situations. Sexual scripts, therefore, delineate the who, what, where, when, how, and why of sexual behavior (DeLamater, 1987; Gagnon, 1990; Gagnon & Simon, 1973; McCormick, 1987; Rosen & Leiblum, 1988). They also depict the sequence in which behaviors are expected to occur within sexual interactions. Individuals may improvise and express their own personalities and preferences while still adhering to the guidelines prescribed by the script.

Sexual scripts are learned through socialization. The sexual script that is most pervasive in North America has been termed the traditional sexual script (TSS), and it contains very different expectations for men's and women's behavior and attitudes in sexual situations. It is these prescribed gender differences which are hypothesized to link adherence to the TSS and sexual coercion (cf. Brownmiller, 1975; Byers, 1990; Clark & Lewis, 1977; Crooks & Baur, 1993; Korman & Leslie, 1982; LaPlante, McCormick & Brannigan, 1980; Peplau, Rubin & Hill, 1977). In the following list, I have summarized the gender differences in expected behaviors and attitudes within the TSS that have been theorized to be particularly important to the occurrence of sexual coercion. As the TSS prescribes that sexual relationships be heterosexual, the following discussion describes only male-female interactions.

(1) The TSS depicts men as "oversexed" and women as "undersexed." As such, men are described as having strong sexual needs, being obsessed with sex, being highly motivated to engage in sexual activity, and willing to exploit or pursue any sexual opportunity made available by a woman. Women, on the other hand, are depicted as having few sexual needs, being sexually reluctant, seeing sex as a means of procuring love or commitment, being slow to arouse, and being difficult to satisfy sexually.

(2) Women's perceived worth and status are seen as being decreased by sexual experience whereas men's worth and status are seen as being enhanced. That is, for men, sexual experience is perceived by society and by their peers as reflecting positive characteristics such as masculinity, virility, and attractiveness. For women, on the other hand, sexual experience is attributed to undesirable characteristics such as nonselectivity, promiscuity, emotional disturbance, and lack of values.

(3) The TSS casts men as the initiators in sexual situations and women as the recipients of the initiations. Thus, because of their supposed large sexual appetites, men are expected to initiate and vigorously pursue dates with women, all sexual interactions, and increasingly intimate sexual activities within any given sexual interaction. Women are expected to adopt a passive, defensive stance in order to protect their perceived worth. They are expected to be prepared for and to respond cautiously to these initiations.

(4) Because women are depicted as not "really" interested in sex and as having their worth decreased by being "too" sexually available or seeming "too" interested in sex, the TSS prescribes that women are expected to place limits on the level of sexual activity in which they engage with their male partner. Thus, women are expected to counteract, forcefully, men's continual pressure to increase sexual intimacy. Even when they are interested in engaging in sexual activity, women are expected to offer at least initial token resistance to the man's advances. It should be noted that forceful resistance is inconsistent with women's gender role scripts, which dictate that women should be passive, submissive, and unassertive. On the other hand, men are expected to try to remove women's restrictions to enhance their own worth and meet their own sexual needs. As such, the TSS legitimizes men's use of a variety of coercive and noncoercive influence strategies in attempting to overcome the woman's reluctance to engage in the sexual activity. This expectation is similar to behavioral expectations within men's gender role script, which prescribes that men be active and aggressive. Use of these strategies is further justified by widespread belief in women's use of token refusal. As such, men who accept the woman's refusal and stop their sexual advances may be perceived as not sufficiently masculine to gain sexual access (Muehlenhard, 1988; Muehlenhard & Hollabaugh, 1988).

Two additional aspects of the TSS have been described as contributing to sexual coercion but are not limited to sexual situations.

(5) The dating and gender role scripts dictate that women's worth is enhanced by being in a romantic relationship. Thus, within the TSS, a woman is expected to restrict sexual access but to do so in a way that does not cause the man to decrease his romantic interest in her. To accomplish this, she should not be too assertive or aggressive in refusing sexual advances, she must appear sexy, and she must convey (through willing participation in low levels of sexual activity) that satisfying sex will occur in the future if the man remains in the relationship.

(6) Women are expected to be emotional, sensitive, and nurturing in interpersonal relationships, whereas men are expected to be unemotional, relatively insensitive, and self-focused. The prescription for women to be nurturing and consider the other person's need before their own is in conflict with the aspect of the TSS that calls for women to restrict access to her sexuality. The latter would require that the woman place her needs and wants before those of her male partner. The prescription that men be unemotional and put their own needs first suggests that, in pursuing their sexual goals, men need not take into account the woman's feelings or reluctance to engage in the sexual activity.

In summary, the TSS pits the oversexed, aggressive, emotionally insensitive male initiator who is enhanced by each sexual conquest and taught not to accept "no" for an answer against the unassertive, passive woman who is trying to protect her worth by restricting access to her sexuality while still appearing interested, sexy, and concerned about the man's needs. Sexual coercion is believed to be learned and maintained through widespread socialization for this behavioral sexual script, traditional gender roles, and attitudes and beliefs that support, condone, and legitimize sexual coercion in at least some circumstances. These attitudes are themselves a consequence of socialization.

An important question that social scientists need to address, then, is whether the TSS is the normative sexual script in North American dating relationships. Other questions that need to be addressed are: How accurate are the gender role stereotypes described in the TSS? To what extent are aspects of the TSS related to the use and experience of sexual coercion? We addressed these broad questions in a series of studies that are reviewed in the following sections.

IS THE TRADITIONAL SEXUAL SCRIPT THE NORMATIVE SEXUAL SCRIPT?

Two predictions based on the TSS have been examined repeatedly in the literature: attitudes supportive of sexual coercion are widespread, and women commonly experience sexual coercion by men within dating relationships. Our results are in keeping with these predictions and with research conducted in the United States (Burt, 1980; Craig, 1990). We found that many Canadian university students hold these beliefs and attitudes (Byers & Eno, 1991; Grenier & Byers, 1990). In addition, we found that a substantial proportion of Canadian university women reported having experienced sexual coercion and Canadian university men reported having engaged in sexual coercion (Byers & Eno, 1991; Finkelman, 1992; O'Sullivan, 1991).

However, these findings do not establish that sexual coercion is the normative or typical sexual script; that is that "the socialization of both men and women takes coercive sexuality as the normal standard of sexual behavior" (Clark & Lewis, 1977, p. 140). To establish that TSS is the normative script, it is necessary to go beyond the finding that many women have experienced male sexual coercion. Rather, it is necessary to demonstrate that the roles described by the TSS are the typical or usual behavior in sexual interactions. Therefore, we examined the normativeness of several aspects of the TSS.

Initiations and restrictions of sexual activity. The TSS defines clearly differentiated gender roles for men and women in sexual situations, some of which are believed to provide the framework within which sexual coercion can occur. "Oversexed" men's greater interest in sex is believed to be expressed by their role as initiator and in their willingness to seize every available sexual opportunity. In contrast, "undersexed" women's lesser interest in sex is thought to be reflected in their roles as recipient of initiations and restrictor of sexual activity. Using a self-monitoring technique, Lucia O'Sullivan and I investigated whether these stereotypes are accurate or normative for dating couples (O'Sullivan & Byers, 1992).

Consistent with descriptions of the TSS, the men initiated sex more than the women did. However, initiations by the women were not rare, albeit only about half as frequent as initiations by the men in the study. In fact, the majority of participants reported one or more sexual initiations by the woman during a two-week period. Of interest, initiations by women were more likely to occur within a steady dating relationship. Thus, the sexual script that designates men as the initiators appears to apply more strongly in casual relationships. Other researchers have found that men's overt sexual advances are usually preceded by women's signals communicating sexual interest and that women are more likely than men to begin sexual encounters (Moore, 1985; Moore & Butler, 1989; Perper, 1989; Perper & Weis, 1987). Moreover, in contrast to predictions based on the TSS, after controlling for the number of initiations, the women were no more likely to refuse a sexual initiation by their partner than were the men. Only a minority of initiations by the men or the women (20%) resulted in a refusal by the partner, calling into question the view that most sexual interactions between men and women are adversarial. The results also indicate that in the typical sexual interaction, and particularly within steady dating relationships, women are not serving a restrictive function, and men do not feel obliged to accept every available sexual opportunity. In so far as the TSS and its stereotypes regarding initiation and restriction of sexual activity are used to explain sexual coercion, the explanation is likely to be inadequate, incomplete, or inaccurate.

Men's compliance with women's refusals. Based on the argument that the TSS is the normative sexual script, we predicted that men typically would wish to engage in a higher level of sexual activity than would women (that is, that adversarial sexual relationships are normative). We also predicted that, given a situation in which the man wants to engage in a higher level of sexual activity than the woman does, men typically would use some form of verbal or physical coercion to try to gain sexual access (i.e., use of coercion by men to overcome resistance is normative). To test these predictions, Kim Lewis and I asked unmarried college men and women to self-monitor their dating and sexual experiences over four weeks (Byers & Lewis, 1988). Respondents recorded whether they had been on a date, whether any level of sexual activity had occurred on that date, and whether the man had desired to engage in a higher level of sexual activity than did the woman. If respondents experienced a disagreement, they recorded the words and actions used to communicate about the differing levels of desired sexual intimacy. Descriptions of the man's behavior following the woman's refusal of his sexual advance were coded in terms of the degree of the man's compliance or noncompliance with the woman's refusal.

Although 47% of respondents reported experiencing one or more disagreements in which the man desired to engage in a higher level of sexual intimacy than did the woman over the four-week period, disagreements occurred on only 7% of all dates. This finding indicates that even though disagreements are a common part of sexual dating relationships, agreement about the desired level of sexual activity is more common and normative than is disagreement. This finding is contrary to the TSS.

Although sexual coercion will not occur if dating partners agree about the desired level of sexual activity, disagreements do not inevitably lead to sexual coercion. Therefore, in this study Lewis and I also examined men's compliance with the woman's refusal of their sexual advances in these disagreement situations (Byers & Lewis, 1988). According to the TSS, as men are in pursuit of ever-increasing levels of sexual intimacy, they should typically respond to refusals of their sexual advances by using strategies, including coercive strategies, to "persuade" the reluctant woman to engage in the disputed sexual activity. Contrary to this prediction, we found that the majority of participants (64% of the men and 58% of the women) reported that when the woman indicated her nonconsent, the man immediately stopped his sexual advances without questioning her. Twenty percent and 13% of the men and women, respectively, described behavior in which the man stopped his advances and questioned, in a non-coercive fashion, the woman's reasons for her reluctance. An additional 8% and 7% of the men and the women, respectively, indicated that the man stopped his advances and tried to persuade the woman to engage in the activity—responses that were not coercive but that indicated the man's reluctance to accept the woman's refusal. Finally, according to the women, 7% of the men stopped their advances but expressed displeasure or anger, and 16% continued the unwanted advances—responses that are clearly indicative of sexual coercion. The percentage of men who reported behaving in these coercive ways were 4% and 4%, respectively.

I found similar results in two studies I conducted using role-play scenarios (Byers, 1988; Byers & Wilson, 1985). For example, Paula Wilson and I asked college men to role-play their initial responses to women's refusals of their sexual advances. In their role-play responses, the majority of the men complied with the woman's refusal without using coercive tactics. However, 6% continued their advances, and 9% complied in a way that indicated that they were angry or upset with the woman—both indications of sexual coercion. An additional 18% complied but tried to persuade the woman to continue, an indication of reluctance but not necessarily of coercion. Although the degree to which these results can be generalized from the role-play situation to a real situation is not known, most men rated their responses as being an accurate representation of how they would behave in a similar real situation, supporting the validity of the data.

To understand better the motivation behind men's behavioral responses, Wilson and I asked the men to interpret what the woman "really" meant when she said "no" to the sexual advance, after they had role-played their responses to the woman's refusal (Byers & Wilson, 1985). The majority of the men reported that they believed that the woman wanted the man to stop what he was doing (34%) or to try again on another date (22%), interpretations that are consistent with their behavioral compliance in the role-play. However, 15% of the men did not believe the woman's refusal, as they reported that the woman wanted the man to try again right away (6%) or that she wanted him to continue (9%)—both interpretations that might account for the 15% of the men whose role-play responses were sexually coercive. Finally, 29% of the men reported that they believed that the woman really wanted the man to try again later that evening, an interpretation that suggests that these men believed she could be "persuaded" to engage in the sexual activity. Similarly, in a study I conducted with Dorothy Price, we found that when men were asked to rate how effective each of a number of different refusals would be in stopping their sexual advances, they indicated that they were not completely certain that even the most definite responses would stop their unwanted sexual advances (Byers, Giles, & Price, 1987). These results suggest that a substantial proportion of the men who participated in these studies subscribed to the belief in women's token refusals of men's sexual advances. Other research has also provided evidence for widespread belief in women's use of token resistance (Muehlenhard, 1988; Muehlenhard & Hollabaugh, 1988).

Summary. There is considerable evidence from our research and that of other researchers that the TSS is a common dating script and thus represents a frequently employed framework for heterosexual dating interactions. In fact, findings of the commonness of women's experiences with male sexual coercion in dating relationships that led, in part, feminists and others to conclude that sexual interactions between men and women typically are adversarial and contain coercive elements. However, our research has failed to support some aspects of the TSS as being normative or typical of sexual interactions in dating relationships. Contrary to predictions based on the TSS, we did not find that, in these sexual interactions, men *typically* attempt to extend the sexual boundaries, women *typically* try to serve a restrictive function, or men *typically* attempt to coerce the sexually reluctant woman to engage in the disputed sexual activity. Rather, we found that men and women typically agree about the desired level of sexual activity. When a disagreement does arise, it is most typical for men to accept a woman's refusal of more intimate sexual involvement without questioning her and to believe that she indeed did not wish to engage in the sexual activity at that time. Although the TSS appears to be common, there are either other equally or more common sexual dating scripts or the TSS as articulated is not sufficiently complex. In either case, the TSS as described does not appear to be the normative dating script.

HOW ACCURATE ARE DEPICTIONS OF GENDER ROLES IN SEXUAL INTERACTIONS?

The TSS is gender-specific. The gender roles are considered to be quite distinct: certain roles are assigned to men; others are assigned to women. In some of our research, we examined the extent to which these gender differences accurately characterize sexual dating interactions.

Men as the reluctant sexual partner/women as the "ardent" partner. The TSS casts men as the coercers and women as the coerced in sexual situations. Early researchers adopted this assumption and only investigated male sexual coercion of women. In keeping with recent research using U.S. college students (Muehlenhard & Cook, 1988; Struckman-Johnson, 1988), we have found evidence that a substantial percentage of Canadian male college students report having experienced sexual coercion by a woman (O'Sullivan, 1991; Finkelman, 1992). However, in both studies, a larger percentage of women than men reported having been coerced to engage in unwanted sexual activity within a one-year period. For example, Larry Finkelman, Lucia O'Sullivan, and I found that 17% of male respondents compared to 36% of the female respondents reported having had an unwanted sex experience because of sexual coercion by their heterosexual dating partner during one year of university (Finkelman, 1992). Of particular interest with regard to critiquing the validity of the TSS, in both studies some women reported having used sexual coercion against a reluctant male partner.

In keeping with the TSS, our early research on disagreement situations only examined situations in which the man desired to engage in a higher level of sexual activity than did the woman (Byers & Lewis, 1988). However, in a recent study, O'Sullivan and I examined situations in which the woman desired to engage in a higher level of sexual activity than did her male dating partner (O'Sullivan & Byers, 1993). We also extended past research by examining the range of influence strategies used in disagreement situations by the "ardent" partner, not just the negative or coercive strategies that have been studied in the past. We found that 56% of participants reported having experienced a disagreement situation in which the woman desired the higher level of sexual intimacy during the previous year, most often within a steady dating relationship. The majority of participants described responses to the man's refusal that indicated that the woman had complied with the refusal. However, 20% described noncompliant responses by the woman. Further, 97% of respondents indicated that the woman in some way had tried to influence the man to engage in the sexual activity after he had refused. Women typically used positive, noncoercive strategies. These findings are clearly inconsistent with the TSS in several ways. First, they demonstrate that women regularly assume the role of initiator and demonstrate their interest in sex in various ways, rather than solely assuming the role of passive recipient to men's demonstrations of sexual ardor. Second, these findings do not support the stereotype that men will exploit any indication of sexual receptivity on the part of women. Instead, respondents described disagreement situations that resulted from men indicating reluctance to engage in sexual activity desired by their female partner. This is consistent with our findings regarding men's and women's responses to the sexual initiations of their partner (O'Sullivan & Byers, 1992). Third, the findings demonstrate that women are active in removing restrictions placed on sexual intimacy by their male partners by trying to influence them to engage in disputed sexual activities. Finally, they demonstrate that some women use coercive strategies to attempt to engage in sexual activity. The TSS does not account for these behaviors by women. Because these disagreements occurred most frequently within the context of steady dating relationships, these findings may indicate that women and men are less likely to adhere to the TSS within steady relationships. It should also be noted, however, that the TSS is accurate in the sense that these behaviors are in general more characteristic of men than they are of women (O'Sullivan & Byers, 1996). Further, these data do not address whether the negative impact of experiencing sexual disagreements or sexual coercion is the same for men as it is for women.

Expressiveness and instrumentality. There has been a good deal of research supporting differences between men and women in their gender role descriptions–men as more instrumental ("masculine") and less expressive ("feminine"), women as more expressive and less instrumental (cf. Bem, 1974; Hiller & Philliber, 1985; Spence & Helmreich, 1978). The TSS suggests that men and women also follow these gender roles in sexual situations both in terms of emotionality, sensitivity, and nurturance (expressive behaviors) as well as in terms of initiation and responses aimed at influencing a sexually reluctant partner (instrumental behaviors). To determine whether gender roles in sexual situations follow these stereotypes, Kelli-an Lawrance, David Taylor, and I asked undergraduate men and women to provide four gender role descriptions (Lawrance, Taylor, & Byers, 1990). Participants described their gender role behavior/characteristics both globally and in a sexual situation. Participants also described their perception of the ideal gender role for men and the ideal gender role for women in sexual situations. We found that the male and female students agreed in their descriptions of how they believed men and women should ideally behave in sexual situations. In keeping with the TSS, these descriptions followed traditional gender lines, with men being described as ideally more instrumental than women and women as ideally more expressive than men. However, although always less so than the women, the men's global gender role was found to be least expressive, their sexual gender role more expressive, and their ideal sexual gender role most expressive. Thus, expressive behavior was not only seen as desirable for men in sexual situations, but the men were also more expressive in sexual than in nonsexual situations. The women described themselves as equally and highly expressive globally and in sexual situations. Further, they perceived this same level of expressiveness as the ideal for a woman in a sexual situation. With respect to instrumental traits/behaviors, the women and the men described the ideal gender roles in sexual situations as more instrumental than their own gender role in a sexual situation but as less instrumental than their own global gender role.

Overall, these results suggest men behave in less gender-typed ways in sexual situations than globally, and they do so because they believe that this type of behavior represents the ideal for men. Women are less instrumental in sexual situations than they are globally, but they did not see this behavior as ideal. Again, these results provide partial support for the TSS. Women were found to be more expressive and men more instrumental, as suggested. However, although men and women are not always able to live up to their sexual ideal, in sexual situations these roles may be converging.

Summary. The gender roles described in the TSS are accurate in describing behavior that is more characteristic of men or of women. Thus, men more often than women take the role of initiator, use coercion, and engage in other instrumental behaviors. Women are more expressive than are men. However, there is also evidence of considerable overlap in men's and women's roles in sexual situations, as well as of convergence in what is perceived as ideal behavior for men and women. In emphasizing gender differences, the TSS may not sufficiently describe gender similarities (Hyde, 1985, 1994).

WHAT FACTORS ARE ASSOCIATED WITH SEXUAL COERCION?

To establish that socialization to the TSS is a causal factor in sexual coercion, it is necessary (although not sufficient) to establish a link between aspects of the TSS and engaging in or experiencing sexual coercion. To test the completeness of the TSS as an explanation for sexual coercion, it is necessary to demonstrate that factors outside those proposed in the TSS are not related to the use of sexual coercion. We have investigated a number of factors that have been proposed to be related to sexual coercion. Because the TSS is limited to depicting men as the coercers and women as the coerced, we only examined factors thought to influence whether men use sexual coercion or women experience sexual coercion.

Predicting men's use of coercion. Based on the TSS, Ray Eno and I predicted that men who subscribe more strongly to beliefs that support and condone sexual coercion would be more likely to report having been sexually coercive in a dating situation. We also predicted that men who were more active daters would be more likely to report having used sexual coercion because of their increased likelihood of being in situations in which they desire a higher level of sexual intimacy than their female partner, thus having more opportunities to use coercion to gain sexual access (Byers & Eno, 1991). We also tested the hypothesis that men who use sexual coercion adopt a hypererotic script. In contrast to theorists who locate the cause of sexual aggression in the TSS, Kanin (1985) has argued that, compared to other men, "date rapists" undergo a differential sexual socialization process that results in a hypererotic orientation. To test this hypothesis, we investigated the relationships between men's sexual responsiveness and their use of sexual coercion.

In keeping with predictions based on the TSS, in two studies we found that men who reported having engaged in both consenting and nonconsenting sex tended to hold more traditional views of women's roles as well as to subscribe more strongly to coercion-supportive beliefs (Byers & Eno, 1991; Grenier & Byers, 1990). Similarly, in the role-play study of men's responses to women's refusals of their sexual advances, Wilson and I found that men who had more liberal attitudes toward women's roles were more compliant with the woman's refusals (Byers & Wilson, 1985). These findings are in keeping with the results of several other studies (Koss, Leonard, Beezley & Oros, 1985; Muehlenhard & Linton, 1987; Rapaport & Burkhart, 1984). Also in keeping with predictions based on the TSS, more active daters were more likely to have experienced consenting intercourse and to have used verbal coercion (Byers & Eno, 1991). However, contrary to predictions, more active daters were less likely to have used physical force, even though they would, presumably, have experienced more disagreements in which the use of force to "persuade" the reluctant woman to engage in the sexual activity was a response option. These results suggest that, whereas the use of verbal coercion may be part of the TSS, the script does not dictate use of physical force as the next step when verbal coercion is unsuccessful. Rather, in sexual situations in which there is a discrepancy in the desired level of sexual intimacy, only men with certain characteristics—for example, men who hold strongly to particular beliefs or men with a hypererotic orientation—may cross the line between use of verbal pressure and use of physical force. This view has also been proposed by Rapaport and Burkhart (1984) and Lisak and Roth (1988). This interpretation is supported by two other findings from this research (Byers & Eno, 1991). First, use of verbal coercion and use of physical force were not significantly related to each other. Second, violence-supportive attitudes and dating experience each uniquely predicted sexual coercion. These results suggest that verbal coercion and physical force are not two manifestations of a continuum of coercive behavior within the same dating script.

Eno and I also identified a second pattern linking attitudes and use of sexual coercion by men (Byers & Eno, 1991). When traditional and coercion-supportive attitudes were controlled, men who described themselves as highly sexually arousable and accepting of interpersonal violence, but who were also relatively more erotophobic and less accepting of adversarial sexual beliefs, were more likely to report having used physical force. However, they were not more likely to report having engaged in consenting intercourse or having used verbal coercion. That is, at least some men who use physical force experience themselves as getting highly aroused in sexual situations and may have difficulty talking about sex because of their erotophobia (Fisher, Byrne, White, & Kelley, 1988). Thus, they may act according to their beliefs that force is an expected and accepted means of resolving discrepancies in the desired level of sexual intimacy. These characteristics are similar to Kanin's (1985) description of hypererotic date rapists who hold an exaggerated view of the importance of engaging in extensive sexual activity and conquest and who also believe that their peers would support their aggressive behavior.

Taken together, these results suggest that the TSS contributes to sexual coercion in that both coercion-supportive and traditional gender role beliefs, as well as active dating, were independently associated with coercive sexual behavior. However, the data also suggest, in keeping with the results of the self-monitoring study of sexual disagreement situations, that use of physical force is *not* part of the typical sexual script for dating men (Byers & Lewis, 1988). In addition, in at least some instances, factors that are not part of depictions of the TSS apparently are related to men's use of physical force.

Predicting women's experience of sexual coercion. We have conducted a number of studies to examine women's behavior in situations in which there is a discrepancy in the level of sexual intimacy desired by women and by their male partners. We did so to test predictions based on the TSS and not to suggest that women should be held responsible, in any way, for their own victimization.

The TSS prescribes roles for women in sexual situations that might put them at risk for experiencing sexual coercion or, at least, reduce their effectiveness in responding to unwanted sexual advances. For example, the TSS prescribes that women behave unassertively with men, particularly if they want to keep the man's romantic interest in them, and that, to avoid being devalued, they should agree only to engage in lower levels of sexual intimacy. Thus, women would be expected to be more definite in their refusals of higher level sexual activities than of lower level sexual activities and in their refusals of advances by men in whom they had less romantic interest. Barbara Giles and I tested these predictions using role-play scenarios (Byers et al., 1987). Each scenario described the man making one of three sexual advances, indicated the woman's level of romantic interest in her date, and instructed the female participants that they did not want to engage in that activity. The women then role-played how they would communicate their nonconsent to their date. In keeping with predictions based on the TSS, the verbal refusals of the women were less definite in the scenarios in which they were described as having greater romantic interest in their date. The women were also less verbally definite in the scenarios describing a lower level of sexual activity than in the scenes involving higher levels of sexual activity.

I used an extended role-play paradigm to determine how women's responses change in situations in which the man does not comply with their initial refusal (Byers, 1988). As with the role-play procedure described above, women were asked to role-play their refusal of a man's unwanted sexual advances. They were then informed that the man did not comply with their wishes and were asked to role-play what they would do and/or say next. Most women increased the definiteness of their refusal from their first to their second response. Increasing the definiteness of the refusal is likely to be an effective strategy for avoiding sexual coercion. However, despite the fact that few women were as definite in their responses as they could have been, one quarter of the women did not become more definite in the second role-play. This finding is in keeping with predictions from the TSS—even when women are aware that the man is not complying with their refusal, many women do not communicate their reluctance as clearly as they could. Some men may interpret the lack of increase in definiteness as evidence that the woman's response constitutes a token refusal. In addition, women with higher acceptance of rape myths tended to be more definite in their refusals of the unwanted sexual advances than women who had lower acceptance of rape myths. Many rape myths place the blame on the woman for her victimization. This suggests that women who accept these views are more aware of how nonassertive behavior may be misinterpreted by men and thus are less likely to behave in ways that leave them open to claims that they are responsible for their sexually coercive experiences.

Effects of women's behavior on men's compliance. The definiteness of women's refusals of men's sexual advances is only important to the extent that it affects men's behavior. Therefore, we examined the relationship between the definiteness of women's refusals and men's responses to their refusals. In one study, Dorothy Price and I asked college men to rate the effectiveness in stopping their sexual advances of verbatim transcripts of women's role-play responses which varied in their definiteness (Byers et al., 1987). Less definite verbal responses were rated by the men as being less effective in stopping their advances, supporting the validity of our definiteness ratings. Similarly, in our self-monitoring study of disagreement situations, Lewis and I found that, according to the women, more definite refusals by women who were romantically interested in their date and had dated him regularly in the past resulted in more compliance with the refusal by the male partner (Byers & Lewis, 1988). In addition, using an extended role-play paradigm, I had men who were not unquestioningly compliant with a woman's initial refusal of their sexual advances role-play their response to a second verbal refusal by the woman. Most (61%) of these men were more compliant with the woman's second refusal (Byers, 1988). Given the pervasiveness of men's belief in women's use of token resistance, a second refusal may be interpreted by men as a clearer indication of a woman's actual lack of interest. These findings suggest that women who act unassertively to conform to the TSS may be at higher risk for experiencing sexual coercion. Low intimacy situations, as well as situations in which the woman is romantically interested in her date, are most likely to produce less definite refusals and thus put women at the greatest risk. However, even though less definite refusals may put women at greater risk, more definite refusals will not necessarily protect women from experiencing sexual coercion. Three of the men who engaged in the extended role-play became less compliant and three other men ignored both of the women's refusals and continued their advances even after the second refusal (Byers, 1988). The remaining 26% of the men did not become either more or less compliant in response to the second refusal. Moreover, 31% of the men indicated that they would initiate the refused advance again the same evening, suggesting that they believed that the woman's refusals were insincere. Needless to say, even if a woman's less assertive behavior puts her at greater risk to experience male sexual coercion, she is still not in any way responsible or to blame for her own victimization.

CONCLUSION

The traditional sexual script has proven useful as a framework for understanding coercion in heterosexual dating interactions. It has met the most important criterion for a theory in that it has provided a framework from which to generate hypotheses and make predictions about men's and women's behavior in sexual dating situations in general and sexually coercive situations in particular. However, as with most theories, it is unable to explain all of the facts with which it is confronted. Thus, proponents must be amenable to making modifications to the theory. The results of my research program demonstrate mixed support for the TSS. Men and women often follow the tenets of the TSS as guidelines for acceptable, societally-condoned behavior. Unfortunately, these guidelines often lead to male sexual coercion of women. However, they also often, and perhaps more often, adopt only parts of the TSS. For example, they may adopt male sexual initiation but not female restriction, or male initiation and female restriction, but not male coercion. At times, men and women stray from these guidelines altogether, apparently adopting a different script.

For example, they may adopt female sexual initiation, male restriction, and female coercion. Our research calls into question the assertion that the TSS is *the* normative script for dating interactions. Rather, it may be one of a number of common and traditional scripts. Moreover, our research has demonstrated that the sharp distinctions between appropriate behavior for men and women in sexual dating situations are missing. Men's and women's roles in sexual interactions overlap considerably, particularly in established relationships.

Even though notions of appropriate behavior for men and women in sexual situations may be evolving, the concept of the TSS and its role in sexual coercion should not be abandoned. The TSS has proven valuable for furthering our understanding of sexual coercion between men and women. It also provides a framework within which to develop interventions designed to prevent sexual coercion in dating relationships. Nonetheless, the results of our program of research demonstrate that the TSS as it is currently formulated needs some revision.

REFERENCES

Bem, S. (1974). The measurement of psychological androgeny. *Journal of Consulting and Clinical Psychology, 42*, 155-162.

Brownmiller, S. (1975). *Against our will.* New York: Simon & Schuster.

Burt, M. R. (1980). Cultural myths and support for rape. *Journal of Personality and Social Psychology, 38*, 217-230.

Byers, E. S. (1988). Effects of sexual arousal on men and women's behavior in sexual disagreement situations. *The Journal of Sex Research, 25*, 235-254.

Byers, E. S. (1990, November). *Research on the traditional sexual script.* Symposium presented at the meeting of the Society for the Scientific Study of Sex, Minneapolis.

Byers, E. S., & Eno, R. (1991). Predicting men's sexual coercion and aggression from attitudes, dating history, and sexual response. *Journal of Psychology & Human Sexuality, 4*, 55-69.

Byers, E. S., Giles, B. L., & Price, D. L. (1987). Definiteness and effectiveness of women's responses to unwanted sexual advances: A laboratory investigation. *Basic and Applied Social Psychology, 8*, 321-338.

Byers, E. S., & Lewis, K. (1988). Dating couples' disagreements over the desired level of sexual activity. *The Journal of Sex Research, 24*, 15-29.

Byers, E. S., & Wilson, P. (1985). Accuracy of women's expectations regarding men's responses to refusals of sexual advances in dating situations. *International Journal of Women's Studies, 4*, 376-387.

Clark, L., & Lewis, D. (1977). *Rape: The price of coercive sexuality.* Toronto: The Woman's Press.

Craig, M. E. (1990). Coercive sexuality in dating relationships: A situational model. *Clinical Psychology Review, 10*, 395-423.

Crooks, R., & Baur, K. (1993). *Our sexuality* (5th ed.). Redwood City, CA: Benjamin/Cummings.

DeLamater, J. (1987). Gender differences in sexual scenarios. In K. Kelley (Ed.), *Females, males and sexuality: Theories and research* (pp. 127-139). Albany, NY: SUNY Press.

Finkelman, L. (1992). *Report of the survey of unwanted sexual experiences among students of UNB-F and STU.* Unpublished manuscript, University of New Brunswick, Fredericton, NB.

Fisher, W. A., Byrne, D., White, L. A., & Kelley, K. (1988). Erotophobia-erotophilia as a dimension of personality. *The Journal of Sex Research, 25,* 123-151.

Gagnon, J. H. (1990). The explicit and implicit use of the scripting perspective in sex research. In J. Bancroft (Ed.), *Annual review of sex research, 1,* 1-43.

Gagnon, J. H., & Simon, W. (1973*). Sexual conduct: The social sources of human sexuality.* Hinsdale, IL: Dryden Press.

Grenier, G., & Byers, E. S. (1990, November). Patterns of coercive sexual behaviour in men. In E. S. Byers (Chair), *Research on the traditional sexual script.* Symposium presented at the meeting of the Society for the Scientific Study of Sex, Minneapolis.

Hiller, D., & Philliber, W. (1985). Internal consistency of the Bem Sex Role Inventory. *Social Psychology Quarterly, 48,* 373-380.

Hyde, J. S. (1994). *Understanding human sexuality* (5th ed.). New York: McGraw Hill.

Hyde, J. S. (1985). *Half the human experience: The psychology of women* (3rd ed.). Lexington, MA: D.C. Heath.

Kanin, E. J. (1985). Date rapists: Differential sexual socialization and relative deprivation. *Archives of Sexual Behavior, 14,* 219-231.

Korman, S. K., & Leslie, G. R. (1982). The relationship of feminist ideology and date expense sharing to perceptions of sexual aggression in dating. *The Journal of Sex Research, 18,* 114-129.

Koss, M. P., Leonard, K. I., Beezley, D. A., & Oros, C. J. (1985). Nonstranger sexual aggression: A discriminant analysis of the psychological characteristics of undetected offenders. *Sex Roles, 12,* 981-992.

LaPlante, M. M., McCormick, N., & Brannigan, G. G. (1980). Living the sexual script: College students' views of influence in sexual encounters. *The Journal of Sex Research, 16,* 338-355.

Lawrance, K., Taylor, D., & Byers, E. S. (1990, November). Variations in global, sexual, and ideal-sexual gender role descriptions. In E. S. Byers (Chair), *Research on the traditional sexual script.* Symposium presented at the meeting of the Society for the Scientific Study of Sex, Minneapolis.

Lisak, D., & Roth, S. (1988). Motivational factors in nonincarcerated sexually aggressive men. *Journal of Personality and Social Psychology, 55,* 795-801.

McCormick, N. B. (1987). Sexual scripts: Social and therapeutic implications. *Sexual and Marital Therapy, 2,* 3-27.

Moore, M. M. (1985). Nonverbal courtship patterns in women. *Ethology and Sociobiology, 6,* 237-247.

Moore, M. M., & Butler, D. L. (1989). Predictive aspects of nonverbal courtship behavior in women. *Semiotica, 76,* 205-215.

Muehlenhard, C. L. (1988). "Nice women" don't say yes and "real men" don't say no: How miscommunication and the double standard can cause sexual problems. In E. Cole & E. D. Rothblum (Eds.), *Women & Therapy,* (pp. 95-108). New York: The Haworth Press, Inc.

Muehlenhard, C. L., & Cook, S. W. (1988). Men's self-reports of unwanted sexual activity. *The Journal of Sex Research, 24,* 58-72.

Muehlenhard, C. L., & Hollabaugh, L. C. (1988). Do women sometimes say no when they mean yes? The prevalence and correlates of women's token resistance to sex. *Journal of Personality and Social Psychology, 54,* 872-879.

Muehlenhard, C. L., & Linton, M. A. (1987). Date rape and sexual aggression in dating situations: Incidence and risk factors. *Journal of Counseling Psychology, 34,* 186-196.

O'Sullivan, L. (1991). *Women's use of sexual influence in heterosexual dating relationships.* Unpublished Master's thesis, University of New Brunswick, Fredericton, NB.

O'Sullivan, L., & Byers, E. S. (1990, November). Female use of sexual influence strategies in dating relationships. In E. S. Byers (Chair), *Research on the traditional sexual script.* Symposium presented at the meeting of the Society for the Scientific Study of Sex, Minneapolis.

O'Sullivan, L., & Byers, E. S. (1992). College students' incorporation of initiator and restrictor roles in sexual dating interactions. *The Journal of Sex Research, 29,* 435-446.

O'Sullivan, L., & Byers, E. S. (1993). Eroding stereotypes: College women's attempts to influence reluctant male sexual partners. *The Journal of Sex Research, 30,* 270-282.

O'Sullivan, L., & Byers, E. S. (1996). Gender Differences in Responses to Discrepancies in Desired Level of Sexual Intimacy. *Journal of Psychology & Human Sexuality, 8,* 49-67.

Peplau, L. A., Rubin, Z., & Hill, C. J. (1977). Sexual intimacy in dating relationships. *Journal of Social Issues, 33,* 86-109.

Perper, T. (1989). Theories and observations on sexual selection and female choice in human beings. *Medical Anthropology, 11,* 409-454.

Perper, T., & Weis, D. L. (1987). Proceptive and rejection strategies of U.S. and Canadian college women. *The Journal of Sex Research, 23,* 455-480.

Rapaport, K., & Burkhart, B. R. (1984). Personality and attitudinal characteristics of sexual coercive college males. *Journal of Abnormal Psychology, 93,* 216-221.

Rosen, R. C., & Leiblum, S. R. (1988). A sexual scripting approach to problems in desire. In S. R. Leiblum & R. C. Rosen (Eds.), *Sexual desire disorders* (pp. 168-191). New York: Guilford Press.

Spence, J., & Helmreich, R. (1978). *Masculinity and femininity: Their psychological dimensions, correlates, and antecedents.* Austin: University of Texas Press.

Struckman-Johnson, C. (1988). Forced sex on dates: It happens to men, too. *The Journal of Sex Research, 24,* 234-241.

An Examination of the Attitudes Underlying Sexual Coercion Among Acquaintances

Jacquelyn W. White, PhD
Patricia L. N. Donat, PhD
John A. Humphrey, PhD

SUMMARY. Analyses of rape-supportive attitudes, with few exceptions, have not included conceptual or operational definitions of attitudes, and analysts have not explicitly examined the affective, cognitive, and behavioral components of attitudes toward rape. The purposes of the present article are to (a) use a social psychological framework for the analysis of attitudes toward rape and (b) examine the usefulness of distinguishing between the affective and cognitive components of attitudes toward rape. Three studies are presented. In Study 1, items from 14 published attitudes-toward-rape scales were categorized as affective, cognitive, or behavioral. Results revealed that 1.1% of the items were identified as behavioral; 52.2% of the items were categorized as cognitive and 46.7% as affective. Second-

---

Jacquelyn W. White is Professor in the Department of Psychology, Patricia L. N. Donat is Research Associate in the School of Nursing and an Instructor in the Department of Psychology, and John A. Humphrey is Professor in the Department of Sociology, all at the University of North Carolina at Greensboro (UNCG).

Address correspondence to Jacquelyn W. White, Department of Psychology, 296 Eberhart Building, University of North Carolina at Greensboro, Greensboro, NC 27412-5001.

[Haworth co-indexing entry note]: "An Examination of the Attitudes Underlying Sexual Coercion Among Acquaintances." White, Jacquelyn W., Patricia L. N. Donat, and John A. Humphrey. Co-published simultaneously in *Journal of Psychology & Human Sexuality* (The Haworth Press, Inc.) Vol. 8, No. 1/2, 1996, pp. 27-47; and: *Sexual Coercion in Dating Relationships* (ed: E. Sandra Byers, and Lucia F. O'Sullivan) The Haworth Press, Inc., 1996, pp. 27-47. Single or multiple copies of this article are available from The Haworth Document Delivery Service [1-800-342-9678, 9:00 a.m. - 5:00 p.m. (EST)].

ary analyses of published data revealed the respondents reported more disagreement with affectively-based rape attitude items than cognitively-based rape attitude items. In Study 2, we further examined the distinction between affective and cognitive components of attitudes using Burt's (1980) Rape Myth Acceptance Scale. Data collected from college men confirmed the affective-cognitive distinction. Furthermore, affectively-based attitudes, but not cognitively-based attitudes, were correlated with level of self-reported sexual coercion. In Study 3, we compared affective and cognitive components using a factor-analytically derived attitude measure. These analyses replicated the findings from Study 2. Together, these results support the importance of attending to the separate components of attitudes. In particular, the affective component of attitudes toward rape may have more predictive utility than the cognitive component. *[Article copies available from The Haworth Document Delivery Service: 1-800-342-9678.]*

The relationship between rape-supportive attitudes and sexually coercive behavior is central to our understanding of sexual coercion. Based on this conceptual relationship, it frequently is assumed that rape-supportive attitudes may influence a man's perceptions and facilitate sexually coercive behavior (Burt, 1980, 1991; Shotland, 1989, 1992). Researchers consistently have identified statistically significant relationships between the endorsement of rape-supportive attitudes and self-reported sexually coercive behavior. Self-reported sexually coercive men are more accepting of traditional sex roles, interpersonal violence, adversarial relationships, and rape myths (Adler, 1985; Koss & Leonard, 1984; Koss, Leonard, Beezley, & Oros, 1985). The link between attitudes and coercive behavior is supported further by the observed correlation between attitudes toward rape and self-reported likelihood of raping a woman (Malamuth, 1981, 1983), self-reported level of sexually coercive behavior (Koss et al., 1985; Koss & Dinero, 1988), and physical aggression against women in a laboratory setting (Malamuth, 1981, 1983).

The attitudes-toward-rape literature, however, suffers from inadequacies in the psychometric properties of the measures used in the field (Lonsway & Fitzgerald, 1994). Lonsway and Fitzgerald concluded that many measures used to study rape-supportive attitudes lack content validity because of inexplicit definitions of key concepts (e.g., consent, force). Few studies to establish criterion-related validity have been conducted. Additionally, the wording of many attitude items may include either more than one concept or words and phrases that may have different meanings for different people. These difficulties may account for the numerous inconsistencies in findings relating attitudes toward rape and factors such as educational/occupational level, ethnicity, age, knowledge/awareness of rape, and knowing a rape victim. Lonsway and Fitzgerald's critique indicates further work is needed to address the conceptual and psychometric inadequacies of the measures used to study rape-supportive attitudes.

In this article, we argue that previous researchers have not applied a theoretical understanding of the attitude construct to rape attitudes. In this article, the substantial attitudes-toward-rape literature is examined in the context of psychological theories and research on attitudes. Particular attention is given to the affective and cognitive components of attitude items found in the attitudes-toward-rape literature. The usefulness of distinguishing these components in the prediction of self-reported sexually coercive behavior in college men is also explored.

SOCIAL PSYCHOLOGICAL THEORIES OF ATTITUDES

Historically, social psychologists have conceptualized an attitude as a tricomponent evaluation consisting of affective, cognitive, and behavioral intention components (e.g., Allport, 1935; Kramer, 1949; Thurstone, 1928). Each component is measured on an evaluative continuum from extremely negative to extremely positive. The cognitive dimension includes thoughts and beliefs about the attitude object. The affective dimension includes feelings or emotions in relation to the attitude object. The behavioral component encompasses intentions or overt behavior toward the attitude object.

Although these components (cognitive, affective, and behavioral) may be interdependent, they also have a large degree of independence (Zajonc, 1980, 1984). Therefore, behaviors associated with some attitudes may be consistent across response classes, whereas others are less consistent (Eagly & Chaiken, 1993). A person may hold strong beliefs in regard to an attitude object, but have feelings that may contradict that belief. For example, a person may believe that women have rape fantasies but feel that sexually coercive behavior is morally reprehensible.

AFFECT-BASED AND COGNITION-BASED ATTITUDES

The distinction between affective and cognitive components has been central to the historical discussion of attitudes (Insko & Schopler, 1967; Krech & Crutchfield, 1948; Rosenberg & Hovland, 1960). Empirical evidence also supports the distinction between these components (Abelson,

Kinder, Peters, & Fiske, 1982; Breckler & Wiggins, 1989; Crites, Fabrigar, & Petty, 1994; Edwards, 1990, 1992; Millar & Millar, 1990; Millar & Tesser, 1986). Some attitudes are more affectively-based, whereas others are more cognitively-based. For example, Abelson and his colleagues (1982) found that affects associated with presidential candidates were more strongly related to the person's attitudes than judgments about the candidates' traits. Moreover, Abelson et al. (1982) suggested that behavioral prediction might be better when using affective reports because they more strongly reflect behavioral motivation. Affect also may be a more direct reflection of experience than cognition, which may be filtered and altered to maintain consistency among attitude components. Additionally, Zanna and Rempel (1988) suggested that attitudes based primarily on affect may lead to greater selective perceptions and attributions about other peoples' behaviors.

Two views have been proposed to explain the greater predictive ability of one component over the other. It may be that the relation between affective and cognitive attitudinal components and behavior are simply a matter of one component (affective) being better at predicting behavior than another (cognitive). However, Millar and Tesser (1986) have suggested that the relation between attitudes and behavior is more complex. The strength of the attitude-behavior relation is determined by the source on which the attitude is based (i.e., affective or cognitive) and the function of the behavior being measured. Instrumental behavior is cognitively driven. For example, a person who works a puzzle in order to develop analytic abilities is interested in the puzzle's characteristics that facilitate skill-building, not how the puzzle makes the person feel. In contrast, consummatory behavior is affectively driven. For example, a person who works a puzzle simply for fun is interested in the pleasure that the puzzle provides rather than its skill-enhancing characteristics. Therefore, to predict behavior, one must know the type of behavior being predicted and the type of attitudinal component being measured or manipulated.

The distinction between affect-based and cognition-based attitudes has been verified empirically. Researchers have demonstrated that these components are partially independent and their ability to predict behavior depends in part on the basis of attitude formation, how deeply held the attitude is, which component is currently salient, and whether the behavior is instrumental or consummatory.

APPLICATIONS TO THE ATTITUDES-TOWARD-RAPE LITERATURE

Analysts of rape-supportive attitudes, with few exceptions, have not addressed conceptual or operational definitions of attitudes and have not attempted to examine explicitly the affective, cognitive, and behavioral components of attitudes toward rape. However, the literature on attitudes suggests that attention to these components could enable us to better predict sexually coercive behavior and to develop more effective attitude change strategies. Given the hedonistic and dominance motives for engaging in sexual behavior reported by sexually coercive men (Donat, 1990; Malamuth, 1986; White & Farmer, 1988) and the potentially consummatory nature of hostile sexual activity, one might expect that affective attitude statements would be correlated more strongly with self-reported sexual behavior than would cognitive attitude statements.

Thus, in this article we first examine the cognitive, affective, and behavioral intention components of several measures used with college populations to study attitudes toward rape. Second, we examine the usefulness of distinguishing between the affective and cognitive components of attitudes toward rape by looking at their ability to predict sexually coercive behavior. To accomplish these goals, analyses are presented from three studies. In Study 1, all published attitudes-toward-rape scales were identified and examined for behavioral items; remaining items were categorized as affective or cognitive. Then, secondary data analyses on previously published data tested the hypothesis that affective and cognitive components would be endorsed differentially. In Study 2, this hypothesis was tested further. Data from a sample of college men permitted the examination of correlations between the affective and cognitive components as a further test of their partial independence. In Study 2, we also examined the hypothesis that the affective component would better predict sexually coercive behavior in men than would the cognitive component. In Study 3, this hypothesis was further tested using a factor analytically-derived measure of attitudes toward rape (derived from one sample of college students and tested in a new sample).

STUDY 1

Method

Materials. A review of the literature initially identified 20 attitudes-toward-rape scales. This list was narrowed to 14 scales for further examination.[1] For all but two scales (Gilmartin-Zena, 1987; Sandberg, Jackson, & Petretic-Jackson, 1987), some psychometric information was provided. A summary of each scale along with psychometric information is provided in Table 1.

Procedure. The initial examination of the items revealed only two be-

TABLE 1. Scales to measure attitudes toward rape.

Scales	Source	Description[a] (A = affective; B = behavioral intention; C = cognitive)	Psychometric properties
Scales Measuring General Attitude			
Acceptance of Rape Myths Scale	Gilmartin-Zena (1987)	29 items (21 A; 0 B; 8 C)	No psychometric data reported
Attitudes-Toward-Rape	Feild (1978)	32 items (12 A; 0 B; 20 C)	8 factors; Cronbach's alphas ranging from .81 to .89
Attitudes-Toward-Rape Victims Scale	Ward (1988)	25 items (8 A; 17 C)	1 factor; Cronbach's alpha of .83; evidence for validity reported
Belief in Rape Myths	Weidner & Griffitt (1983)	2 items (2 A; 0 B; 0 C)	No psychometric data reported for these items added to the larger Sexual Opinion Survey, which has split-half reliability of .84 and evidence of construct validity.
Beliefs About Rape	Costin (1985)	20 items (8 A; 0 B; 10 C)	3 factors; Cronbach's alphas ranging from .49 to .70
General Attitudes Toward Rape	Larsen & Long (1988)	22 items (9 A; 13 C)	3 factors; Cronbach's alpha of .81
Likelihood to Force Sex and Likelihood to Rape Scales	Malamuth (1981); Malamuth (1989a,b)	2 items (0 A; 2 B; 0 C)	The 6-item Attraction to Sexual Aggression Scale from which these items were taken has 1 factor; Cronbach's alphas ranging from .84 to .91 across administrations; and evidence for construct and discriminant validity reported.
Rape Belief Scale	Bunting & Reeves (1983)	15 items (12 A; 0 B; 3 C)	1 factor; no reliability reported; evidence for validity reported.
Rape Myth Acceptance Scale	Burt (1980)	19 items (7 A; 0 B; 4 C)[b]	1 factor; Cronbach's alpha of .875; construct validity reported by Ashton, 1982

32

Scales	Source	Description[a] (A = affective; B = behavioral intention; C = cognitive)	Psychometric properties
Scales Specific to Dating			
Date Rape Subscale	Dull & Giacopassi (1987)	15 items (3 A; 0 B; 12 C)	1 factor; no reliability reported
Dating Attitude Questionnaire	Sandberg et al. (1987)	13 items (4 A; 0 B; 9 C)	No psychometric data reported
Endorsement of Force Scale	Rapaport & Burkhart (1984)	20 brief descriptions of dating situations (N/A)	1 dimension; Cronbach's alpha of .90
Forcible Date Rape Scale	Goodchilds et al. (1988)	9 circumstances (N/A)	1 factor, verified by Fischer, 1986; no reliability reported

[a] Most scales use a Likert response format. Malamuth et al. (1980, 1981, 1983, 1989a,b) use a 5-point "not at all likely to very likely" scale for his Likelihood items. Goodchilds et al. (1988) use a 5-point "acceptability of force" scale. Sandberg et al. (1987) use a 6-point "never to frequently" scale. Rapaport and Burkhart (1984) use a 7-point "endorsement of use of force on the part of the man to obtain sexual acts" scale.

[b] The last 8 items were not categorized; 2 ask respondents to estimate percentages and 6 ask for ratings of believability of rape reports by best friend, Indian woman, neighborhood woman, young boy, White woman, Black woman

havioral items, the Likelihood to Force Sex and Likelihood to Rape measures by Malamuth and colleagues. Thus, five independent judges, all doctoral students in social or clinical psychology, were asked to categorize all remaining items as affective or cognitive. The judges were provided with operational definitions of affective and cognitive statements along with copies of items from each scale. A cognition was defined as a statement that could be verified, i.e., one that provided information or fact about the attitude object (though the statement did not actually have to be true, such as "the world is flat"), or a statement of belief, with judgment missing (e.g., "there is a god"). Examples of cognitive items from the attitudes-toward-rape scales included "In forcible rape the victim never causes the crime" (Costin, 1985), and "For some females, physical aggressiveness by the male is a necessary prelude to the acceptance of love and affection" (Dull & Giacopassi, 1987). Affective statements were defined as opinions that provided a value judgment, a conclusion about someone's character (i.e., good-bad, worthy-unworthy, right-wrong), or injunctions (i.e., statements indicating how things ought to be). Examples include "Women who get raped while hitchhiking get what they deserve" (Burt, 1980), and "A raped woman is a less desirable woman" (Feild, 1978).

Results. Interrater reliability was high among the independent raters. At least four judges agreed on 78.32% of the 180 items categorized.[2] Three out of five judges agreed on the remaining items. Overall, 1.1% of the items were identified as behavioral, 52.2% of the items were categorized as cognitive, and the remainder as affective.[3] The number of cognitive, affective, and behavioral intention items on each scale is listed in Table 1.

In addition, sufficient data (means and standard deviations) were provided for individual items in the articles by Feild (1978), Dull and Giacopassi (1987), and Ward (1988) to compute means and average standard deviations for the affective and cognitive components of their full scales, as well as for each factor of Feild's and Dull and Giacopassi's scales. Ward reported data separately for women and men in two samples, one from Singapore and one from the United States. Using data from these scales and assuming equal sample sizes, we conducted two-tailed t-tests comparing the mean level of endorsement of the affective and cognitive items.[4] Results revealed that people reported more disagreement with affectively-based rape attitude items than cognitively-based rape attitude items ($p <$ .001). Mean ratings for the affective and cognitive components are presented in Table 2. To determine whether there is a general tendency to respond more extremely to affective items than to cognitive items, we also analyzed items from the nonrape attitude scale developed by Dull and Giacopassi (the Sex and Dating Scale [SDS]). For this scale, in contrast to

TABLE 2. Mean level of disagreement with affective and cognitive components of selected attitude toward rape scales.

	Sample Size	Mean level of disagreement[1]		t[3]
		Affective	Cognitive	
Citation		Mean (deviation score[2])	Mean (deviation score[2])	
Study 1				
Feild (1978)				
Total	1448	4.24 (+0.74)	3.90 (+0.40)	7.26
Factor I		4.66 (+1.16)	4.11 (+0.61)	11.96
Factor III		3.98 (+0.48)	3.89 (+0.39)	1.38
Factor IV		4.22 (+0.72)	3.55 (+0.05)	11.96
Dull & Giacopassi (1987)				
Total	449	2.53 (+0.53)	2.21 (+0.21)	4.21
SDS		1.75 (−0.25)	2.11 (+0.11)	4.83
RS		2.79 (+0.74)	2.35 (+0.35)	5.62
Ward (1988)				
Singapore	411	1.70 (+0.30)	1.17 (+0.83)	5.12
Women	212	1.02 (+0.98)	1.31 (+0.69)	3.47
Men	199	1.35 (+0.65)	1.83 (+0.17)	3.08
U.S.A.	572	.46 (+2.54)	.78 (+2.22)	4.32
Women	359	.42 (+1.58)	.97 (+1.03)	6.53
Men	211	.92 (+1.08)	1.47 (+0.53)	6.52
Study 2				
Burt's RMAS	280	5.60 (+1.60)	4.87 (+0.87)	17.30
Burt's ASB	299	4.42 (+0.42)	4.73 (+0.73)	−5.70
Burt's AIV	298	4.86 (+0.86)	5.35 (+1.35)	−5.80
Study 3				
Rape Factor	278	4.11 (+1.11)	3.82 (+0.82)	7.42

SDS = Sex & Dating Scale; RS = Rape Scale; RMAS = Rape Myth Acceptance Scale; ASB = Adversarial Sex Beliefs; AIV = Acceptance of Interpersonal Violence

[1] Means reported are based on Likert ratings from agree to disagree: Feild, scored 1-6; Dull & Giacopassi, 0-4; Burt, 1-7; White et al., 1-5. Ward's scale is scored 0-4, disagree to agree.

[2] Reporting of deviation scores was necessary because of differences in midpoints across attitude scales. The deviation score is calculated by subtracting each scale's midpoint from the mean reported. Positive deviation scores reflect disagreement with the attitude item.

[3] All t values are significant at $p < .02$. Positive t values indicate greater disagreement with affective than cognitive items.

the attitudes-toward-rape scale, cognitive items were disagreed with more strongly than affective items.

Discussion

In general, attitudes-toward-rape scales currently used in research ignore the behavioral intention component of attitudes. Items from Malamuth's (Malamuth, 1981) Likelihood to Force Sex and Likelihood to Rape scales, and his multi-item Attraction to Sexual Aggression Scale (Malamuth, 1989a, b), were the only items that assessed behavioral intentions. These items, however, are not acknowledged in the literature as attitudinal scales. Rather, they often are used as outcome rather than predictor variables.

Moreover, all the scales we examined mixed affectively- and cognitively-based attitude items. Some were loaded with more cognitive than affective items (Costin, 1985; Dull & Giacopassi, 1987; Feild, 1978; Larsen & Long, 1988; Sandberg et al., 1987; Ward, 1988), whereas others were more affectively laden (Bunting & Reeves, 1983; Burt, 1980; Gilmartin-Zena, 1987; Weidner & Griffitt, 1983). However, level of endorsement of affective and cognitive items differed significantly for the scales for which data were available. Whereas people may accept certain myths and stereotypes about rape, they certainly do not *feel* positively about rape. Additionally, most means are below the center of the rating scales, indicating that differences are in degree of *disagreement* rather than *agreement*. In sum, when ratings of cognitive and affective items are averaged, the differences in *feelings* about rape may be obscured.

Although level of endorsement of affective and cognitive items differed significantly, the differences were small and may reflect the psychometric inadequacy of the scales rather than real differences, as identified by Lonsway and Fitzgerald (1994). Thus, further research is necessary to assess whether affective and cognitive statements about rape necessarily differ in their potency. That is, are affective items more likely to elicit greater disagreement because of people's negative feelings about rape, or do extant scales inadvertently contain affective items with greater potency, hence eliciting a more extreme reaction, than cognitive items? Consideration of our analyses of Dull and Giacopassi's SDS indicates that affective items do not always elicit more extreme responses. This possibility has implications for procedures used to develop new attitudes-toward-rape scales. Researchers would be well-advised to include an equal number of equally valence affective, cognitive, and behavioral intention items when developing new scales (see Crites et al., 1994, for a discussion of measuring affective and cognitive properties of attitudes).

STUDY 2

Although we found statistically significant differences in college students' ratings of cognitive and affective attitudes about rape, it is unclear whether this distinction has practical significance. The distinction between affective and cognitive components of attitudes will be most helpful if it increases the predictive validity of the attitude scales. Though past research indicates that men who report engaging in sexually coercive behavior endorse rape-supportive attitudes more so than others, the strength of the relationships has been weak. These results may be due to the fact that combining affective and cognitive components obscured the relationship between each component and sexually coercive behavior. Thus, in Study 2 we assessed the relative independence of the affective and cognitive components and their predictive power. Also, we tested the hypothesis that affective items will elicit greater disagreement than would cognitive items, using Burt's (1980) Rape Myth Acceptance Scale. Burt's scale was chosen because it is the most widely used attitudes-toward-rape scale. Additionally, we further explored the possibility that affective items, in general, elicit more extreme responses than cognitive items by examining the difference between the affective and cognitive components of two additional scales, Burt's Adversarial Sex Beliefs and Acceptance of Interpersonal Violence.

Method

Participants. Three hundred two undergraduate male college students from a large state university participated in the study in return for credit in an introductory psychology course (referred to as Phase One). As part of a second, unrelated study (referred to as Phase Two), a random sample of 166 men were invited back to complete an additional set of surveys (see White & Farmer, 1988).

Materials. In Phase One, participants completed a self-report questionnaire that consisted of Burt's (1980) Rape Myth Acceptance Scale (RMAS) described in Study 1, Burt's Adversarial Sex Beliefs (ASB), Acceptance of Interpersonal Violence (AIV), and the Sexual Experiences Survey (SES) developed by Koss and Oros (1982). The men who participated in the second phase also completed Malamuth's (1981) Likelihood to Use Force and Rape (LF & LR) measures.

The RMAS is internally consistent (Cronbach's alpha = .875) and is reported to have construct validity (Ashton, 1982). The ASB consists of nine items, with a reliability of .802; the AIV consists of six items with a reliability of .586. All items were categorized as affective or cognitive by the judges used in Study 1.

The SES is a 10-item behavioral survey that categorizes men along a continuum of sexual coercion. Men were asked the frequency with which they had engaged in each behavior listed since the age of 14. Only items subsequently identified by Koss, Gidycz, and Wisniewski (1987) were used to categorize men into five mutually exclusive sexual coercion categories based on the most severe form of sexual coercion reported. These categories were no sexual coercion, unwanted contact, verbal coercion, attempted rape, and rape. Significant correlations have been found between self-report on the SES and men's stated level of coercion in an interview two weeks later ($r = .61$, $p < .001$), lending support for the construct validity of this measure (Koss & Gidycz, 1985). Koss and Gidycz (1985) also reported test-retest reliability of .93 and an internal consistency reliability of .89 using a Cronbach alpha.

Procedure. In both Phase One and Phase Two, participants responded to the questionnaires in large mixed-sex groups. Students completed a large number of unrelated scales during the administration of these measures. Responses were recorded on a computerized answer sheet.

Results

Mean differences. There was a significant difference in mean level of disagreement with the affective and cognitive components of the RMAS, as well as for the ASB and AIV (see Table 2). Students disagreed significantly more with the affective component of the RMAS than with the cognitive component, while disagreeing more with the cognitive components of the ASB and the AIV.

Self-reported sexually coercive behavior. Categorization of respondents, using the SES, indicated that 19.4% reported no experiences with sexual intercourse since the age of 14, whereas 47.6% reported consensual sexual experiences, but no sexually coercive experiences. The remaining 33% reported engaging in some form of sexual coercion since the age of 14: 4.8% used force to engage in unwanted sexual contact (kissing, petting, fondling, but not intercourse); 25.2% admitted to using verbal coercion to obtain intercourse with a woman when she did not want to; and 3.1% admitted to behaviors that meet the legal definition of rape or attempted rape.

Analyses of variance revealed that affectively-based attitudes, $F(4, 272) = 4.23$, $p = .002$, but not cognitively-based attitudes, $F(4, 272) = 1.58$, $p = .18$, were significantly related to level of self-reported sexual coercion. Means comparisons, using a Tukey HSD test ($a = .05$), revealed that men who had engaged in rape or attempted rape were more accepting of the affective items than any other group of men, who did not differ from one another.

Consistent with Malamuth (1986), the frequency of each sexually coercive behavior reported on the SES was summed to produce a total sexual coercion score. To verify that this continuous measure reflects accurately the categorical assignment of respondents to an SES-assessed sexual coercion category, an analysis of variance using sexual coercion as a categorical variable and frequency of sexually coercive acts as the dependent variable was performed. Results revealed a significant relationship, $F(4, 289) = 299.33$, $p < .001$. Men in the unwanted coercion reported the fewest sexually coercive acts ($M = 1.2$), with men in the verbally coercive category reporting slightly more ($M = 1.64$), and men in the rape and attempted rape categories reporting considerably more ($M = 3.56$). Frequency of sexual coercion was correlated with the mean affective and cognitive RMAS scores. A significant correlation for the affective component, $r = .22$, $p < .01$, but not the cognitive component, $r = .11$, was found.

Correlation between components and self-reported coercion. The Pearson product moment correlation between the affective and cognitive components of the RMAS was significant, $r = .565$, $p < .01$. Its moderate size (accounting for 16% of the variance) suggests that the affective and cognitive items tap separate components of rape attitudes.

Because of the significant correlation between the affective and cognitive component of the RMAS, two analyses of covariance were performed on self-reported sexually coercive behavior to ascertain if one component accounted for a significant portion of the variance in sexual coercion after controlling for the other component. Results revealed that after adjustment for cognitive attitude items, self-reported sexual coercion varied significantly with affective attitude item endorsement, $F(4, 285) = 4.88$, $p = .001$. In contrast, after adjustment for affective attitude items, self-reported sexual coercion did not vary significantly with cognitive attitude item endorsement, $F(4, 285) = .89$, $p = .471$.

Relationship to behavioral intentions. Correlations between ratings on Malamuth's Likelihood to Use Force and Likelihood to Rape questions and with the affective and cognitive components of the RMAS indicated (a) the correlation between the likelihood to use force and the likelihood to rape was significant, $r = .504$, $p < .01$, with the likelihood of forcing a woman into sex ($M = 6.26$, range 2-7) being greater than the likelihood of raping ($M = 6.79$, range 4-7, on 1-7 scale where 1 = very likely to 7 = not at all likely); (b) the correlations between these two likelihood measures and the affective and cognitive components were significant and of comparable magnitudes (rs ranged from .32 to .43).

Discussion

These results suggest that, for the RMAS, the affective and cognitive components are distinct and, consistent with the analyses of other attitudes-toward-rape scales, disagreement was greater for affective than cognitive items. Finding that this pattern did not hold up for the ASB and AIV scales suggests that the results were not due to a general tendency for affective items to elicit more extreme responses than cognitive items. Rather, the differences may result from one or more psychological processes, including the basis on which the attitude was formed initially, the salience of the attitudinal components at the time of testing, or the function sexually coercive behavior serves. Clearly, future research is needed to explore the foundations of this difference.

Although both components were correlated with behavioral intention measures, only the affective component discriminated among groups of self-reported sexually coercive and sexually noncoercive men. Men who reported engaging in sexually coercive behavior were more likely to endorse rape-supportive attitudes, particularly the affectively-based items. We suggest that sexually coercive men's feelings about rape, rather than their beliefs, tend to distinguish them from sexually noncoercive men. They hold more negative opinions than do sexually noncoercive men about women who are sexually victimized, although sexually noncoercive men do not appear to differ from the sexually coercive men regarding beliefs about rape.

STUDY 3

The purpose of Study 3 was to confirm conceptually the results of Study 2 by using an independent sample of participants and a different measure of attitudes toward rape. This measure was derived by performing a principle components factor analysis on the RMAS, ASB, and AIV items from Study 2, as part of a larger study testing models of sexual coercion (White & Farmer, 1988).

Method

Participants. Two hundred seventy-eight men enrolled in introductory sociology classes over a two-semester period participated in a voluntary survey administered in large mixed-sex groups.

Materials. Participants filled out a survey containing items selected on the basis of a factor analysis of the responses to the RMAS, ASB, and AIV provided in Study 2, along with a number of unrelated measures. Of interest in the present study was the attitudes-toward-rape factor. There were the nine items; six were cognitive items and three were affective items. The cognitive items had an internal consistency of .624; the affective items had an internal consistency of .683. Participants also completed the Koss and Oros (1982) SES.

Results

Mean differences and relationship to self-reported coercion. Consistent with analyses from the first two studies, the affective items elicited greater disagreement than the cognitive items (see Table 2). Additionally, analyses of variance and Tukey's HSD test for means comparisons revealed a significant difference for mean affective scores, $F(3, 267) = 10.69$, $p < .001$, as well as for mean cognitive scores, $F(3, 267) = 7.93$, $p < .001$, as a function of category of sexual coercion, with men who raped or attempted rape (8% of the sample) endorsing the affective and cognitive items more than nonsexually coercive men (68% of the sample) or men who reported other forms of sexual coercion (13.1% admitted to unwanted contact; 10.9% to verbal coercion).

The correlations between number of sexually coercive behaviors reported (as described in Study 2) and the affective and cognitive components of the factor-analytically derived attitude measure were significant, respective $rs = .225, .206$, $p < .01$. Finally, although the correlation between the affective and cognitive components was significant, $r = .581$, $p < .01$, analyses of covariance confirmed that the affective component accounted for unique variance. After adjustment for cognitive attitude items, self-reported sexual coercion varied significantly with affective attitude item endorsement, $F(3, 266) = 4.15$, $p = .007$, whereas self-reported sexual coercion did not vary significantly with cognitive attitude item endorsement, $F(3, 266) = 1.58$, $p = .194$, after adjustment for the affective items.

Discussion

Results of Study 3 confirmed the hypothesis that the affective component of rape attitudes elicited more disagreement than the cognitive component in an independent sample of college men. Unlike Study 2, these data showed that sexually coercive men differed from sexually noncoercive men on both the affective and cognitive components. However, the analyses of covariance from both studies yielded consistent results, supporting the claim that the components are partially independent. We found that, after controlling for shared variance, the affective component was significantly related to level of sexual coercion, but the cognitive component was not.

Confirmation of Study 2 results is not surprising, in part, because Study 3 defined attitudes toward rape using a factor-analytically determined subset of Burt's items. Thus, to examine the generalizability of these results and to address some conceptual and psychometric problems associated with attitudes-toward-rape measures, future researchers should develop a new rape attitude scale, following standard test construction procedures. The hypotheses considered in the present series of studies should be verified with this new instrument.

GENERAL DISCUSSION

There is overwhelming support for the dynamic interplay between affect and cognition in the precipitation of behavior (Zajonc, 1980). The concept of *attitude* provides a highly useful integration of the influence of affect and cognition on behavior. However, the fact that affective, cognitive, and behavioral responses toward an attitude object are not always highly correlated must be noted. Moreover, a scale's predictive value may be affected by the components an attitudinal instrument actually measures. Thus, the distinctions among affective, cognitive, and behavioral components of an attitude have both theoretical and practical significance.

Our review of the attitudes-toward-rape literature reveals little attention to the definition of attitude and virtually no attention to the affective, cognitive, and behavioral distinctions discussed previously. Furthermore, our analyses indicate that many attitudes-toward-rape scales tend to be loaded with cognitive items; however, affective items tend to better predict sexually coercive behavior than do cognitive items.

Intervention strategies should be based on counterattitudinal advocacy research, which suggests that people think and behave to maintain consistency between attitudes and behavior (Cook & Flay, 1978). In particular, based on Olson and Zanna's (1993) review, intervention strategies must consider whether attitudes are newly-formed or well-entrenched, and whether they are primarily affectively- or cognitively-based. For newly formed, affectively-based attitudes, attitude change should be greater when the persuasive communication is affective rather than cognitive (Edwards, 1990). In contrast, for established attitudes, "mismatch" approaches may be more effective (i.e., using a cognitive appeal with an affectively-based attitude or vice-versa) (Millar & Millar, 1990).

For example, if rape-supportive attitudes are affectively-based and relatively newly-formed, as for adolescents, for instance, it may be best to focus on affective persuasive messages followed by new "affective" experiences, such as role-play. However, this type of intervention may strengthen rape-supportive attitudes in individuals with well-established attitudes. The affect associated with a well-established attitude may be resistant to change (Zajonc, 1980). Challenging one's deeply held feelings may actually strengthen, rather than weaken, them. This may be why some sexual coercion awareness programs backfire (Donnerstein, 1992; Fischer, 1986a). In these cases, intervention strategies need to avoid arousing defensive reactions, perhaps focusing on rationally persuasive messages, with no appeal to feelings. These interventions could provide educational information on women's sexuality, consequences of sexual coercion, social skills training, and other rational arguments against rape (see Linz, Wilson, & Donnerstein, 1992, for a more extensive discussion of intervention strategies).

Our findings suggest that it is crucial for theorists and researchers to attend to the structural characteristics of attitudes when attempting to predict behavior and induce attitude change. Future researchers using attitudinal measures should (a) explicitly address the definition of attitude; (b) be guided by attitude-behavior theories; (c) systematically assess affective, cognitive, and behavioral components toward the attitude object; and (d) consider the implications of the distinction among these components for the prediction of sexual coercion and the success of prevention strategies.

NOTES

1. Several scales found in the literature (e.g., Ellis, O'Sullivan, & Sowards, 1992; Fonow, Richardson, & Wemmerus, 1992; Jenkins & Dambrot, 1987; Mayerson & Taylor, 1987; Spanos, Dubreuil, & Gwynnm, 1991-1992; Thornton, Robbins, & Johnson, 1981) were not included in this review because the scales were composed of items from other scales, primarily Burt (1980), Feild (1978), and Costin (1985), which are included in the present analyses. Additionally, items used by Fischer (1986a, b) were not included because the items, created by Allgeier and Hyde (1979), were not devised for research use (Allgeier, personal communication, September, 1994). Finally, scales assessing attribution of blame for rape were not included (such as Resick & Jackson, 1981).

2. Items from Goodchilds, Zellman, Johnson, and Giarrusso (1988) and Rapaport and Burkhart (1984) could not be classified because they presented vignettes to which respondents were to judge whether forced sex was acceptable.

3. If you need a copy of the categorization of individual items, contact the first author.

4. Only three of Feild's eight subscales could be analyzed in this manner. Three subscales consisted of only cognitive items and two of only affective items.

REFERENCES

Abelson, R. P., Kinder, D. R., Peters, M. D., & Fiske, S. T. (1982). Affective and semantic components in political person perception. *Journal of Personality and Social Psychology, 42,* 619-630.

Adler, C. (1985). An exploration of self-reported sexually aggressive behavior. *Crime and Delinquency, 31,* 306-331.

Allgeier, E., & Hyde, J. S. (1979). *Instructor's manual for understanding human sexuality.* New York: McGraw-Hill.

Allport, G. W. (1935). Attitudes. In C. Murchison (Ed.), *Handbook of social psychology* (pp. 798-844). Worcester, MA: Clark University Press.

Ashton, N. L. (1982). Validation of the Rape Myth Acceptance Scale. *Psychological Reports, 50,* 252.

Breckler, S. J., & Wiggins, E. C. (1989). Affect versus evaluation in the structure of attitudes. *Journal of Experimental Social Psychology, 25,* 253-271.

Bunting, A. B., & Reeves, J. B. (1983). Perceived male sex orientation and beliefs about rape. *Deviant Behavior, 4,* 281-295.

Burt, M. R. (1980). Cultural myths and supports for rape. *Journal of Personality and Social Psychology, 38,* 217-230.

Burt, M. R. (1991). Rape myths and acquaintance rape. In A. Parrot & L. Bechhofer (Eds.), *Acquaintance rape: The hidden crime* (pp. 26-40). New York: John Wiley & Sons.

Cook, T. D., & Flay, B. R. (1978). The persistence of experimentally induced attitude change. In L. Berkowitz (Ed.), *Advances in experimental social psychology (Vol. 11,* pp. 1-57). New York: Academic Press.

Costin, F. (1985). Beliefs about rape and women's social roles. *Archives of Sexual Behavior, 14,* 319-325.

Crites, S. L., Fabrigar, L. R., & Petty, R. E. (1994). Measuring the affective and cognitive properties of attitudes: Conceptual and methodological issues. *Personality and Social Psychology Bulletin, 20,* 619-634.

Donat, P. L. N. (1991, April). *Do attitudes guide behavior: Attitude accessibility in sexually aggressive males.* Poster presented at the Southeastern Psychological Association, New Orleans, LA.

Donnerstein, E. (1992). *Mitigating the effects of mass media sexual violence.* Paper presented at X World Meeting of International Society for Research in Aggression. Siena, Italy, September.

Dull, R. T., & Giacopassi, D. J. (1987). Demographic correlates of sexual and dating attitudes. *Criminal Justice and Behavior, 14,* 175-193.

Eagly, A. H., & Chaiken, S. (1993). *The psychology of attitudes.* Fort Worth: Harcourt Brace Jovanovich.

Edwards, K. (1990). The interplay of affect and cognition in attitude formation and change. *Journal of Personality and Social Psychology, 59,* 202-216.

Edwards, K. (1992). The primacy of affect in attitude formation and change: Restoring the integrity of affect in the tripartite model (Doctoral dissertation, University of Michigan, 1992). *Dissertation Abstracts International, 53,* 2583B.

Ellis, A. L., O'Sullivan, C. S., & Sowards, B. A. (1992). The impact of contemplated exposure to a survivor of rape on attitudes towards rape. *Journal of Applied Social Psychology, 22,* 889-895.

Feild, H. S. (1978). Attitudes toward rape: A comparative analysis of police, rapists, crisis counselors, and citizens. *Journal of Personality and Social Psychology, 36,* 156-179.

Fischer, G. J. (1986a). College student attitudes toward forcible date rape: Change after taking a human sexuality course. *Journal of Sex Education and Therapy, 12,* 42-46.

Fischer, G. J. (1986b). College student attitudes toward forcible date rape: I. Cognitive predictors. *Archives of Sexual Behavior, 15,* 457-466.

Fonow, M. M., Richardson, L., & Wemmerus, V. A. (1992). Feminist rape education: Does it work? *Gender and Society, 6,* 108-121.

Gilmartin-Zena, P. (1987). Attitudes toward rape: Student characteristics as predictors. *Free Inquiry in Creative Sociology, 15,* 175-182.

Goodchilds, J., Zellman, G., Johnson, P., & Giarrusso, R. (1988). Adolescents and their perceptions of sexual interactions. In A. W. Burgess (Ed.), *Rape and sexual coercion (Vol II).* New York: Garland.

Insko, C. A., & Schopler, J. (1967). Triadic consistency: A statement of affective-cognitive-conative consistency. *Psychological Review, 74,* 361-376.

Jenkins, M. J., & Dambrot, F. H. (1987). The attribution of date rape: Observer's attitudes and sexual experiences and the dating situation. *Journal of Applied Social Psychology, 17,* 875-895.

Koss, M. P., & Dinero, T. E. (1988). Predictors of sexual aggression among a national sample of male college students. *Annals of the New York Academy of Sciences, 528,* 113-146.

Koss, M. P., & Gidycz, C. A. (1985). Sexual Experiences Survey: Reliability and validity. *Journal of Consulting and Clinical Psychology, 53,* 422-423.

Koss, M. P., Gidycz, C. A., & Wisniewski, N. (1987). The scope of rape: Incidence and prevalence of sexual aggression and victimization in a national sample of higher education students. *Journal of Consulting and Clinical Psychology, 55,* 162-170.

Koss, M. P., & Leonard, K. E. (1984). Sexually aggressive men: Empirical findings and theoretical implications. In N. Malamuth & E. Donnerstein (Eds.), *Pornography and sexual aggression* (pp. 213-232). New York: Academic Press.

Koss, M. P., Leonard, K. E., Beezley, D. A., & Oros, C. J. (1985). Non-stranger sexual aggression: A discriminant analysis of the psychological characteristics of undetected offenders. *Sex Roles, 12,* 981-992.

Koss, M. P., & Oros, C. J. (1982). Sexual Experiences Survey: A research instrument investigating sexual aggression and victimization. *Journal of Consulting and Clinical Psychology, 50,* 455-457.

Kramer, B. M. (1949). Dimensions of prejudice. *Journal of Psychology, 27,* 389-451.

Krech, D., & Crutchfield, R. S. (1948). *Theory and problems of social psychology.* New York: McGraw-Hill.

Larsen, K., & Long, A. (1988). Attitudes toward rape. *The Journal of Sex Research, 24,* 299-304.

Linz, D., Wilson, B. J., & Donnerstein, E. (1992). Sexual violence in the mass media: Legal solutions, warnings, and mitigation through education. *Journal of Social Issues, 48,* 145-171.

Lonsway, K. A., & Fitzgerald, L. F. (1994). Rape myths: In review. *Psychology of Women Quarterly, 18,* 133-164.

Malamuth, N. M. (1981). Rape proclivity among males. *Journal of Social Issues, 37,* 138-157.

Malamuth, N. M. (1983). Factors associated with rape as predictors of laboratory aggression against women. *Journal of Personality and Social Psychology, 45,* 432-442.

Malamuth, N. M. (1986). Predictors of naturalistic sexual aggression. *Journal of Personality and Social Psychology, 50,* 953-962.

Malamuth, N. M. (1989a). The attraction to sexual aggression scale: Part one. *The Journal of Sex Research, 26,* 26-49.

Malamuth, N. M. (1989b). The attraction to sexual aggression scale: Part two. *The Journal of Sex Research, 26,* 324-354.

Mayerson, S. E., & Taylor, D. A. (1987). The effects of rape myth pornography on women's attitudes and the mediating role of sex role stereotyping. *Sex Roles, 17,* 321-338.

Millar, M. G., & Millar, K. U. (1990). Attitude change as a function of attitude type and argument type. *Journal of Personality and Social Psychology, 59,* 217-228.

Millar, M. G., & Tesser, A. (1986). Effects of affective and cognitive focus on the attitude-behavior relationship. *Journal of Personality and Social Psychology, 51,* 270-276.

Olson, J. M., & Zanna, M. P. (1993). Attitudes and attitude change. *Annual Review of Psychology, 44,* 117-154.

Rapaport, K., & Burkhart, B. R. (1984). Personality and attitudinal characteristics of sexually coercive college males. *Journal of Abnormal Psychology, 93,* 216-221.

Resick, P. A., & Jackson, T. L. (1981). Attitudes toward rape among mental health professionals. *American Journal of Community Psychology, 9,* 481-490.

Rosenberg, M. J., & Hovland, C. I. (1960). Cognitive, affective, and behavioral components of attitudes. In C. I. Hovland & M. J. Rosenberg (Eds.), *Attitude organization and change* (pp. 1-14). New Haven, CT: Yale University Press.

Sandberg, G., Jackson, T. L., & Petretic-Jackson, P. (1987). College students' attitudes regarding sexual coercion and aggression: Developing educational and preventive strategies. *Journal of College Student Personnel, 28,* 302-311.

Shotland, R. L. (1989). A model of the causes of date rape in developing and close relationships. In C. Hendrick (Ed.), *Close relationships* (pp. 247-270). Newbury Park, CA: Sage.

Shotland, R. L. (1992). A theory of the causes of courtship rape: Part 2. *Journal of Social Issues, 48,* 127-143.

Spanos, N. P., Dubreuil, S. C., & Gwynn, M. I. (1991-1992). The effects of expert testimony concerning rape on the verdicts and beliefs of mock jurors. *Imagination, Cognition, and Personality, 11,* 37-51.

Thornton, B., Robbins, M. A., & Johnson, J. A. (1981). Social perception of the rape victim's culpability: The influence of respondent's personal-environmental causal attribution tendencies. *Human Relations, 34,* 225-237.

Thurstone, L. L. (1928). Attitudes can be measured. *American Journal of Sociology, 33,* 529-544.

Ward, C. (1988). The attitudes toward rape victims scale: Construction, validation, and cross-cultural applicability. *Psychology of Women Quarterly, 12,* 127-146.

Weidner, G., & Griffitt, W. (1983). Rape: A sexual stigma. *Journal of Personality, 51,* 152-166.

White, J. W., & Farmer, R. (1988). *Correlates of sexual aggression.* Paper presented at Southeastern Psychological Association, Atlanta, Georgia.

Zajonc, R. B. (1980). Feeling and thinking: Preferences need no inferences. *American Psychologist, 35,* 151-175.

Zajonc, R. B. (1984). On the primacy of affect. *American Psychologist, 39,* 117-124.

Zanna, M. P., & Rempel, J. K. (1988). Attitudes: A new look at an old concept. In D. Bar-Tal & A. W. Kruglanski (Eds.), *The social psychology of knowledge* (pp. 315-334). Cambridge: Cambridge University Press.

Gender Differences
in Responses to Discrepancies
in Desired Level of Sexual Intimacy

Lucia F. O'Sullivan, PhD

E. Sandra Byers, PhD

SUMMARY. The purpose of the current study was to compare reports of discrepancies in the desired level of sexual intimacy in which a man was the reluctant dating partner and those in which a woman was the reluctant dating partner. To obtain information about this type of dating interaction, 139 male and 159 female unmarried heterosexual students completed the Sexual Situation Questionnaire (O'Sullivan & Byers, 1993), which provided information about a situation in which they or their partner refused a sexual advance. A higher percentage of respondents reported having had a disagreement characterized by a reluctant female than a reluctant male in the year preceding the study. However, few differences were noted in the descriptions of male-reluctant and female-reluctant disagree-

---

Lucia F. O'Sullivan is an Instructor in the Department of Natural and Social Sciences, Bowling Green State University, Huron, OH. E. Sandra Byers is Professor in the Department of Psychology and Acting Director of the Muriel McQueen Fergusson Centre for Family Violence Research at the University of New Brunswick, Fredericton, New Brunswick.

Address correspondence to E. Sandra Byers, Department of Psychology, The University of New Brunswick, Fredericton, New Brunswick, Canada E3B 6E4.

Preparation for this article was supported in part by funding from the Department of Psychology at The University of New Brunswick.

These data were presented at the Annual Meeting of The Society for the Scientific Study of Sex, New Orleans, November 1991.

[Haworth co-indexing entry note]: "Gender Differences in Responses to Discrepancies in Desired Level of Sexual Intimacy." O'Sullivan, Lucia F., and E. Sandra Byers. Co-published simultaneously in *Journal of Psychology & Human Sexuality* (The Haworth Press, Inc.) Vol. 8, No. 1/2, 1996, pp. 49-67; and: *Sexual Coercion in Dating Relationships* (ed: E. Sandra Byers, and Lucia F. O'Sullivan) The Haworth Press, Inc., 1996, pp. 49-67. Single or multiple copies of this article are available from The Haworth Document Delivery Service [1-800-342-9678, 9:00 a.m. - 5:00 p.m. (EST)].

49

ments, suggesting that men and women share a common script. Differences in these descriptions typically constituted actor-observer differences, rather than actual differences between the two types of disagreement interactions. Implications for examining men's and women's shared experiences of discrepancies in desired sexual intimacy are discussed. *[Article copies available from The Haworth Document Delivery Service: 1-800-342-9678.]*

Situations in which there is a discrepancy in the desired level of sexual intimacy between heterosexual dating partners can lead to unwanted or nonconsensual sexual activity. Although it is not always the man who desires the higher level of sexual intimacy (O'Sullivan & Byers, 1993), researchers typically have examined only men's use of aggressive behaviors and women's experiences of unwanted sexual advances (e.g., Brickman & Briere, 1984; Koss, Gidycz, & Wisniewski, 1987; Malamuth, Sockloskie, Koss, & Tanaka, 1991; Muehlenhard & Linton, 1987). This perspective corresponds to traditional views about men's and women's sexual motives. Men have been viewed as sexually appetitive, exercising little discrimination with regard to their choice of sexual partners, and at times employing aggressive means to gain sexual access (Check & Malamuth, 1985). In contrast, women have been viewed as sexually reluctant, engaging in sexual activity only after receiving adequate assurance of a partner's commitment to their relationship (Clark & Hatfield, 1989). A substantial number of studies support these differences in sexual motives (e.g., Carroll, Volk, & Hyde, 1985; Christopher & Cate, 1985; Knox & Wilson, 1981).

THE RESEARCH TRADITION

Researchers have documented considerable overlap in men's and women's sexual interactions (Finlay, Starnes, & Alvarez, 1985; Lawson, 1988; Miller & Marshall, 1987; Sherwin & Corbett, 1985). In this context, researchers have recently investigated differences in men's and women's behavior in interactions in which the man and the woman desired different levels of sexual intimacy (Aizenman & Kelley, 1988; Muehlenhard & Cook, 1988; Poppen & Segal, 1988; Stets & Pirog-Good, 1987; Struckman-Johnson, 1988). Again, most of these researchers examined coercive interactions. Typically, the rates of sustained force are higher for women than for men, a greater percentage of men than women reported having forced a partner to engage in intercourse, and the forms of coercion that men and women experience tend to differ (e.g., Aizenman & Kelley, 1988; Mueh-lenhard and Cook, 1988; Poppen & Segal, 1988; Struckman-Johnson, 1988). These findings serve to emphasize the importance of examining men's and women's experiences of sexual encounters separately.

The purpose of the current study was to compare reports of discrepancies in the desired level of sexual intimacy in which the man was the reluctant dating partner and those in which the woman was the reluctant dating partner. Both male and female respondents described either their or their partners' behavior in one of these situations. We investigated whether the initiating partner responded to the reluctant partner with behavior indicating compliance with a refusal, compliance with an attempt to influence a partner, or noncompliance. We predicted that complying with a partner's refusal (with no subsequent attempt to influence) would be reported most frequently because this response was expected to be least disruptive to the relationship for both men and women. However, in keeping with traditional views of men's and women's roles, women were expected to be relatively more likely than were men to comply with a partner's refusal and men were expected to be relatively more likely than were women to use coercion. We predicted that noncompliance would be reported least frequently because disregarding the reluctant partner's refusal by using verbal or physical coercion was expected to precipitate distress. In support of this prediction are the findings of an investigation of disagreements in which the man desired a more intimate level of sexual involvement than did his female dating partner (Byers & Lewis, 1988). The researchers found that, according to respondents' reports, in 61% of the cases the men complied with women's refusals without any attempt to influence their partner to engage in the unwanted sexual activity. We expected a similar pattern of response would characterize both the male-reluctant and female-reluctant disagreements reported in this study.

LIMITATIONS OF PAST RESEARCH

Past studies of dating interactions in which the man and the woman differed in the desired level of sexual intimacy have several limitations. For example, some researchers requested that participants respond to hypothetical sexual encounters, making generalizations to actual sexual encounters uncertain (e.g., Lewin, 1985; McCormick, 1979; Perper & Weis, 1987). Other researchers examined only behaviors used to influence a reluctant partner to engage in sexual intercourse rather than examining a range of sexual activities (e.g., Muehlenhard & Cook, 1988; Mynatt & Allgeier, 1990; Struckman-Johnson, 1988). Further, researchers typically have examined only coercive influence behaviors. The use of a range of other possible influence behaviors has typically been ignored. For instance, most researchers have not examined noncoercive forms of influence, such as flirting and complimenting one's partner, asking for an explanation, or using humor.

Examining both negative or coercive and positive or noncoercive types of influence will aid the investigation of the full range of responses a man or woman can make to a partner's indication of reluctance to engage in sexual activity. If traditional views about men's and women's sexual motives are accurate, men would be more likely than would women to disregard a partner's refusal and use negative forms of influence, such as verbal or physical coercion, to gain compliance. If there is substantial overlap between gender roles for this type of sexual dating interaction, then no differences in the likelihood of using coercive forms of influence for men and women would be apparent.

Most studies of influence behaviors have used a priori categorizations of influence strategies (Christopher & Frandsen, 1990; McCormick, 1979) and may have incorrectly inferred the reactions experienced by the respondents to the use of influence. O'Sullivan and Byers (1993) had respondents indicate from a list of 44 influence strategies which strategies (if any) were used in an attempt to overcome the reluctant partner's resistance to sexual advances. Then respondents rated the impact on the reluctant partner of each influence strategy reported. Strategies could be rated as positive (i.e., pleasing to the reluctant partner), negative (i.e., displeasing to the reluctant partner), or neutral. No influence strategy was rated as having a consistent impact on the reluctant partner in each case, indicating the futility in attempting to infer the likely impact. Thus, a similar procedure was used in the current study. We examined differences in men's and women's use of influence strategies and expected that men would be more likely than would women to use all forms of influence, particularly negative forms, in accordance with traditional expectations of men's and women's sexual behavior.

OVERVIEW OF THE CURRENT STUDY

This study was undertaken as a comparison of male and female college students' experiences of discrepancies in the level of sexual intimacy desired by themselves and their dating partners. We examined the prevalence and characteristics of these two types of disagreements, the extent to which men and women complied with refusals, their attempts to influence their reluctant partners to engage in sex, as well as the emotional and relational consequences associated with men's and women's use of influence. Finally, actor-observer differences in men's and women's reports of disagreement situations were examined. We expected a response bias to be apparent, similar to the bias noted in studies of sexual coercion in which self-reported victimization rates are consistently higher than self-reported perpetration rates (e.g., Koss et al., 1987). Results related to women's use of influence with a reluctant male sexual partner have been reported elsewhere (O'Sullivan & Byers, 1993).

METHOD

Subjects

Subjects were 139 male and 159 female unmarried heterosexual students enrolled in introductory psychology classes at a midsized Canadian university. All students had grown up in Canada or the United States. Students volunteered to participate in the study called "Sexual Dating Behavior" as part of a research participation option for course credit. The average age of the subjects was 19.2 years (range 17 to 35).

Measures

Sexual Situation Questionnaire (SSQ). The SSQ constitutes a modification of a similar instrument used successfully by Byers and Lewis (1988). The model instrument has demonstrated reliability and validity (Byers & Lewis, 1988; Byers & Wilson, 1985). Respondents completed either a male-reluctant or female-reluctant version of the SSQ. The male-reluctant version consisted of items assessing the most recent interaction experienced within the year preceding the study in which the man did not want to engage in as high a level of sexual intimacy as did his female partner. The female-reluctant version assessed situations in which the woman was reluctant to engage in the higher level of sexual intimacy. Thus, subjects provided information about either their or their partner's behavior, depending on the version of the questionnaire that they were assigned. *Sexual activity* was defined for subjects as including all levels of sexual activity, not just sexual intercourse. Also, the term *disagreement* was defined as a situation in which one partner indicated a desire to engage in a higher level of sexual intimacy than his or her partner wanted at that time.

Subjects who had experienced the assigned type of disagreement situation responded to questions concerning their dating relationship (e.g., type of relationship, number of previous dates, romantic interest in their partner), where they were at the time of the disagreement, the disputed level of sexual activity (i.e., ranging from unwanted hugging to unwanted anal intercourse), whether they had engaged in the sexual activity with their partner on a previous occasion, and the consensual sexual activities preceding the disagreement (if any). Respondents also provided the reasons why they or their partner did not want to engage in the initiated sexual activity.

Detailed information regarding the communication about the disputed sexual activity was obtained. Respondents provided the verbal and/or nonverbal behaviors used by (a) the man or woman to indicate his or her desire to engage in the sexual activity (i.e., initiation behaviors), (b) the non-initiating partner to indicate reluctance (i.e., response behaviors), and (c) the initiator in response to this show of reluctance (i.e., influence behaviors). Respondents rated how clearly the initiator had indicated a desire for the sexual activity and how clearly the partner had indicated reluctance on 6-point scales ranging from 1 (extremely unclearly) to 6 (extremely clearly). To obtain even greater detail about men's and women's attempts to resolve the discrepancy in the desired level of intimacy, respondents indicated from a list of 44 strategies those strategies (if any) used to influence the reluctant partner to engage in the unwanted sexual activity (termed *influence strategies*, p. 61). For each strategy endorsed, respondents indicated whether the impact on the reluctant partner was positive (i.e., pleasing), negative (i.e., displeasing), or neutral (i.e., neither pleasing nor displeasing).

Respondents then reported whether they had engaged in the disputed level of sexual activity following the disagreement. They also rated the pleasantness associated with the disagreement interaction both at the time of disagreement and the time of the study on 6-point scales ranging from 1 (extremely unpleasant) to 6 (extremely pleasant) and the amount of romantic interest felt toward their dating partner both before and after the disagreement interaction on 5-point scales ranging from 1 (no romantic interest) to 5 (extremely romantically interested).

Using an open-ended format, respondents were given the opportunity to provide additional information about the interaction they had described. Finally, they rated their confidence in the accuracy of their responses on a 6-point scale ranging from 1 (very unsure) to 6 (very sure). The average confidence rating was 5.2 (mode = 5), providing support for the validity of the instrument.

The format of the SSQ was primarily multiple choice, although a few open-ended items were included throughout. These items included location, reasons for reluctance to engage in the disputed level of sexual activity, and the verbal and nonverbal components of the disagreement. Operational definitions of these categories are available from the authors. The mean interrater agreement for these variables was .87 (range .83 to 1.00), indicating good reliability. Where disagreements arose, the rating assigned by a third rater determined the final coding in all cases.

Background and Dating History Questionnaire. A self-administered questionnaire was used to collect demographic information such as age and gender. Other items concerned the extent of dating experience (e.g., current dating status, number of dates in the month preceding the study) and sexual experience (e.g., experience with intercourse, number of sexual partners in the past).

Procedure

Subjects were tested in groups of fewer than 10 people. Subjects were informed of the general purpose of the study and the procedures involved. All subjects indicated willingness to participate in the study, and written informed consent was obtained. Subjects were randomly assigned to complete either a male-reluctant or female-reluctant version of the SSQ. Subjects completed the background questionnaire then the SSQ. Ninety male and 111 female subjects completed the male-reluctant version of the SSQ, and 49 male and 48 female subjects completed the female-reluctant version of the SSQ. Thirty-one subjects were dropped from the study because they did not complete the questionnaires properly or else reported a male- or female-reluctant interaction that occurred more than a year preceding the study.

RESULTS

Equal numbers of subjects (47.7%) reported being in a steady dating relationship as not being in a steady dating relationship at the time of the study. The remaining subjects (4.6%) reported being in a cohabiting relationship. Subjects reported moderately active past sexual/dating histories. To examine gender differences in reports of male- and female-reluctant disagreement situations, 2 (gender of reluctant partner) × 2 (gender of subject) analyses were used throughout.

Prevalence of Discrepancies in Level of Desired Sexual Intimacy

Overall, approximately 66% of the subjects reported having had a disagreement about the desired level of sexual intimacy with a partner in the year preceding the study. An ANOVA indicated that significantly more respondents reported female-reluctant situations (89% of those receiving this version) than male-reluctant situations (56% of those receiving this version), $F(1, 294) = 34.00$, $p < .001$. More male subjects (74%) reported disagreements than did female subjects (60%), $F(1, 294) = 4.08$, $p < .05$. The interaction between gender of reluctant partner and gender of subject, however, was not significant, $F(1, 294) = 0.73$, $p > .05$.

Characteristics of Disagreements About Level of Desired Sexual Intimacy

A series of chi-square analyses was conducted to examine differences in the reported characteristics of male-reluctant and female-reluctant disagreements (see Table 1). A Bonferroni adjustment was made to correct for inflated probability of Type I error, resulting in a significance level of .002. No significant differences were found as a function of either variable for reports of relationship status of the couple, location of the disagreement, whether the couple had engaged in the disputed level of sexual activity on a previous occasion, and whether the couple had engaged in some type of sexual activity prior to the disagreement.

In general, subjects reported that approximately half of the relationships (51.0%) were steady dating relationships. Disagreements occurred most frequently in a room other than a bedroom in one partner's dwellings (73.7%). Somewhat more than half of the subjects (52.0%) indicated that they had engaged in the disputed level of sexual activity with their partner on a previous occasion. Subjects frequently reported that they had engaged in some type of sexual activity with their partner prior to the initiation of the disputed sexual activity, although 21% of the disagreements were not preceded by any sexual interaction. The chi-square analyses revealed two differences in the reports of disagreement characteristics. First, a significantly higher proportion of men than women reported that intercourse constituted the disputed sexual activity for male-reluctant disagreements. No significant differences were found between men's and women's reports for female-reluctant disagreements. However, according to women, intercourse constituted the disputed sexual activity in a greater proportion of female-reluctant disagreements than male-reluctant disagreements. No differences were found in men's reports across disagreement types.

Second, for male-reluctant disagreements, a higher proportion of men than women reported reluctance related to relationship factors, whereas a higher proportion of women than men reported reluctance because of physical or situational factors. Similarly, for female-reluctant disagreements, a higher proportion of women than men reported reluctance be-

TABLE 1. Percent of Men and Women Reporting Various Characteristics of Male-Reluctant and Female-Reluctant Disagreements

Characteristics	Male-Reluctant Disagreements		Female-Reluctant Disagreements		Chi-Square (df = 1)			
	Men (n = 58)	Women (n = 54)	Men (n = 45)	Women (n = 41)	Male-Reluctant by Subject	Female-Reluctant by Subject	Males by Type	Females by Type
Steady dating relationship	39.7	59.3	60.0	46.3	4.3	1.5	4.3	1.6
Disagreement in bedroom	25.9	33.3	24.4	19.5	0.7	0.2	0.0	2.2
Dispute over intercourse	82.8[a]	42.6[ab]	66.7	80.5[b]	19.3*	2.2	3.5	13.7*
Past shared sex. experience	43.1	72.2	51.1	39.0	9.5	1.3	0.6	10.4
Consensual sexual activity	75.9	68.5	88.9	87.8	0.8	0.0	2.8	4.8
Reasons for reluctance[a]								
Relationship issues	65.5[ac]	20.4[ad]	26.7[bc]	73.2[bd]	23.2*	19.5*	16.4*	2.5*
Physical or situational	24.1[e]	51.8[eg]	40.0[f]	9.8[fg]				
Other	10.4	27.8	33.4	17.1				

Note: Means with the same superscript differ significantly. * p < .002.
a df = 2.

cause of relationship factors, whereas a higher proportion of men than women reported reluctance because of physical or situational factors. In a like manner, both men and women were more likely to provide relationship-related reasons when they were the reluctant partner, and women (but not men) were more likely to provide physical or situational reasons when their partner was reluctant compared to when they were reluctant.

In summary, few differences in men's and women's descriptions of male-reluctant and female-reluctant disagreements were found. For those differences in descriptions that were apparent, men's and women's descriptions of the disagreements appear to constitute actor-observer reporting differences, rather than actual differences between the two disagreement types per se.

Behavioral Responses to Disagreements About Desired Level of Sexual Intimacy

The behavioral responses to the disagreements can be found in Table 2. Sixty subjects (30.3% of all subjects) who reported a disagreement interaction did not provide the verbal and nonverbal behaviors used in response

TABLE 2. Behavioral Responses to Male-Reluctant and Female-Reluctant Disagreements as Reported by Men and Women[a]

Characteristics	Male-Reluctant Situations		Female-Reluctant Situations		Overall
	Men (%)	Women (%)	Men (%)	Women (%)	(%)
Response to refusal					
Compliance using no influence behaviors	35.5	52.5	86.4	70.0	60.1[b]
Compliance using influence behaviors	35.4	37.5	8.7	13.3	23.2
Noncompliance	28.8	10.0	4.3	16.6	16.7[c]

Note: Responses were categorized post-hoc.
[a] Based on the 138 subjects who reported verbal and/or nonverbal response behaviors; $n = 45$ men and $n = 40$ women (male-reluctant condition) and $n = 23$ men and $n = 30$ women (female-reluctant condition)
[b] Reported more frequently than expected
[c] Reported less frequently than expected

to the reluctant partner's indication of unwillingness. The analyses related to the responses to a partner's refusals were based on the 138 subjects who did report this information. These behaviors were categorized as compliance with no attempt to influence one's partner, compliance with an attempt to influence one's partner, and noncompliance. First, a 2 (gender of reluctant partner) × 2 (gender of subject) × 3 (type of behavioral response) loglinear analysis was conducted to determine the relative frequencies of men's and women's use of compliance, compliance with influence, and noncompliance, as reported by male and female subjects. The main effect for type of response was significant, $\chi^2(2) = 34.38$, $p < .001$, as was one of the two-way effects (type of response × gender of reluctant partner), $\chi^2(2) = 16.37$, $p < .001$. The other two-way effects (type of response × gender of subject and gender of reluctant partner × gender of subject) were not significant, $\chi^2(2) = 1.23$ and $\chi^2(1) = 0.87$, $ps > .05$, respectively. However, the three-way effect (type of response × gender of reluctant partner × gender of subject) was significant, $\chi^2(2) = 6.58$, $p < .05$.

A logit analysis was conducted next to identify differences in reports. For the main effect of type of response, respondents were more likely than expected by chance alone to report compliance without subsequent use of influence (60%, $z = 6.15$), and less likely than expected by chance alone to report noncompliance in response to a refusal (17%, $z = -3.36$). For type of response × gender of reluctant partner, the analysis revealed that men were more likely than were women to comply with their partner's refusal without using any type of influence (79% and 44%, respectively, $z = 3.73$), and less likely than were women to comply while making an attempt to influence their partner (11% and 36%, respectively, $z = -2.21$). No differences in men's and women's use of coercion were noted in reports (11% and 20%, respectively, $z = -0.69$). The three-way effect for type of response × gender of reluctant partner × gender of subject was significant for compliance without influence ($z = 2.37$) and noncompliance ($z = -2.36$). Compared to women, men reported greater discrepancies in the proportion of men and women who complied with their partner's refusal without any attempt to influence, as well as between the proportion of men and women who did not comply with a partner's refusal.

An ANOVA was conducted to assess differences in the likelihood of engaging in the disputed level of sexual activity for male- and female-reluctant situations. The main effect for gender of reluctant partner was significant, $F(1, 194) = 18.79$, $p < .001$. Subjects were more likely to report engaging in the disputed level of sexual activity after male-reluctant disagreements than after female-reluctant disagreements ($Ms = .31$ and .07, respectively). The main effect for gender of subject was not significant, $F(1, 194) = 0.68$, $p > .05$, nor was the interaction of gender of reluctant partner and gender of subject, $F(1, 194) = 0.01$, $p > .05$.

Use of Influence to Resolve Discrepancies in Desired Intimacy

Impact of the influence strategies employed. Another source of information about men's and women's attempts to influence a reluctant partner was the list of 44 influence strategies. Subjects indicated which influence strategies, if any, were employed during the disagreement interaction, then rated those used as having had a positive, negative, or neutral impact on the reluctant partner. The modal response for positive, negative, and neutral influence strategies was zero in each case. However, of particular note, all but 10 subjects reported the use of at least one influence strategy by the partner desiring the higher level of sexual intimacy. An ANOVA was conducted to assess whether men and women differed in the total number of strategies they employed. The main effect for gender of subject was not significant, $F(1, 188) = 0.53$, $p > .05$, but the main effect for gender of reluctant partner was significant, $F(1, 188) = 4.54$, $p < .05$. Subjects reported the use of more influence strategies by women during male-reluctant interactions than by men during female-reluctant interactions (Ms = 8.03 and 6.57, respectively). However, this main effect is qualified by the significant interaction between gender of subject and gender of reluctant partner, $F(1, 188) = 6.21$, $p < .05$. Women reported similar numbers of influence strategies for male- and female-reluctant interactions (Ms = 7.00 and 7.30, respectively); however, men reported the use of more influence strategies by the women than the men reported for themselves (Ms = 8.95 and 5.85, respectively).

To examine differences in the reported impact of influence strategies used by the men and the women, a $2 \times 2 \times 3$ ANOVA was conducted, with gender of reluctant partner and gender of subject as between-subjects variables and impact of strategy (i.e., positive, negative, or neutral) as a repeated measure within-subject variable. The main effect for impact was significant, $F(2, 193) = 34.11$, $p < .001$. Overall, subjects reported the use of more positive than negative or neutral influence strategies (Ms = 3.81, 1.48, and 1.70, respectively). The main effects for gender of reluctant partner and gender of subject were not significant, $F(1, 194) = 3.87$, and $F(1, 194) = 0.20$, $ps > .05$, respectively, nor were the interactions of gender of reluctant partner by impact of strategy and gender of subject by impact of strategy, $F(2, 193) = 1.70$ and $F(2, 193) = 0.51$, $ps > .05$, respectively.

However, the three-way interaction of gender of reluctant partner, gender of subject, and impact was significant, $F(2, 193) = 6.22$, $p < .01$. The follow-up analyses revealed that the interaction was significant for reports of negative and neutral influence strategies, $F(1, 194) = 9.12$, $p < .01$ and $F(1, 194) = 4.64$, $p < .05$, respectively. Compared to the women, the men reported the use of more negative influence strategies during male-reluctant interactions ($Ms = 2.22$ and 0.78, respectively) and fewer negative strategies during female-reluctant interactions ($Ms = 1.78$ and 1.38, respectively). Similarly, compared to the women, the men reported the use of more neutral influence strategies during male-reluctant interactions ($Ms = 1.43$ and 2.16, respectively), and the use of fewer negative influence strategies during female-reluctant interactions ($Ms = 1.78$ and 1.38, respectively). Moreover, compared to female subjects, male subjects tended to report the use of more negative and neutral strategies on behalf of women ($Ms = 0.78$ and 1.43 versus 2.22 and 2.16, respectively) and fewer negative and neutral strategies for themselves ($Ms = 2.32$ and 1.78 versus 0.58 and 1.43, respectively).

Most commonly reported types of influence strategies. Eight influence strategies from the list of 44 influence strategies were reported by more than 25% of the subjects. These strategies were flirting (50.8%), touching/stroking partner (48.4%), making positive comments about partner's appearance (45.2%), complimenting partner on body or sexuality (45.0%), asking partner to explain his or her reluctance (41.5%), tickling (37.0%), pouting/sulking (34.9%), and talking about feelings toward partner (33.3%). To analyze differences in the types of influence strategies reportedly used by men and women, an ANOVA was conducted with these strategies as repeated measures. The main effect for type of influence strategy was significant, $F(7, 178) = 2.48$, $p < .05$. Flirting was reported more frequently than was pouting/sulking and talking about one's feelings ($Ms = .51$, $.35$, and $.34$, respectively), $F(1, 184) = 4.13$, $p < .05$ and $F(1, 184) = 9.84$, $p < .01$, and touching/stroking was also reported more frequently than was talking about one's feelings ($Ms = .48$ and $.34$, respectively), $F(1, 184) = 4.85$, $p < .05$.

The main effects for gender of reluctant partner and gender of subject were not significant, $F(1, 184) = 1.70$ and $F(1, 184) = 0.65$, $ps > .05$. The interactions of gender of reluctant partner by gender of subject and gender of subject by type of influence strategy were also not significant, $F(1, 184) = 1.70$ and $F(7, 178) = 1.71$, $ps > .05$. However, the interaction of gender of reluctant partner and type of influence strategy was significant, $F(7, 178) = 2.81$, $p < .01$. Subjects reported the use of flirting as an influence strategy more often for male-reluctant disagreements than for female-reluctant disagreements ($Ms = .60$ and $.38$, respectively), whereas asking one's partner about their unwillingness was more often reported for female-reluctant disagreements than for male-reluctant disagreements ($Ms = .52$ and

.33, respectively). However, this interaction was qualified by the significant three-way interaction of gender of reluctant partner by gender of subject by type of influence strategy, $F(7, 178) = 2.80, p < .01$. According to the women, flirting was used more often ($Ms = .63$ and $.33$, respectively) and asking partner less often within male-reluctant compared to female-reluctant disagreements ($Ms = .63$ and $.26$, respectively). In summary, men and women did not tend to differ significantly in their use of these common types of influence strategies; however, women reported differences in the likelihood with which men as compared to women used flirting and asking one's partner to explain his or her reluctance.

Consequences Associated with Discrepancies in Level of Desired Sexual Intimacy

To assess differences in the ratings of the consequences associated with male-reluctant and female-reluctant situations, a MANOVA was conducted with ratings of pleasantness at the time of the disagreement and change in romantic interest as dependent variables. This analysis revealed that the interaction between gender of reluctant partner and gender of subject was not significant, *multivariate* $F(2, 193) = 2.51, p > .05$, nor were the main effects for gender of reluctant partner and gender of subject, *multivariate* $F(2, 193) = 1.09, p > .05$, and *multivariate* $F(2, 193) = 2.65, p > .05$, respectively, indicating that the emotional and relational factors related to discrepancies in the desired level of intimacy characterized by a reluctant male or a reluctant female dating partner did not differ significantly, according to both male and female subjects. For the most part, subjects indicated that interactions with their partner concerning discrepancies in preferred level of sexual intimacy were somewhat unpleasant ($M = 2.28$, $SD = 1.53$) on a 6-point scale. However, subjects reported experiencing a moderate amount of romantic interest in their dating partner both before and after the disagreement ($M = 3.41, SD = 1.27$, and $M = 3.11$ and $SD = 1.44$, respectively).

DISCUSSION

Prevalence and Profiles of Disagreements

Discrepancies in the desired level of sexual intimacy are common experiences for heterosexual dating men and women. Overall, 66% of the respondents reported that they had experienced either a male- or female-reluctant disagreement within the year preceding the study. The higher prevalence of disagreements in which the woman was the reluctant partner compared to disagreements in which the man was the reluctant partner corresponds to the traditional script designating men as the initiators and aggressors in sexual encounters. However, the substantial proportion of women and men reporting men as reluctant and women as attempting to influence their reluctant partner to engage in sexual activity clearly challenges the stereotypes of women as passive recipients of men's sexual advances and men as assuming an "ever-ready" posture with regard to sex.

Of particular interest, we found that men and women employ a similar script when attempting to influence a reluctant partner. The two types of disagreements were characterized by similar profiles with regard to relationship status, shared sexual histories, and situational factors. However, reluctant men were more likely than were reluctant women to end up participating in the disputed level of sexual activity. As being reluctant is discordant with the prescriptions of appropriate behavior for men, it may be more difficult for men than for women to continue their resistance when faced with a partner who continues to indicate sexual interest. As such, men may be more easily influenced by an ardent partner.

Alternately, it may be that men are somewhat more likely to accept women's refusals than women are to accept men's refusals because of increases in campus preventive efforts and media attention given to the issue of women's experiences of sexual assault. Men tended to report the use of more influence strategies by women than by themselves, suggesting that women made a stronger attempt to overcome a partner's reluctance by employing a wider repertoire of influence behaviors. Further, according to both women and men, women were less likely than were men to comply with a partner's refusal without any attempt to influence. Women may be less likely to perceive their partner's refusal as legitimate and therefore may continue to try to influence him, stopping short of coercion. If women believe the cultural myth that a man is always interested in and ready to engage in sex (Zilbergeld, 1992), they may also believe that it is impossible to victimize male sexual partners.

Actor-Observer Differences in Reports

The results reflect a tendency to view one's behavior in more positive terms than one's partner's behavior. For example, women were less likely to report that intercourse, a high level of sexual intimacy, constituted the disputed sexual activity for male-reluctant disagreements compared to female-reluctant disagreements. Men reported more noncompliance with a reluctant partner's refusal by women than for themselves. Moreover, both men and women attributed the use of more negative influence strategies to the other gender than to themselves. This self-enhancing trend may be related to the response bias noted in studies of men's sexual coercion of women in which self-reported victimization rates are consistently higher than self-reported perpetration rates (e.g., Koss et al., 1987). These findings extend earlier research as they demonstrate that both men and women may be prone to this self-enhancing response bias.

The self-enhancing trend may have been a result of respondents' lack of awareness regarding the impact of their influence behaviors on their partner. If so, this trend has important implications for interpreting past coercion research, in that low self-reported perpetration rates may truly represent a failure to recognize or acknowledge one's coercive actions. In support of this hypothesis, respondents were found to attribute their reluctance to relationship-related reasons and their partner's reluctance to situational factors. Attributing situational factors to their partner's reluctance may serve to minimize the impact of the negative event (i.e., refusal of one's sexual advance) and help to enhance and maintain satisfaction with the relationship (Baucom, Sayers, & Duhe, 1989; Bradbury & Fincham, 1992). Respondents may have attributed personal or relational factors for their reluctance because of differences in the information they possess (i.e., covert thoughts and feelings, information about their behavioral variability over time and situations).

Resolution of Discrepancies in Desired Sexual Intimacy

The discrepancies in the desired level of sexual intimacy were resolved most frequently by compliance with the refusal and least frequently by noncompliance on behalf of the more "ardent" partner. This corresponds to the findings of Byers and Lewis (1988) in their investigation of disagreements characterized by ardent male and reluctant female dating partners. Clearly, most discrepancies in the desired levels of sexual intimacy do not result in the use of coercion. This finding suggests a need to reexamine assumptions guiding some coercion researchers about the inherently detrimental nature of disagreements about sexual intimacy. Even though most respondents indicated that these interactions were somewhat unpleasant, discrepancies in desired sexual intimacy were not associated with lessened romantic interest in one's partner. Contrary to our prediction, women were no more likely to comply than were men and men were no more likely to coerce than were women. Men's and women's reactions to the disagreements did not differ in any notable way, although differences in reactions may have been noted had we investigated less benign interactions.

CONCLUSION

Both men and women experience discrepancies in desired sexual intimacy, and at times attempt to influence a reluctant dating partner to engage in unwanted sexual activity. Of particular interest, men's and women's behavior appears to be quite similar when a person is faced with a reluctant sexual partner, indicating substantial overlap of gender roles and endorsement of a similar script. Coercion, an extreme form of influence, is not a typical aspect of this sexual script. For the most part, discrepancies in desired sexual intimacy were not related to severe negative emotional consequences or the introduction of discord in heterosexual relationships. Thus, traditional perspectives regarding the use of sexual influence appear to be of limited use, calling into question the veracity of the stereotypes guiding past researchers.

A limitation of the current study was that it was retrospective, thus introducing potential error from faulty recall of events. In the future, researchers should employ a prospective type of methodology when studying discrepancies in desired intimacy, such as a diary-type format, which has been used successfully in the past (Byers & Heinlein, 1989; O'Sullivan & Byers, 1992). Caution should be exercised when assuming that the men and the women were describing the same domain of events as the men and the women in the current study were not known to be dating each other and overlap in their descriptions may be coincidental. A comparison of couples' reports could be useful in examining further the discrepancies in reports of disagreements. Furthermore, researchers need to examine how discrepancies in the desired level of sexual intimacy are resolved in relationships characterized by different ages, ethnic groups, and orientations.

REFERENCES

Aizenman, M., & Kelley, G. (1988). The incidence of violence and acquaintance rape in dating relationships among college men and women. *Journal of College Student Development, 29,* 305-311.

Baucom, D. H., Sayers, S. L., & Duhe, A. (1989). Attributional style and attributional patterns among married couples. *Journal of Personality and Social Psychology, 56,* 596-607.

Bradbury, T. N., & Fincham, F. D. (1992). Attributions and behavior in marital interaction. *Journal of Personality and Social Psychology, 63,* 613-628.

Brickman, J., & Briere, J. (1984). Incidence of rape and sexual assault in an urban Canadian population. *International Journal of Women's Studies, 7,* 195-206.

Byers, E. S., & Heinlein, L. (1989). Predicting initiations and refusals of sexual activities in married and cohabiting heterosexual couples. *The Journal of Sex Research, 26,* 210-231.

Byers, E. S., & Lewis, K. (1988). Dating couples' disagreements over the desired level of sexual intimacy. *The Journal of Sex Research, 24,* 15-29.

Byers, E. S., & Wilson, P. (1985). Accuracy of women's expectations regarding men's responses to refusals of sexual advances in dating situations. *International Journal of Women's Studies, 4,* 376-387.

Carroll, J. L., Volk, K. D., & Hyde, J. S. (1985). Differences between males and females in motives for engaging in sexual intercourse. *Archives of Sexual Behavior, 14,* 131-139.

Check, J. V. P., & Malamuth, N. (1985). An empirical assessment of some feminist hypotheses about rape. *International Journal of Women's Studies, 8,* 414-422.

Christopher, F. S., & Cate, R. M. (1985). Anticipated influences on sexual decision-making for first intercourse. *Family Relations, 34,* 265-270.

Christopher, F. S., & Frandsen, M. M. (1990). Strategies of influence in sex and dating. *Journal of Social and Personal Relationships, 7,* 89-105.

Clark, R. D., & Hatfield, E. (1989). Gender differences in receptivity to sexual offers. *Journal of Psychology and Human Sexuality, 2,* 39-55.

Finlay, B., Starnes, C. E., & Alvarez, F. B. (1985). Recent changes in sex-role ideology among divorced men and women: Some possible causes and implications. *Sex Roles, 12,* 637-653.

Knox, D., & Wilson, K. (1981). Dating behaviors of university students. *Family Relations, 30,* 255-258.

Koss, M. P., Gidycz, C. A., & Wisniewski, N. (1987). The scope of rape: Incidence and prevalence of sexual aggression and victimization in a national sample of higher education students. *Journal of Consulting and Clinical Psychology, 55,* 162-170.

Lawson, A. (1988). *Adultery.* New York: Basic Books.

Lewin, M. (1985). Unwanted intercourse: The difficulty of saying no. *Psychology of Women Quarterly, 9,* 184-192.

Malamuth, N. M., Sockloskie, R. J., Koss, M. P., & Tanaka, J. S. (1991). Characteristics of aggressors against women: Testing a model using a national sample of college students. *Journal of Consulting and Clinical Psychology, 59,* 670-681.

McCormick, N. B. (1979). Come-ons and put-offs: Unmarried students' strategies for having and avoiding sexual intercourse. *Psychology of Women Quarterly, 4,* 194-211.

Miller, B., & Marshall, J. C. (1987). Coercive sex on the university campus. *Journal of College Student Personnel, 28,* 38-47.

Muehlenhard, C. L., & Cook, S. W. (1988). Men's self-reports of unwanted sexual activity. *The Journal of Sex Research, 24,* 58-72.

Muehlenhard, C. L., & Linton, M. A. (1987). Date rape and sexual aggression in dating situations: Incidence and risk factors. *Journal of Counseling Psychology, 34,* 186-196.

Mynatt, C. R., & Allgeier, E. R. (1990). Risk factors, self-attributions, and adjustment problems among victims of sexual coercion. *Journal of Applied Social Psychology, 20,* 130-153.

O'Sullivan, L. F., & Byers, E. S. (1992). College students' incorporation of initiator and restrictor roles in sexual dating interactions. *The Journal of Sex Research, 29,* 435-446.

O'Sullivan, L. F., & Byers, E. S. (1993). Eroding stereotypes: College women's attempts to influence reluctant male sexual partners. *The Journal of Sex Research, 30,* 270-282.

Perper, T., & Weis, D. L. (1987). Proceptive and rejective strategies in U.S. and Canadian college women. *The Journal of Sex Research, 23,* 455-480.

Poppen, P. J., & Segal, N. J. (1988). The influence of sex and sex role orientation on sexual coercion. *Sex Roles, 19,* 689-701.

Sherwin, R., & Corbett, S. (1985). Campus sexual norms and dating relationships: A trend analysis. *The Journal of Sex Research, 21,* 258- 274.

Stets, J. E., & Pirog-Good, M. A. (1987). Violence in dating relationships. *Social Psychology Quarterly, 50,* 237-246.

Struckman-Johnson, C. (1988). Forced sex on dates: It happens to men, too. *The Journal of Sex Research, 24,* 234-241.

Zilbergeld, B. (1992). *The new male sexuality.* New York: Bantam Books.

Coercive Heterosexual Sexuality in Dating Relationships of College Students: Implications of Differential Male-Female Experiences

Matthew Hogben, MA
Donn Byrne, PhD
Merle E. Hamburger, PhD

SUMMARY. Although it has generally been assumed that most instances of coercive sexual acts involve male coercion against female targets, recent data (appearing in the literature beginning in the late 1980s) suggest that the reverse experience is also common. In the present investigation, the Ross and Allgeier Sexual Experience Questionnaire was administered to 214 university students (113 women and 101 men) who reported past interactions in which they

Matthew Hogben, Donn Byrne, and Merle E. Hamburger are all affiliated with The University at Albany, State University of New York.

Address correspondence to Donn Byrne, Department of Psychology, University at Albany, State University of New York, Albany, NY 12222.

The authors thank Kathryn Kelley for her suggestions at various points during the investigation and for her comments on this article; Ronald R. Ross and Elizabeth Rice Allgeier for providing them with the measuring instrument they developed; E. R. Allgeier, William A. Fisher, Marty Klein, Naomi B. McCormick, Eleanor Smith, and Cindy Struckman-Johnson for their very helpful corrections and comments; Stephanie McGowan for her assistance in locating references; and Steve Flores, Mary Ann D'Agostino, and Donyale Washington for gathering data, scoring protocols, and entering data for analysis.

[Haworth co-indexing entry note]: "Coercive Heterosexual Sexuality in Dating Relationships of College Students: Implications of Differential Male-Female Experiences." Hogben, Matthew, Donn Byrne, and Merle E. Hamburger. Co-published simultaneously in *Journal of Psychology & Human Sexuality* (The Haworth Press, Inc.) Vol. 8, No. 1/2, 1996, pp. 69-78; and: *Sexual Coercion in Dating Relationships* (ed: E. Sandra Byers, and Lucia F. O'Sullivan) The Haworth Press, Inc., 1996, pp. 69-78. Single or multiple copies of this article are available from The Haworth Document Delivery Service [1-800-342-9678, 9:00 a.m. - 5:00 p.m. (EST)].

engaged in sexual coercion, were the targets of such coercion, both, or neither. The findings ($p < .001$) were consistent with widely held assumptions that men more often coerce, whereas women are more often the targets of these acts. It also appears that, although men behave more coercively than women, both genders report coercing and being coerced when investigators ask the appropriate questions of both men and women. Empirical reports indicating similar or even reversed male-female coercion may be attributable to methodological variations involving the specific wording of questions about coercion and differences in the interpretation of such questions by male and female research participants. The implications of gender-specific coercive tactics, reasons for compliance, and the effects of having been coerced are discussed. *[Article copies available from The Haworth Document Delivery Service: 1-800-342-9678.]*

Sexual interaction ideally involves mutual consent, but sexual acts quite often include attempts by one individual to gain the behavioral compliance of a partner who is unwilling or disinterested. In one study of male and female college students, almost half described sexual disagreements with a date, and in each instance the man wanted to engage in a given sexual act, but the woman did not (Byers & Lewis, 1988). Most men simply accept this kind of refusal as definitive, but some men attempt to reverse the woman's decision. The resulting coercive activity can be verbal, physical, or both (Struckman-Johnson & Struckman-Johnson, 1994). Coercion is often ordered along a continuum with force or threat of force on one extreme and verbal ploys (false professions of love, persistent persuasive arguments, threats to end the relationship, etc.) on the other (Christopher & Frandsen, 1990).

Implicit in this information is the traditional assumption–long accepted by most investigators of sexuality–that almost all sexually coercive acts are perpetrated by men against women. The perceived scenario of male sexual aggressors and female targets has emerged over almost four decades from numerous investigations in which women reported being coerced by men or men reported having coerced women (Craig, 1990).

The assumption that only men coerce was first questioned in the late 1980s when new data indicated that substantial percentages of men are sexually coerced by women. In one investigation, 22% of the women and 16% of the men reported that they had been forced to engage in sexual intercourse on a date at least once (Struckman-Johnson, 1988). In a second investigation, male students were asked about their experiences as targets of coercion since age 16; 24% described the use of pressure or force by women, 4% by men, and 6% by both (Struckman-Johnson & Struckman-

Johnson, 1994). In a third study, Aizenman and Kelley (1988) reported that 29% of the women and 14% of the men reported having been forced to have intercourse against their will in a dating relationship. Even more surprisingly, in a fourth study (Muehlenhard & Cook, 1988), most women (97.5%) *and* most men (93.5%) reported having engaged in unwanted sexual activity. Further, *more* men (62.7%) than women (46.3%) said they had engaged in unwanted sexual intercourse. Such data were seemingly inconsistent with existing assumptions and theories, and the authors of these papers were appropriately cautious in interpreting their findings. Others were not.

Quoting these findings, some nonscientists–following specific ideological agendas–casually dismissed the dangers of date rape and the necessity of programs designed to protect women. For example, the data were touted as evidence bolstering one aspect of the *Playboy* editorial view that male and female college students are simply experimenting with sex as amateurish equal partners (The paradox . . ., 1990) and that "college courtship rituals" should be accepted as normative behavior rather than condemned and criminalized as coercive sexuality (Forum, 1991, p. 42). Columnist George Will (1994, p. A-12) stated that federal funding to study sexual assaults on campuses is ". . . a monument to the feminist fiction that in a world infested with predatory males, women students risk life and limb just walking from dorms to libraries, not to mention the terrors of dating." He concluded that the proposed Violence Against Women Act in President Clinton's crime bill ". . . genuflects at every altar in the feminist church."

Despite this hyperbole, if both genders are active in pressuring partners to comply with their sexual demands, and if both may become the targets of such pressure, this new information would obviously require a rethinking of current conceptions of sexual interactions in dating relationships. The pitfall in jumping to radical conclusions is the fact that research and its interpretation are inseparable from values and politics (Byrne & Kelley, 1989; Muehlenhard, Harney, & Jones, 1992). Before jumping, therefore, we felt compelled to attempt to replicate and perhaps explain these new findings. How might one account for data indicating that coercive sexual acts are not exclusively under male proprietorship?

A crucial observation is that in most past research, men were not asked about being sexual targets and women were not asked about their sexual coerciveness (Struckman-Johnson, 1988). Possibly, then, the seemingly ubiquitous sex differences were an unintended artifact of research methodology guided by the unquestioned assumptions prevailing among investigators. Even in the original Kinsey studies beginning in the 1940s, women were asked about being sexually assaulted by men, but men were not asked the analogous question (Sarrel & Masters, 1982). Obviously, the same questions must be asked of both genders to determine whether their responses are similar or different, and that is done in the present investigation. It is also possible, of course, that sexual mores have undergone rapid changes in recent years. Consistent with this suggestion is the finding of a substantial increase between 1979 and 1988 in pornographic movie scenes depicting reluctant males being sexually pressured by persuasive females (Brosius, Weaver, & Staab, 1993). It is conceivable that female coercion of male targets may have become a common experience in dating interactions during the past decade (O'Sullivan & Byers, 1993), resulting in post-1987 findings of much more coercion of men by women than was commonly assumed. These methodological and temporal possibilities are examined in this investigation.

METHOD

Subjects

The initial pool of research participants consisted of 250 University at Albany students enrolled in the introductory psychology course in 1992. They took part in this study by voluntarily signing up for an investigation surveying sexual experiences, as partial fulfillment of a class requirement. As a result of errors made in administering the questionnaire and of subjects' self-described sexual orientation as homosexual, 36 individuals were dropped from the study, leaving a final total of 214 (113 women and 101 men) for analysis. All students (aged 18 to 23) completed the survey anonymously in small groups of 10-20 persons in widely separated seats in a large lecture room (to ensure privacy), and each student had the opportunity to discontinue participation at any time without loss of research credit.

Sexual Experience Questionnaire

A revised version of the Sexual Experience Questionnaire (Ross & Allgeier, 1991) was given to each subject. The original measuring instrument asked male participants to estimate the number of their successful and unsuccessful attempts to engage in eight specific sexual behaviors when the partner was not willing. These acts ranged from "kissing" and "putting your hand on a woman's chest" to "engaging in vaginal intercourse" and "engaging in anal intercourse." There are no behavioral overlaps among any of the acts assessed, although any or all might occur within a single encounter. Thus, responses consist of real-number estimates that are added to obtain an index of coercive acts.

The revised questionnaire asked both male and female students about (a) experiences as the unwilling target of such activity, (b) experiences as the initiator of each activity with an unwilling partner, and (c) whether each coercion attempt was successful or unsuccessful. Coefficient alphas of .77 for the respondent's coercion attempts and .81 for attempts by others to coerce the respondent indicate satisfactory internal consistency.

RESULTS

For both genders, the number of successful self-initiated coercive attempts correlated substantially with the number of unsuccessful self-initiated coercive attempts: for men, $r(99) = .50$, $p < .001$, and for women, $r(111) = .82$, $p < .001$. These correlations suggest a relatively consistent pattern of coercive sexuality across partners; that is, a person's characteristic pattern of coercive behavior sometimes leads to success and sometimes to failure in securing a partner's compliance. Also, for both men and women, the number of experiences as the target of successful coercion attempts by partners correlated significantly with the number of experiences as the target of unsuccessful coercion attempts: for men, $r(99) = .36$, $p < .001$, and for women, $r(111) = .46$, $p < .001$. We concluded that combining the successful and unsuccessful categories was justified both for coercing and for being the target of coercion.

These data were first examined in terms of how many individuals had or had not ever coerced and how many had or had not ever been coerced, yielding gender differences parallel to those of Struckman-Johnson (1988) and others. As hypothesized, a higher proportion of men (41%) than of women (24%) reported having at least once coerced a partner sexually, $\chi^2(1) = 27.42$, $p < .001$. Also, a higher proportion of women (79%) than of men (52%) reported having at least once been coerced by a partner sexually, $\chi^2(1) = 22.18$, $p < .001$.

A second analysis dealt with the cumulative coercion scores. The means and standard deviations of the self-reported incidents of sexual coercion are shown in Table 1.[1] Again, gender differences were found for type of sexually coercive experience. A between-within analysis of variance with repeated measures indicated a significant interaction between gender of subject and coercion by self versus coercion by partner, $F(1,211) = 23.3$, $p < .001$. More specifically, men reported more attempts to coerce

TABLE 1. Means and Standard Deviations of Self-Reported Sexual Coercion

	Women (n = 113)		Men (n = 101)	
Variable	M	SD	M	SD
Subject's successful and unsuccessful attempts to coerce others	2.34	11.06	13.55	30.25
Others' successful and unsuccessful attempts to coerce subject	21.16	30.28	6.95	17.93

women sexually, compared with the frequency of such reported attempts by women to coerce men, $F(1,212) = 13.52$, $p < .001$, whereas women reported having more often been the target of coercion attempts by men, compared with male reports of being the target of coercion attempts by women, $F(1,212) = 16.93$, $p < .001$.

Both analyses indicate greater coerciveness by men than by women, but both also indicate that a substantial proportion of male college students are the targets of coercion by their female dating partners.

DISCUSSION

Altogether, recent findings indicating both male and female coerciveness are confirmed, as were more traditional findings of gender differences in frequency. There is clearly no indication of dramatic temporal changes in gender-based sexual insistence. Why, then, have investigations differed in indicating greater male coerciveness, greater female coerciveness, or gender-equal coerciveness?

A plausible reason is that the investigators who study coercion have used a variety of measuring instruments (Porter & Critelli, 1992). As a result, the devices Aizenman and Kelley (1988), Muehlenhard and Cook (1988), Struckman-Johnson (1988), and Struckman-Johnson and Struckman-Johnson (1994) used to assess coercion differ somewhat from each other and from those used in other research, including the current study. For example, most past research has relied on the Sexual Experiences

Survey (Koss & Oros, 1982) with questions that take the form, "Has a woman given in to sex play when she didn't want to because she was overwhelmed by your continual arguments and pressure?" On the Coercive Sexuality Scale (Rapaport & Burkhart, 1984), the wording is, "How many times have you had intercourse with a woman against her will?" Lott, Reilly, and Howard (1982) asked a large sample of both men and women about "sexual assault" (use of force, threatened force, or a weapon) and found extreme sex differences in that 97% of those assaulted were female, and 97% of the assaulters were male. Similar results were obtained by Poppen and Segal (1988), who asked both sexes about the use of physical force and verbal arguments. As noted earlier, the Sexual Experience Questionnaire used here refers to the frequency of engaging in specific behaviors when the partner "was not willing" to do so and the acts of a partner "when you were not willing."

In contrast, Muehlenhard and Cook (1988) asked their participants if they had engaged in "unwanted sexual activity" for any of 13 possible reasons. With the benefit of hindsight, it seems very likely that "unwanted" is interpreted more benignly by respondents than "unwilling" or "didn't want to." Further, those authors reported that the specific coercive actions of a man tend to include forceful verbal or physical attempts to achieve compliance, but the coercive actions of a woman tend to involve enticement, as when she unbuttons or removes some of her clothing. Additionally, the reasons for complying differ. Women said they feared male aggression, the ending of the relationship, and the consequences of unmet male needs. Men said their compliance was based on self-esteem and interpersonal concerns, such as assumptions about peer expectancies, the belief that compliance would enhance their popularity, and the possibility that refusal would result in their being perceived as gay, shy, or inexperienced.

The Struckman-Johnson results and those of Aizenman and Kelley are less easily explained on the basis of item wording. The former investigator asked respondents about the number of times "you have been forced to engage in sexual intercourse while on a date" and the number of times "you forced someone to engage in sexual intercourse while on a date," and the latter investigators asked whether respondents had been "forced to have intercourse against their will." Perhaps "forced" isn't interpreted literally, especially by men. When asked, male targets tend to describe force as psychological pressure; female targets describe physical force (Muehlenhard & Cook, 1988; Struckman-Johnson, 1988). When Struckman-Johnson and Struckman-Johnson (1994) asked men specifically about being "pressured" (psychological coercion) or "forced" (physical coercion), the vast majority (88%) of female coercive activity was described as pressure. In addition, the self-reported aftereffects of coercion are found to be gender-specific. Struckman-Johnson (1988) reported that most coerced women (88%) in her sample were emotionally upset by the experience and that the negative effects were long-term (78%); most of the coerced men felt good (27%) or neutral (46%) about the experience, and most (69%) reported no long-term impact. Similarly, the typical man in the Struckman-Johnson and Struckman-Johnson (1994) study indicated only minimal impact from being coerced by a woman.

Investigators who ask both men and women about coercing *and* being coerced have revealed new aspects of sexual interactions as well as gender differences in how one goes about obtaining the sexual compliance of a partner, the reasons for that person's compliance, and the psychological consequences of complying (O'Sullivan & Byers, 1993). Even if men and women coerce in different ways, however, one need not conclude either that male coerciveness should be ignored or that female sexual pressure is an irrelevant or trivial phenomenon.

Findings of gender differences do not eliminate judgmental questions or provide ready answers to them (Muehlenhard, Friedman, & Thomas, 1985). Consider a few examples.

1. Should physical coercion be differentiated from verbal coercion? An extreme view has been expressed by Catherine MacKinnon and others who equate verbal coercion with physical violence. If such equations are reasonable, most women and a sizable segment of the male population have been sexually assaulted. We disagree with such overinclusive blurring and trivializing. Different standards are ordinarily applied to words and deeds, and we believe that a very important distinction should be made between an individual who "feels violated" by unacceptable words and another who is physically raped.

2. Should force and the threat of force be evaluated more harshly than enticement as a coercive technique? We believe so, as do most research participants (Struckman-Johnson & Struckman-Johnson, 1991). Perhaps the difference is analogous to a more negative evaluation of an armed robber than of a charming swindler, each of whom illegally obtains money from victims.

3. How should one judge the use of force in an unequal heterosexual interaction in which men are likely to have a physical, economic, and political advantage over women? Because threats and acts based on actual power are especially credible and effective, we conclude that they should be evaluated as especially offensive.

4. Is compliance to a partner's demands based on fear of threatened physical actions more emotionally damaging than compliance based on fear of tarnishing one's self-image? We think so, but this judgment may simply reflect cultural predilections. Empirical evidence for this proposed difference is needed.

The final answers to all such questions do not lie in emotional assertions but, rather, in the attempt to obtain relevant empirical evidence and in a thoughtful examination of complex, value-laden issues.

NOTE

1. Given the relatively large standard deviations, it seemed prudent to determine the possible effect of "outliers" on the results. We found that removal of extreme scores (> 2.5 *SD*) on each variable did not significantly alter any reported findings.

REFERENCES

Aizenman, M., & Kelley, G. (1988). The incidence of violence and acquaintance rape in dating relationships among college men and women. *Journal of College Student Development, 29,* 305-311.

Brosius, H.-B., Weaver, J. B., III, & Staab, J. F. (1993). Exploring the social and sexual "reality" of contemporary pornography. *The Journal of Sex Research, 30,* 161-170.

Byers, E. S., & Lewis, K. (1988). Dating couples' disagreements over the desired level of sexual intimacy. *The Journal of Sex Research, 24,* 15-29.

Byrne, D., & Kelley, K. (1989). Basing legislative action on research data: Prejudice, prudence, and empirical limitations. In D. Zillmann & J. Bryant (Eds.), *Pornography: Research advances and policy considerations* (pp. 363-385). Hillsdale, NJ: Lawrence Erlbaum Associates.

Christopher, F. S., & Frandsen, M. M. (1990). Strategies of influence in sex and dating. *Journal of Social and Personal Relationships, 7,* 89-105.

Craig, M. E. (1990). Coercive sexuality in dating relationships: A situational model. *Clinical Psychology Review, 10,* 395-423.

Forum. (1991, February). *Playboy* (p. 42).

Koss, M. P., & Oros, C. J. (1982). Sexual experiences survey: A research instrument investigating sexual aggression and victimization. *Journal of Counseling and Clinical Psychology, 50,* 455-457.

Lott, B., Reilly, M. E., & Howard, D. R. (1982). Sexual assault and harassment: A campus community case study. *Journal of Women in Culture and Society, 8,* 296-319.

Muehlenhard, C. L., & Cook, S. W. (1988). Men's self-reports of unwanted sexual activity. *The Journal of Sex Research, 24,* 58-72.

Muehlenhard, C. L., Friedman, D. E., & Thomas, C. M. (1985). Is date rape justifiable? The effects of dating activity, who initiated, who paid, and men's attitudes toward women. *Psychology of Women Quarterly, 9,* 297-310.

Muehlenhard, C. L., Harney, P. A., & Jones, J. M. (1992). From "victim-precipitated rape" to "date rape": How far have we come? *Annual Review of Sex Research, 3,* 219-253.

O'Sullivan, L. F., & Byers, E. S. (1993). Eroding stereotypes: College women's attempts to influence reluctant male sexual partners. *The Journal of Sex Research, 30,* 270-282.

Paradox, the: The double standard is alive. (1990, November). *Playboy* (p. 55).

Poppen, P. J., & Segal, N. J. (1988). The influence of sex and sex role orientation on sexual coercion. *Sex Roles, 19,* 689-701.

Porter, J. F., & Critelli, J. W. (1992). Measurement of sexual aggression in college men: A methodological analysis. *Archives of Sexual Behavior, 21,* 525-542.

Rapaport, K., & Burkhart, B. (1984). Personality and attitudinal characteristics of sexually coercive college males. *Journal of Abnormal Psychology, 93,* 216-221.

Ross, R. R., & Allgeier, E. R. (1991, August). *Correlates of males' femininity with sexually coercive attitudes and behavior.* Paper presented at the meeting of the American Psychological Association, San Francisco, CA.

Sarrel, P. M., & Masters, W. H. (1982). Sexual molestation of men by women. *Archives of Sexual Behavior, 11,* 117-131.

Struckman-Johnson, C. (1988). Forced sex on dates: It happens to men, too. *The Journal of Sex Research, 24,* 234-241.

Struckman-Johnson, C., & Struckman-Johnson, D. (1994). Men pressured and forced into sexual experience. *Archives of Sexual Behavior, 23,* 93-114.

Struckman-Johnson, D., & Struckman-Johnson, C. (1991). Men and women's acceptance of coercive sexual strategies varied by initiator gender and couple intimacy. *Sex Roles, 25,* 661-676.

Will, G. (1994, July 14). Clinton's anti-crime bill will increase for the law. *Albany Times Union,* p. A-12.

Post-Traumatic Stress Disorder Among College Student Victims of Acquaintance Assault

Catalina M. Arata, PhD
Barry R. Burkhart, PhD

SUMMARY. Post-traumatic stress disorder symptomatology was evaluated among 316 college women who reported coercive sexual experiences. History of victimization, attributions of blame, and current symptoms were assessed. Acquaintance assault victims reported significantly higher levels of Post-Traumatic Stress Disorder (PTSD) symptoms than non-victims, and one-third exceeded criteria for clinical levels of distress. Situational variables, including the type of assault, were not associated with PTSD status or symptoms. Cognitive appraisals, however, were significantly associated with PTSD symptomatology. Attributions of blame were all associated with PTSD status, with characterological self-blame also being associated with level of current symptomatology. The results document the negative psychological consequences of acquaintance assaults among college students and help to focus the efforts of treatment programs for acquaintance assault victims. In addition, the results highlight the importance of cognitive appraisals in mediating effects of sexual victimization. *[Article copies available from The Haworth Document Delivery Service: 1-800-342-9678.]*

In the past 20 years, the study of sexual assault has come full circle. No longer ignored, talk of incest, rape, and date rape are everyday occurrences

Catalina M. Arata is affiliated with the University of South Alabama. Barry R. Burkhart is affiliated with Auburn University.

[Haworth co-indexing entry note]: "Post-Traumatic Stress Disorder Among College Student Victims of Acquaintance Assault." Arata, Catalina M., and Barry R. Burkhart. Co-published simultaneously in *Journal of Psychology & Human Sexuality* (The Haworth Press, Inc.) Vol. 8, No. 1/2, 1996, pp. 79-92; and: *Sexual Coercion in Dating Relationships* (ed: E. Sandra Byers, and Lucia F. O'Sullivan) The Haworth Press, Inc., 1996, pp. 79-92. Single or multiple copies of this article are available from The Haworth Document Delivery Service [1-800-342-9678, 9:00 a.m. - 5:00 p.m. (EST)].

in the media and have even become litmus tests for cultural critics. Although public and professional recognition and acceptance of the magnitude of these social problems has increased tremendously, the research base in many ways is still in its infancy. Early research on sexual assault, though often anecdotal, began to reveal the significant, damaging effects suffered by victims. An important task for researchers has been to further describe these effects, particularly with hidden victims (Koss & Oros, 1982).

It is now known that sexual assault at any age can have extremely negative effects on the life of the victim (see Briere & Runtz, 1993, and Resick, 1993, for reviews). Although early researchers focused primarily on identified victims reporting to rape crisis centers, more recent researchers have examined hidden victims. Many women sexually assaulted by acquaintances not only do not report the assault but may not even label it as such (Mandoki & Burkhart, 1991).

ACQUAINTANCE RAPE

Bechhofer and Parrot (1991) defined acquaintance rape as sexual assault that occurs between people who know each other. The study of acquaintance assaults has focused on college student samples, both because they are a high-risk group for this crime because of both their age and social circumstances and because they are a group accessible to researchers (Koss, 1993). Much of the early research on acquaintance assaults has been directed primarily toward identifying its prevalence and the variables that are associated with being a victim or a perpetrator. There has been little research, however, regarding the psychological consequences of acquaintance assaults.

Whether the findings from the broader sexual assault literature can be applied to acquaintance assaults is not clear. Much of this research has focused specifically on victims of rape. Katz (1991) reviewed the research on stranger versus acquaintance rape and found that no consistent pattern of findings has emerged, with relationship status at times mediating effects of rape and at other times having no effect (see also Katz & Mazur, 1979; Ruch & Chandler, 1983). Katz (1991) theorized that rather than one being worse than the other, stranger rape would have different effects from acquaintance rape and the effect may be more evident over time rather than in the initial crisis phase. Katz (1991) found, consistent with her hypotheses, that the level of pre-rape closeness to the perpetrator prior to the assault was associated with increased self-blame and with a longer recovery process.

POST-TRAUMATIC STRESS DISORDER

Researchers studying the effects of sexual assault among community and rape-crisis center samples have frequently identified Post-Traumatic Stress Disorder (PTSD) as a common consequence of sexual assault (Burge, 1988; Resnick, Kilpatrick, Best, & Kramer, 1992; Rothbaum, Foa, Riggs, Murdok, & Walsh, 1992). PTSD is a diagnostic category that was first identified among veterans of wars, but it also characterizes the symptom response of many sexual assault victims. PTSD is characterized by reexperiencing symptoms (i.e., nightmares, flashbacks), avoidance symptoms (i.e., numbing, avoidance of reminders), and increased arousal (i.e., hypervigilance, sleep disturbance) related to a specific traumatic event and reminders of that event (American Psychiatric Association, 1987). Researchers have found PTSD rates among female crime victims to range from 21% (Resnick et al., 1992) to 60% (Kilpatrick, Saunders, Amick-McMullen, Best, and Veronen, 1987). In a recent national survey, Kilpatrick, Edmunds, and Seymour (1992) reported that 31% of all rape victims developed PTSD at some point during their lives.

Given the high rates of PTSD found among community samples of victims, it seems probable that PTSD would also be prevalent among a college sample of acquaintance assault victims; however, no researcher has directly addressed this issue.

COGNITIVE APPRAISALS

Both situational and cognitive variables have been identified as correlates of PTSD among victims of sexual assault. Kilpatrick et al. (1987) found that experiencing a completed rape, perceiving life threat, and experiencing physical injury increased the risk among crime victims of developing PTSD. Resick (1993), on the other hand, reported that cognitive beliefs were associated with different symptoms of PTSD. In a prospective, longitudinal study of rape victims, Rothbaum, Foa, Riggs, Murdok, and Walsh (1992) found that women with persistent PTSD symptoms had exhibited more severe symptoms initially.

The results of these studies suggest that a number of variables mediate risk for development of PTSD following sexual assault, including initial distress, cognitive appraisals and situational variables. The role of cognitive appraisals is consistent with the literature on stress and coping that suggests that the long-term cognitive appraisal a person makes of a situation may effect his or her ability to cope with a particular stressor (Lazarus & Folkman, 1984), and therefore may help explain differences in adjustment.

In relation to sexual assault, Janoff-Bulman (1979) proposed that appraisals of self-blame are common consequences. She suggested that some rape victims blamed their character or some enduring quality of themselves (characterological self-blame) while others blamed their behavior (behavioral self-blame). She suggested that persons blaming their character would experience more distress than women who blamed their behavior. Consistent with Janoff-Bulman's theory, several researchers have identified self-blame as a cognitive appraisal associated with higher levels of distress following sexual assault (Katz, 1991; Mandoki & Burkhart, 1989).

The purpose of this study was to examine the effects of sexual assault among a sample of college women, particularly evidence of PTSD and the role of self-blame in mediating effects. There were a number of hypotheses regarding the possible effects:

a. Victims of sexual assaults by acquaintances would display symptoms of PTSD.
b. Forcible rape victims would be more likely to have symptoms of PTSD than victims of other types of sexual assaults.
c. Attributions of blame would be associated with PTSD, with women exhibiting greater self-blame being more likely to exhibit symptoms of PTSD.
d. Situational variables, such as the relationship between the perpetrator and victim, use of drugs/alcohol, and method of coercion and resistance, would be associated with PTSD status.

METHOD

Subjects

Eight hundred twenty-eight women were recruited from undergraduate psychology courses at a major university in the southeastern portion of the United States. Subjects were recruited from March 1988 through November 1988. Subjects were told that the study would involve completing anonymous questionnaires regarding previous sexual experiences, as well as their feelings and beliefs about these experiences. Written informed consent was obtained from subjects prior to completing the questionnaire. Students received extra credit for their participation.

Whenever possible, incomplete questionnaires were included in the analyses; however, the data for 15 subjects were not included because of excessive errors or missing data. Subjects ranged in age from 17 to 34, with a mean age of 19.3.

Materials

Demographic data. Subjects were questioned regarding their current age and their year in school.

Victimization measure. The Sexual Experiences Survey (SES; Koss & Oros, 1982) was revised to identify victims of coercive sexual experiences. The SES is an eight-item questionnaire that asks behaviorally specific questions regarding past coercive sexual experiences, ranging from engaging in sexual behavior (kissing or petting) because of a man's verbal coercion to engaging in intercourse because of threats or use of physical force. The questionnaire was revised by grouping questions to make four questions (see Table 1). The questionnaire was revised to shorten the total time involved in completing the entire questionnaire and to focus more on victims of rape, rather than victims of other types of sexual assaults. Although this format has not been previously used, the same types of experiences that are examined on the SES were included.

Subjects responded to the four questions concerning their experiences with sexual victimization after the age of 14. The questions were ordered from least to most intrusive in terms of the type of coercion used. For the most intrusive type of coercion reported on the revised SES, subjects were asked to respond to a number of questions surrounding the circumstances related to this victimization experience. Situational variables assessed in-

TABLE 1. Revised Sexual Experiences Survey

1. Have you had sex play (fondling, kissing, or petting, but not intercourse) when you didn't want to because of a man's continual arguments or pressure or because a man threatened or used some degree of physical force (twisting your arm, holding you down, etc.)?

2. Have you had a man attempt sexual intercourse (get on top of you, attempt to insert his penis) when you didn't want to by threatening or using some degree of force (twisting your arm, holding you down, etc.) but intercourse did *not* occur?

3. Have you had sexual intercourse when you didn't want to because a man had used his position of authority (boss, teacher, camp counselor, supervisor), or because a man gave you alcohol or drugs?

4. Have you had anal, oral, or sexual intercourse when you didn't want to because a man threatened or used some degree of physical force (twisting your arm, holding you down, etc.)?

cluded the length of time since the assault, the relationship with the perpetrator, the use of alcohol or drugs by either the victim or perpetrator, the methods of coercion (arguments, threats of physical force, twisting your arm, hitting, choking, weapon) and resistance (nothing, turn cold, reason, cry, scream, run away, physically struggle), prior intimacy with the perpetrator, and prior sexual experiences of the victim.

Victimization Groups

Subjects were divided into groups based on the most intrusive level of victimization reported on the revised SES. Of 813 subjects, 316 (39%) reported some type of coercive sexual experiences. The Molestation group included 88 (11%) subjects who reported experiencing sexual activity (fondling, kissing, or petting) when they did not want to because of a man's continual pressure or threatened or actual force. Attempted Rape victims included 73 (9%) women who reported having had a man attempt sexual intercourse against their will by threatening or using some degree of force. Coerced Rape victims included 84 (10%) women who reported having had sexual intercourse because of verbal coercion or a man's use of authority or because a man gave them alcohol or drugs. The Forcible Rape group consisted of 71 (9%) women who reported having had sexual intercourse or sex acts (e.g., anal or oral intercourse) against their will through threats or use of physical force.

Attributions of blame. The subjects' attributions of responsibility for the assault were assessed using questions devised by Meyer and Taylor (1986). Subjects were asked to rate 24 statements according to their importance in helping to explain why the coercive sexual experience they described had occurred. The coercive experience was the last question to which they had responded "yes" on the revised SES. Items were designed to assess self-blame ("I am too trusting") and blame on uncontrollable factors, society, or others ("People are too scared to get involved"). The items were factor-analyzed for this sample to produce three subscales: characterological self-blame (blame on enduring qualities of oneself), behavioral self-blame (blame on one's behavior), and societal blame (blame focused on society's attitudes and behavior). The characterological self-blame scale had nine items with a coeffecent alpha of .80. The behavioral self-blame scale had four items with a coeffecent alpha of .67, and the societal blame scale had seven items with a coeffecent alpha of .88. These scales were similar to those obtained by Meyer and Taylor (1986).

Responses were made on a scale from -2 to $+2$. Negative scores indicated the statement was false, and positive scores indicated the statement was true, with 0 being neutral. The responses were summed for each of the scales, yielding three scores. The characterological self-blame scale had a possible range of scores from − 18 to +18. The behavioral self-blame scale had a possible range of scores from − 8 to +8, and the societal blame scale had a possible range of scores from − 14 to +14.

Post-Traumatic Stress Disorder symptoms. The presence of PTSD symptomatology was assessed by having subjects complete the Symptoms Checklist 90–Revised (SCL90-R; Derogatis, 1977). Prior to completing any other measures, subjects were asked to complete the SCL90-R for the two-week time period prior to the time of the study. The SCL90-R is a 90-item self-report inventory through which individuals rate on a scale from 0 to 4 the degree to which they have experienced a number of psychiatric symptoms in the past two weeks. Derogatis (1977) reported adequate test-retest and internal consistency reliability and concurrent and discriminant validity for the SCL90-R.

Using the SCL90-R, Saunders, Arata, and Kilpatrick (1990) devised a 28-item subscale to assess Crime-Related Post-Traumatic Stress Disorder symptomatology (CR-PTSD). The scale is scored by summing the responses to the items on the SCL90-R CR-PTSD scale and dividing by 28. Thus, the CR-PTSD total score can range from 0 to 4. Saunders et al. (1990) found that subjects scoring above 0.89 on the CR-PTSD scale were highly likely to meet DSM-III diagnostic criteria (American Psychiatric Association, 1980) for PTSD. This cut-off score was successful in discriminating 89% of crime victims who did or did not have PTSD.

Subjects' scores on the CR-PTSD scale were used as a measure of PTSD symptomatology. The women's responses to the SCL90-R were used to obtain a score on the CR-PTSD scale. Reliability analyses for this sample indicated a coefficient alpha of 0.92 for the scale, with a correlation of 0.96 between the CR-PTSD score and the Global Severity Index of the SCL90-R.

Procedure

Subjects completed the questionnaires in classrooms in groups of 25 to 50 subjects. Subjects sat in every other seat and the questionnaires were anonymous in order to increase privacy. Prior to completing the questionnaire, subjects were told the purpose of the study and signed a consent form which described risks and benefits of the study. Subjects were told this was a study on sexual behavior and adjustment in which they would be asked about coercive sexual experiences. They were informed that they need not complete any questions that they did not wish to complete. At the conclusion of the questionnaire, subjects were given a debriefing sheet that described in greater detail the purposes of the study and resources for counseling.

All questionnaires were given in the same order because of the need for certain information to follow others. The questionnaires were given in the following order:

1. Demographic data,
2. Symptom Checklist 90–Revised,
3. Revised SES,
4. detailed questions regarding the sexual assault, and
5. attributions of blame.

RESULTS

Post-Traumatic Stress Disorder Symptoms

The first hypothesis, that sexual assault victims would display symptoms of PTSD, was examined first by comparing victims to non-victims on the CR-PTSD scale. An analysis of variance indicated that, overall, victims of all types of sexual assaults scored higher than non-victims on the CR-PTSD scale, $F(1, 808) = 19.8$, $p < .00001$, therefore supporting Hypothesis 1. However, the second hypothesis, that rape victims would be more likely to have symptoms of PTSD, was not confirmed. There was no significant variation between the different levels of victimization on the total score for the CR-PTSD scale, $F(3, 312) = .38$, $p = .77$.

Hypotheses 1 and 2 were also evaluated by examining percentages of subjects scoring above the clinical cutoff (.89) of the CR-PTSD scale. First, victims versus non-victims were examined. Overall, 34% (108) of women experiencing sexual assaults scored above the cutoff on the CR-PTSD scale, compared to 22% (111) of non-victims. This difference between the groups was significant, χ^2 $(1, N = 810)$, $p < .0004$.

The percentage of victims scoring above the cutoff on the CR-PTSD was identified for each level of victimization. The percentages of PTSD-positive women did not differ significantly for the different levels of victimization, χ^2 $(3, N = 316) = 1.38$, $p < .71$.

Attributions of Blame

The third hypothesis was that self-blame would be positively associated with greater symptoms of PTSD. Given that different levels of victimization were not associated with differences in risk of PTSD, the analyses of PTSD-positive versus PTSD-negative women were completed using all women reporting coercive sexual experiences. One-way analysis of variance was used to evaluate the attributions of blame in relation to PTSD status. All three cognitive variables (characterological, behavioral blame, and societal blame) were associated with PTSD status. Women in the PTSD-positive group reported more characterological self-blame, more societal blame, and more behavioral self-blame (see Table 2). All subjects scored in the negative range on societal and characterological blame, although they scored in the positive range on behavioral self-blame. This indicated that, overall, regardless of PTSD status, women did not tend to blame their character or society, but they did attribute blame to their behavior.

Situational Variables

The third hypothesis, that situational variables would be associated with PTSD status, was evaluated through Chi-square analyses. The length of time since the assault, the victim's relationship with the perpetrator, the use of alcohol/drugs by the victim or perpetrator, the method of resistance,

TABLE 2. Attributions of Blame Scores Between PTSD Positive and Negative Subjects

Scale	PTSD Positive[a] M (SD)	PTSD Negative[b] M (SD)	F	p
Characterological Self-Blame[c]	− 4.26 (7.14)	− 8.75 (6.86)	29.7	.0001
Behavioral Self-Blame[d]	2.49 (3.66)	1.37 (3.98)	5.9	.016
Societal Blame[e]	− 0.93 (7.25)	− 3.43 (6.83)	9.1	.003

[a]$n = 108$ [b]$n = 209$
[c]range of scores: − 18 to 18
[d]range of scores: − 8 to +8
[e]range of scores: − 14 to 14

the method of coercion, and previous intimacy with the perpetrator were all examined. None of these variables was significantly different for PTSD-positive versus PTSD-negative subjects.

Multiple Regression

To further examine the role of attributions of blame and situational variables in mediating PTSD symptoms, stepwise multiple regression analyses were done using only victims of sexual assault. The situational and cognitive variables were entered in stepwise fashion to predict the subjects' scores on the CR-PTSD scale. Characterological self-blame was the only variable that had a significant contribution to the CR-PTSD score, with higher levels of PTSD symptoms being reported by women who tended to blame themselves for the assault, $R = .38$, $p < .00005$. Thus, self-attribution of blame did predict adjustment, whereas, in this sample, situational variables related to the assault did not.

DISCUSSION

The primary purpose of this study was to further the understanding of the psychological consequences of sexual assault among a college sample. A self-report inventory was used to assess symptoms of PTSD, a common consequence of sexual assault among community samples. Efforts were made to predict differences in current adjustment among sexual assault victims.

There were several striking findings in this study, some consistent with our hypotheses, with some surprising contrary findings. As predicted, victims of sexual assaults by acquaintances did display significant levels of PTSD symptoms. In fact, one third of the women reporting coercive sexual experiences reported significant levels of PTSD symptomatology. What was striking was the fact that the type of assault was not associated with PTSD status. That is, women experiencing molestations as well as attempted rape were as likely as women experiencing completed rape to score above the cutoff on the CR-PTSD scale.

As predicted, attributions of blame were significantly associated with PTSD symptoms. Cognitive variables were consistently associated with group differences in both the overall score on the CR-PTSD scale and in characterizing those who scored above the clinical cutting score. Subjects in the PTSD-positive group were more likely to believe that they somehow deserved the sexual assault because of an internal quality of themselves or their behavior, or they believed that the nature of society caused the victimization. The regression analyses indicated blaming one's character was the only variable that had a significant impact on total CR-PTSD scores. That is, women who blamed themselves for the assault tended to report higher levels of PTSD symptomatology.

The finding that PTSD symptoms were associated more by cognitive attributions than by features of the assault, including whether the assault was completed, is consistent with findings by Katz (1991) that self-blame was associated with a longer recovery time. Similarly, Koss and Burkhart (1989) suggested that predicting long-term outcomes to rape would require understanding the cognitive processes of appraisal, attributions, and accommodations. The present data confirm these early conceptual notions and fit well with the recent cognitive models of trauma and coping (McCann & Pearlman, 1990; Resick & Schnicke, 1992).

In understanding the cognitive processes involved, it is important to note that the majority of subjects scored in the negative range on characterological and societal blame. This finding suggests that most subjects do not absolutely blame themselves or society; however, the strength of their relative sense of blame is predictive of PTSD status. Thus, the less that women blame themselves or society, the fewer symptoms of PTSD they report and the less likely they are to score in the clinically significant range on the CR-PTSD scale.

An analysis of the items making up the characterological self-blame and societal blame scale helps to understand this process. The attributions included on these scales suggest causes of the sexual assault that are difficult to change or prevent. Clinical qualities of PTSD have to do with fear and feelings of reexperiencing the event which may potentiate a fear of the same thing happening again. As such, the belief that one cannot prevent future sexual assault would fit with the clinical pattern of PTSD.

The hypothesis that situational variables would be associated with PTSD status was not supported. Overall, assault-related situational variables had very little effect on post-rape symptomatology. In particular, even the level of victimization was not associated with whether an individual experienced PTSD-like symptoms. The lack of significance of situational variables is contrary to what has been found in community samples and what might be expected from the perspective of "common sense." In community samples, experiencing a completed rape, perceiving life threat, and physical injury have been found to predict an increased risk of developing PTSD (Kilpatrick et al., 1987). It may well be that, for this sample of young women, exposure to sexual aggressiveness, per se, is sufficiently stressful to potentiate distress. Whether the assault is completed apparently has less effect than the fact that an assault was attempted.

Several important limitations to this study should be considered with any possible interpretations of the findings. Most importantly, the only measure of PTSD symptoms was the CR-PTSD scale, which alone is not sufficient to diagnose PTSD. Therefore, the findings only suggest possible correlates of PTSD symptoms, as opposed to the actual diagnostic category. In retrospect, a second limitation was the failure to obtain more life history and personality data. As situational variables were not associated with differences in adjustment, it is difficult to understand what other variables are associated with adjustment. Prior life experiences, particularly prior victimization, may be more important in predicting differences in adjustment and cognitive appraisals than the actual experience. For example, women with a history of victimization might be more likely to blame some unchangeable aspect of themselves or society for their victimization. It is also possible that prior life experiences could be causal factors in current symptoms; therefore, one must be careful in assuming that the current distress is in fact caused by the assaults reported, when other variables could be causing the current distress.

Acquaintance rape and other coercive sexual experiences are a serious and common problem among college students. A substantial portion of the women in this study who were sexually assaulted reported clinically significant levels of PTSD symptoms. It is quite alarming that one-third of sexual assault victims in a "normal" sample reported such high levels of distress. The impact of sexual assault among less adjusted populations might be even more devastating. Clearly, these results highlight the significant, negative impact of sexual assaults among college students, as well as defining these subjects as in need of treatment from an epidemiological perspective.

These results also demonstrate that, in identifying victims in need of treatment, it appears that the events do not, by themselves, predict degree of distress, but rather the cognitive appraisals of the victims mediate the degree of emotional distress. Additionally, Koss and Burkhart's (1989) suggestion that treatment should focus on cognitive processes seems wise. Continued research to understand the nature and origin of these cognitive appraisals, as well as their responsiveness to treatment, is needed.

REFERENCES

American Psychiatric Association. (1980). *Diagnostic and statistical manual of mental disorders (3rd ed.)*. Washington, DC: American Psychiatric Association.

American Psychiatric Association. (1987). *Diagnostic and statistical manual of mental disorders (3rd ed.)*. Washington, DC: American Psychiatric Association.

Bechhofer, L., & Parrot, A. (1991). What is acquaintance rape? In A. Parrot & L. Bechhofer (Eds.), *Acquaintance rape: The hidden crime* (pp. 9-25). New York: Wiley.

Briere, J., & Runtz, M. (1993). Childhood sexual abuse: Long-term sequelae and implications for psychological assessment. *Journal of Interpersonal Violence, 8,* 312-330.

Burge, S. (1988). Post-Traumatic Stress Disorder in victims of rape. *Journal of Traumatic Stress, 1,* 193-210.

Derogatis, L. R. (1977). *SCL90-R: Administration, scoring, and procedure manual-I for the R (revised) version.* Baltimore: Johns-Hopkins University School of Medicine.

Janoff-Bulman, R. (1979). Characterological versus behavioral self-blame: Inquiries into depression and rape. *Journal of Personality, 50,* 180-191.

Katz, B. (1991). The psychological impact of stranger versus nonstranger rape on victims' recovery. In A. Parrot & L. Bechhofer (Eds.), *Acquaintance rape: The hidden crime* (pp. 251-269). New York: Wiley.

Katz, S., & Mazur, M. A. (1979). *Understanding the rape victims: A synthesis of research findings.* New York: Wiley.

Kilpatrick, D. G., Edmunds, C. N., & Seymour, A. K. (1992). *Rape in America: A report to the nation.* Arlington, VA: National Victim Center.

Kilpatrick, D. G., Saunders, B. E., Amick-McMullen, A., Best, C., & Veronen, L. J. (1987). *Factors affecting the development of crime-related Post-Traumatic Stress Disorder: A Multivariate Approach.* Paper presented at the 21st Annual Association for the Advancement of Behavior Therapy Convention, November 13, 1987, Boston, Massachusetts.

Koss, M. P. (1993). Detecting the scope of rape: A review of prevalence research methods. *Journal of Interpersonal Violence, 8,* 198-222.

Koss, M. P., & Burkhart, B. R. (1989). A conceptual analysis of rape victimization: Long-term effects and implications for treatment. *Psychology of Women Quarterly, 9,* 193-212.

Koss, M. P., & Oros, C. J. (1982). Sexual experience survey: A research instrument investigating sexual aggression and victimization. *Journal of Consulting and Clinical Psychology, 50,* 455-457.

Lazarus, R. S., & Folkman, S. (1984). *Stress, appraisals, and coping.* New York: Springer.

Mandoki, C. A., & Burkhart, B. R. (1989). *Coping and adjustment to rape.* Paper presented at the annual meeting of the American Psychological Association, August, 1989, New Orleans, Louisiana.

Mandoki, C. A., & Burkhart, B. R. (1991). Women as victims: Antecedent and consequences of acquaintance rape. In A. Parrot and L. Bechhofer (Eds.), *Acquaintance rape: The hidden crime* (pp. 176-191). New York: Wiley.

McCann, I. L., & Pearlman, L. A. (1990). *Psychological trauma and the adult survivor: Theory, therapy, and transformation.* New York: Brunner/Mazel.

Meyer, C. B., & Taylor, S. D. (1986). Adjustment to rape. *Journal of Personality and Social Psychology, 50,* 1226-1234.

Resick, P. A. (1993). The psychological impact of rape. *Journal of Interpersonal Violence, 8,* 223-255.

Resick, P. A., & Schnicke, M. K. (1992). Cognitive processing therapy for sexual assault victims. *Journal of Consulting and Clinical Psychology, 60,* 748-756.

Resnick, H. S., Kilpatrick, D. G., Best, C. L., & Kramer, T. L. (1992). Vulnerability-stress factors in development of Posttraumatic Stress Disorder. *The Journal of Nervous and Mental Disease, 180,* 424-430.

Rothbaum, B., Foa, E. B., Riggs, D. S., Murdok, T., & Walsh, W. (1992). A prospective examination of Post-Traumatic Stress Disorder in rape victims. *Journal of Traumatic Stress, 5,* 455-475.

Ruch, L. O., & Chandler, S. M. (1983). Sexual assault trauma during the acute phase: An exploratory model and multivariate analysis. *Journal of Health and Social Behavior, 24,* 174-185.

Saunders, B. E., Arata, C. M., & Kilpatrick, D. G. (1990). Development of a crime-related Post-Traumatic Stress Disorder scale for women within the Symptom Checklist 90–Revised. *Journal of Traumatic Stress, 3,* 439-448.

College Men's Reactions to Hypothetical Forceful Sexual Advances from Women

David Struckman-Johnson, PhD
Cindy Struckman-Johnson, PhD

SUMMARY. A sample of 263 college men read a vignette in which they were to imagine receiving a forceful sexual advance from a woman. Initiator relationship was varied by describing the woman as a relative stranger, an acquaintance, a recent non-sexual dating partner, or a steady dating partner with whom the subject has already had sexual intercourse (sexual date). The sexual intimacy of the act attempted–genital touch, oral sex, and sexual intercourse–was varied in the vignette. Subjects gave ratings for social acceptability, positive reaction, feelings of violation, and negative impact of the situation, and indicated if they would consent to sex with the initiator. Results revealed a significant effect for relationship. Men had generally negative responses to the advance of a stranger and positive responses to the advance of a sexual date. Reactions to acquaintance and recent date advances were more positive than those for a stranger, but less positive than responses to the sexual date. The results add further support to a model that proposes that men will respond favorably to female sexual coercion when conditions are optimal for perceiving the event as a sexual opportunity. To date, conditions known to promote positive reactions to hypothetical sexual advances are low force, high initiator sexual desirability, and a high level of romantic

David Struckman-Johnson and Cindy Struckman-Johnson are both affiliated with the Department of Psychology, University of South Dakota.

[Haworth co-indexing entry note]: "College Men's Reactions to Hypothetical Forceful Sexual Advances from Women." Struckman-Johnson, David, and Cindy Struckman-Johnson. Co-published simultaneously in *Journal of Psychology & Human Sexuality* (The Haworth Press, Inc.) Vol. 8, No. 1/2, 1996, pp. 93-105; and: *Sexual Coercion in Dating Relationships* (ed: E. Sandra Byers, and Lucia F. O'Sullivan) The Haworth Press, Inc., 1996, pp. 93-105. Single or multiple copies of this article are available from The Haworth Document Delivery Service [1-800-342-9678, 9:00 a.m. - 5:00 p.m. (EST)].

relationship with the initiator. *[Article copies available from The Haworth Document Delivery Service: 1-800-342-9678.]*

A prevailing stereotype in the literature is that sexual coercion occurs only between male perpetrators and female recipients. In reality, men are sometimes the target of coercive sexual advances of female strangers, acquaintances, and intimate partners. Although the research to date is limited, it has been found that as many as 32% to 45% of college men have experienced coercive kissing, fondling, and sexual intercourse with a female initiator (Lottes, 1991; Poppen & Segal, 1988; Sandberg, Jackson, & Petretic-Jackson, 1987; Struckman-Johnson & Struckman-Johnson, 1994a).

Most men who have had coercive sexual contact with women were either verbally pressured (e.g., by persistent arguments or emotional appeals) and/or were too intoxicated to control the situation (Lottes, 1991; Sandberg et al., 1987; Struckman-Johnson & Struckman-Johnson, 1994a). However, some male victims have reported the use of outright force or threats of harm. For example, Anderson and Aymami (1993) found that of 128 college men, 16% had sexual contact with a woman initiated by physical force, 15% by threat of force, and 5% by use of a weapon. In other studies, the percentages of men reporting physically forceful sexual contact with a woman range from 1% (Murphy, 1988; Struckman-Johnson & Struckman-Johnson, 1994a) to 14% (Poppen & Segal, 1988).

Our research has focused on the question of how men are affected by the coercive advances of women. Although it is well-documented that women have strong negative responses to any level of coercive sexual contact with men (e.g., Christopher, 1988), little is known about men's reactions in the reverse situation. In our first study of a small sample of men who reported forced sexual intercourse on dates (Struckman-Johnson, 1988), almost half of the victims categorized their reactions as "neutral." Surprisingly, equal numbers of men rated their reactions as "bad" and as "good." In a more recent study, 80% of 42 male victims of female coercion indicated that the incident had little negative impact (Struckman-Johnson & Struckman-Johnson, 1994a).

Other researchers have reported evidence of men's variable and ambivalent reactions to coercive contact with women. Long and Muehlenhard (1987) found that men who had experienced unwanted sexual contact with women had a mix of negative feelings (sad, uncomfortable) and positive reactions (feeling cared for, confident of manhood). Siegel, Golding, Burnam, and Sorenson (1990) documented that male victims of sexual assault in a community setting were significantly less likely than women to report "life-affecting" emotional reactions. About one-fourth to one-third of the men reported feelings of anger, sadness, and guilt.

These findings have led us to develop a framework for explaining why men may experience a range of positive to negative reactions to coercive sexual contact with women. In our view, men's reactions are mediated by a gender role script that prescribes that young men seek and initiate sexual interactions with potential female partners (Simon & Gagnon, 1986). When confronted with a woman who aggressively makes a sexual advance, a man is likely to view it as a positive opportunity to engage in sex, not a violation of will (Smith, Pine, & Hawley, 1988; Struckman-Johnson & Struckman-Johnson, 1991). Because the woman is clearly signaling that she wants sex, the man can participate without the responsibility or risks associated with sexual initiation.

We have proposed that a man's response to a woman's forceful sexual advance may be influenced by at least four factors: (1) the degree to which the advance violates his sexual standards, (2) the level of force used by the woman, (3) the degree to which the woman is sexually desirable or creates sexual arousal by her actions, and (4) the extent to which a romantic relationship with the woman justifies the act (Struckman-Johnson & Struckman-Johnson, 1994b.) In our model, we predicted that men will respond favorably when conditions are optimal for viewing the event as a positive sexual opportunity. This will occur when levels of sexual standard violation and coercion are low and levels of sexual desirability and romantic relationship are high.

The sexual opportunity model is based upon a series of vignette studies in which we asked college men to tell us how they would react if a woman attempted to initiate sex with them in a variety of ways. In the first study, subjects rated the negative impact of a hypothetical situation in which a nonromantic acquaintance unexpectedly touched their genitals during a study session (Struckman-Johnson & Struckman-Johnson, 1993.) We predicted that men would have a stronger negative reaction when the touch was described as forceful (being pushed down on the couch) as compared to when the touch was described as gentle. Male subjects, however, perceived both situations as having little negative impact. We speculated that if the vignette had portrayed a significantly more forceful act by the woman, men would have had a negative reaction.

In a follow-up study (Struckman-Johnson & Struckman-Johnson, 1994b), men rated their reactions to a female study partner who touched their genitals in one of four different ways: a gentle touch (low force), a push down on the couch (moderate force), a push and a verbal threat of harm (high force), and a push, a verbal threat, and wielding of a knife (very high force). As predicted, men anticipated significantly more negative effects from the two high force conditions as compared to the low and moderate force conditions.

A second factor investigated in the study was sexual desirability of the initiator. In each force condition, the woman was described as either "very attractive" or "very unattractive." Results showed a "beauty bias" in that men responded more positively (or less negatively) to an attractive initiator than to an unattractive woman in all force conditions. Men had generally negative reactions to advances by an unattractive initiator, regardless of force level used. Overall, the results showed that two factors from our model had predictable influences on men's reaction to sexual coercion. When conditions of force were low to moderate and initiator sexual attractiveness were high, most men viewed the situation as a positive sexual opportunity.

PURPOSES AND HYPOTHESES OF THE PRESENT STUDY

The primary purpose of the present study was to examine the effects of a third factor from the model—the level of romantic relationship with the initiator. In our first studies, we assessed men's reactions to a forceful advance of a nonromantic acquaintance. We wondered how men would react if the woman were described as a romantic partner such as a new date or a steady girlfriend. We speculated that if the man were already in a romantic relationship with the initiator, he would perceive her actions as a novel or playful form of seduction. Thus, the romantic relationship would provide a justification or an explanation for the woman's behavior. The same actions by a stranger, however, would likely be perceived as inappropriate and aggressive.

In the present study, this question was investigated by assessing men's reactions to a forceful sexual advance scenario in which the woman was described as a relative stranger, or a friend-acquaintance, or a recent dating partner who had not yet had sex with the subject (recent date), or a steady dating partner who had already had sex with the subject (sexual date). It was hypothesized that subjects' reactions would be increasingly positive as the level of romantic relationship increased. Specifically, it was predicted that men would anticipate strong negative responses to the stranger's advance as measured by ratings of social acceptability, positive reaction, feelings of violation, and negative impact, and a willingness to engage in further sexual activity. Responses to the acquaintance situation were expected to be somewhat neutral, and reactions to the recent and sexual date advances were predicted to be positive.

The second factor investigated in the study was the degree of sexual intimacy of the act attempted by the initiator. In our first studies, men were asked how they would react to a woman who touched their genital area. We wondered if it would make a difference if the woman attempted a more sexually intimate act that would create greater sexual arousal. To investigate this question, the attempted sexual act in the study vignette was described as a genital touch, or oral sex, or mounting for sexual intercourse. We speculated that men's reactions to the intimacy level of the act would depend upon the relationship with the initiator. If a man already had an established romantic relationship with a woman, he would respond more positively to acts of increasing intimacy. However, if he had no relationship with her, he would respond more negatively to acts of increasing intimacy. Therefore, it was hypothesized that for the recent date and sexual date conditions, men would give more positive responses for all measures to the acts of oral sex and sexual intercourse than to a genital touch. For the stranger and acquaintance conditions, it was expected that men would give more negative ratings to the acts of oral sex and intercourse than to a genital touch.

METHODS

Subjects

The subjects were 265 men attending a Midwestern state college in fall semester 1994. The 8,000 students on campus are predominantly White and middle-class. After excluding two subjects who did not complete numerous measures, the final sample consisted of 263 men (*M* age = 20.7, range = 18-40 years).

Instrument

Sexual advance vignette. Subjects were instructed to "Please put yourself in the following situation. Imagine that the scene described below happens to you. Please describe how you would feel and react to this event in your answers to the questions that follow." Subjects then read *one* of twelve variations of a vignette about a study session in which a woman used physical coercion to initiate a sexual act with the subject. The basic vignette read as follows: "Imagine that you are studying with a female college student. [Insert initiator relationship level.] During a break, she unexpectedly and in a physically forceful way (using her arms and weight to hold you down) [insert sexual intimacy level]." Initiator relationship was varied by inserting the following descriptions:

Stranger: The woman is a relative stranger whom you have only known a few hours.

Acquaintance: The woman is a friend-acquaintance whom you have known for several months. You have never dated or had sexual intercourse with her.

Recent Date: The woman is someone whom you have recently dated several times. You have not yet had sexual intercourse with her.

Sexual Date: The woman is someone whom you have dated steadily during the last several months. You have already had sexual intercourse with her.

To vary sexual intimacy, the *Genital Touch* phrase read "begins to touch your genitals." The *Oral Sex* phrase was "begins to give you oral sex (fellatio)." In the *Sexual Intercourse* condition, the phrase read "stimulates you to erection and positions herself to begin sexual intercourse with you."

The vignette initiator was explicitly described as using "physical force" to hold the man down so that her actions would be viewed as mildly to moderately forceful, but not as overtly threatening.

Dependent Measures

Five dependent measures, interspersed among 13 other questions, followed the vignette. Four measures were adopted from our previous vignette studies. Questions for *social acceptability* (How socially acceptable is this behavior?) and *violation* (How much would you feel that you have been physically violated?) were rated on scales ranging from (1) Not at all to (7) Very Much. The item for *negative impact* was "Please rate the extent that this event would have a negative impact upon you." The scale ranged from (1) Would have no negative effect upon me to (7) Would have a severe negative effect upon me. For *expected sexual outcome,* the question read "What do you think would be the outcome if this situation really happened to you? Check only one." The consent alternative read "You would willingly let her touch you and you would willingly engage in further sexual activity." Four other alternatives indicated that the subject would not willingly engage in further sexual activity with the initiator.

A new dependent measure was added to assess subjects' negative or positive *reaction* to the vignette. The item was "Using the scale below, rate your reaction to this situation." The scale was anchored by: (1) Very Negative Reaction and (7) Very Positive Reaction.

A manipulation check measure for the perceived level of *force* used by the vignette initiator read: "How much do you believe that force was being used in this situation?" The scale ranged from (1) Not At All to (7) Very Much. The final measure for subjects' *personal opinion* was "In your own words, explain how you would feel and react to this situation if it actually happened to you."

Procedures. The researchers entered five psychology classes to solicit volunteer subjects. They gave a brief description of the study at the beginning of class and invited interested students to take a questionnaire and consent form on their way out of class. Students were instructed to complete the anonymous survey privately at home and to return it to the next class, where consent forms and surveys would be collected in separate boxes. The 12 versions of the vignette-questionnaire were arranged in sequential order in the stacks for even distribution among participants. Participants were given extra credit points for their psychology courses.

RESULTS

Manipulation Check for Force Level

A manipulation check was made to determine if subjects perceived the force level of the initiator's actions as low to moderate in all vignette conditions. A four (relationship level) by three (sexual intimacy level) ANOVA was conducted on the ratings for the degree of force used by the initiator. Relationship and intimacy were between-subjects factors. Because cell sizes were unequal, SAS Type III sums of squares were used to interpret effects. A significant main effect was found for relationship, $F(11, 249) = 5.33$; $p < .001$. The main effect for intimacy and the interaction were not significant.

According to a Duncan's paired comparison test, force ratings for the stranger ratings ($M = 4.4$) were significantly higher than those for the recent date ($M = 3.4$) and sexual date ($M = 3.1$) vignettes, $p < .05$. Force level ratings for the acquaintance situation ($M = 3.9$) were significantly higher than those for the sexual date condition, $p < .05$. Based upon a seven-point scale, subjects viewed the action of being pinned down as moderately forceful in the stranger and acquaintance conditions and as between low and moderately forceful in the recent and sexual date conditions. The overall mean force rating for the action was in the moderate range.

Responses to Sexual Advance Vignettes

A four (relationship) by three (sexual intimacy) between-subjects MANOVA was conducted on ratings of acceptability, reaction, violation, and negative impact of the advance situation. Significant main effects were found for relationship, Wilks' Lambda = .807, $F(12, 648) = 4.57; p < .001$, and for sexual intimacy, Wilks' Lambda = .922, $F(8, 490) = 2.52; p < .01$. The interaction was not significant. The significant effects found for the MANOVA permitted the conduct of univariate analyses for the dependent measures.

A series of four (relationship) by three (sexual intimacy) ANOVAs revealed a significant relationship main effect for social acceptability, $F(11, 248) = 10.95; p < .001$; reaction, $F(11, 248) = 9.36; p < .001$; violation, $F(11, 248) = 9.65; p < .001$; and negative impact $F(11, 248) = 12.63; p < .001$. The main effect for intimacy and the interaction were not significant in any analysis. The means and standard deviations for the four dependent measures by relationship condition are in Table 1.

Duncan's paired comparison tests were used to interpret the differences

TABLE 1. Means of Ratings for Social Acceptability, Reaction, Violation and Negative Impact by Levels of Relationship

Dependent Variable	Level of Relationship				
	Relative Stranger	Acquaintance	Recent Date	Sexual Date	Across Levels
Social Acceptability	2.10[a]	3.06[b]	3.33[b]	3.61[b]	3.03
	(1.28)	(1.60)	(1.85)	(1.62)	(1.68)
Reaction	3.67[a]	4.69[b]	4.84[b]	5.35[b]	4.64
	(1.90)	(1.92)	(1.95)	(1.68)	(1.95)
Violation	3.88[a]	3.08[b]	2.89[b]	2.19[c]	3.00
	(1.96)	(2.13)	(1.83)	(1.53)	(1.96)
Negative Impact	3.50[a]	2.93[b]	2.72[b]	1.88[c]	2.75
	(1.63)	(1.76)	(1.77)	(1.22)	(1.70)

Note: Values in parentheses are standard deviations. Cell *N*s range from 61 to 69. Ratings are on a seven-point scale. For each variable, means with the same superscript are not significantly different at alpha = .05.

among means for relationship conditions for each dependent measure. The alpha level was set at .05 for all Duncan's tests. For the measure of social acceptability, ratings of the stranger condition were significantly lower than those for all other conditions. The acceptability ratings for an advance by a stranger were in the very low to low range of the scale, whereas ratings for all other conditions were in the moderately low to moderate range.

For the reaction measure, ratings for the stranger's action were significantly lower than ratings for all other conditions. Subjects' reaction ratings for the stranger vignette were in the low to moderately negative range whereas ratings for all other initiators approached the moderately positive range of the scale.

The Duncan's test for the violation measure revealed that ratings for the stranger condition were higher than for all other conditions. Ratings for the sexual date vignette were lower than for all other conditions. Subjects' feelings of violation were in the moderate range for the stranger vignette, the moderately low range for the acquaintance and recent date conditions, and in the very low to low range for the sexual date condition.

A similar pattern was found for the negative impact measure. Ratings for the stranger condition were significantly higher than for all other conditions. Ratings for the sexual date vignette were significantly lower than for all other situations. Subjects' estimates of negative impact approached the moderate range for the stranger vignette, were low for the acquaintance and recent date conditions, and were very low to low for the sexual date vignette.

The intimacy effect, found to be significant in the MANOVA but not in follow-up ANOVAs, was further investigated by a canonical discriminant analysis. The effect was found to be significant, Wilks' Lambda $(8, 508) = 2.54$; $p < .01$. According to the means of the canonical variables, subjects' responses in the touch condition were different than those in the oral sex and intercourse conditions. However, the four dependent measures in combination accounted for only 7% of the variance of the analysis.

The percentages of subjects who said they would consent to further sexual activity with the vignette initiator by relationship condition were 29% (19/66) for a stranger, 54% (33/61) for an acquaintance, 56% (36/64) for a recent date and 81% (58/72) for a sexual date. A Chi-square analysis revealed significant differences among the distributions of subjects who said they would consent or not consent to sex by relationship conditions, $\chi^2 = 37.4$; $p < .001$. According to the Chi-square contributions by individual cells, the largest departures from expected frequencies were the small number of subjects who said they would consent to the stranger and the large number of subjects who said they would consent to the sexual date. A similar analysis of consent rates for subjects by sexual intimacy conditions revealed no significant differences.

CONCLUSION AND DISCUSSION

The results indicated that men's anticipated reactions to a forceful sexual advance were more positive for increasing levels of romantic relationship with the female initiator. The most conclusive finding of the study is that a majority of men had a negative reaction to the idea of being pinned down for a sexual interaction by a woman whom they had only known for two hours. They judged this action as very socially unacceptable and anticipated low to moderate levels of violation and negative impact from the incident. Fewer than one-third of the subjects said they would consent to engage in further sexual activity with the stranger. Overall, they tended to evaluate the event as an unpleasant but not a traumatic event. Our explanation is that men viewed the actions of a stranger as inappropriate sexual coercion because there was no romantic context to explain or justify her behavior. Supporting this interpretation, the results of the manipulation check indicated that the subjects perceived the actions of the stranger as significantly more forceful than actions of the recent and sexual date initiators.

According to written opinions of subjects in the stranger condition, most viewed the advance as a shocking, forceful, and somewhat upsetting event. One wrote "It would make me really uncomfortable. Yeah sex is cool in any form, but I prefer to know the person for quite awhile . . . I feel that sort of thing to be a complete disrespectful act and a violation of my rights." A majority said that they would stop her actions, such as one man who wrote "I would feel disgusted. The girl is probably a tramp and could not get a man any other way. I would resist the come-on to full extent of my powers." Other men said they would calmly explain to the woman that this was not the way to get their romantic attention.

Subjects who indicated that they would consent to sex with the stranger often qualified their response by saying that she would have to be attractive. One wrote "If I was attracted to her I would tell her to lay off the force-there is no need for it. If I was not attracted to her I would tell her to get the hell off of me." Several men wrote that they would be pleased to have sex with her, but they would use condoms in case she had an STD.

A second conclusion is that subjects were most receptive to the forceful sexual advance of a woman described as a steady dating partner with whom they had already had sexual intercourse. Men judged this advance as only slightly unacceptable and anticipated minimal feelings of violation and negative impact from the incident. Eighty percent of the men said they would consent to further sex with her. This consent rate was substantially higher than the 56% rate for the recent date initiator.

According to comments of subjects in the sexual date condition, a majority viewed the advance as an act of seduction, not coercion. They typically wrote that they would be surprised but pleased and aroused by this display of sexual interest from a steady girlfriend. Some men surmised that the woman was showing extreme sexual desire, whereas others thought she was trying a new sexual technique. One wrote ". . . it would be refreshing for the girl to make the first move and show her feelings in a straight forward way instead of the subtle ways they usually do." However, some men said they would feel "used," "violated," and "turned off" by the woman's use of force.

A third finding is that men's reactions to the forceful sexual advances of an acquaintance and recent date were viewed more positively than those of a stranger but less positively than those of a steady sexual date. Although we had hypothesized that men would have neutral reactions to the advance of an acquaintance, subjects had a slightly positive reaction to the advances of both the acquaintance and a recent date. Over half of the subjects said they would consent to sex with either type of initiator.

The comments of subjects in the acquaintance and recent date conditions indicated that they would feel quite confused and uncertain about the appropriate response. Many men indicated that their response would depend upon their attraction to the woman. For example, one wrote "I think if I were attracted to this girl, I would welcome her advances with intense erotic feelings. If I didn't feel anything for this person I would tell them to stop . . . if they continued I would probably consider it rape." Some men said that this type of advance would jeopardize their friendship with the woman. One man wrote "I would be a little angry because the female just ruined a perfect friendship." However, many men simply viewed it as a positive sexual opportunity. One wrote "At first (the 1st 15-25 seconds) I'd feel embarrassed, but after that my hormones (I wish I didn't have as many as I do) would kick in and the rest of the time we would engage in sex."

A final outcome of the study is that we were unable to find an interpretable relationship between the level of intimacy of the sexual act described in a scenario and men's responses to the dependent measures. Results of a discriminant analysis suggested that men responded differently to scenarios involving a genital touch than they did to those describing oral sex or intercourse. In light of the small amount of variance accounted for in this analysis, we conclude that men's reactions to the sexual advance scenarios were not strongly influenced by the sexual intimacy variable.

To summarize our research to date, we have established that three conditions of the sexual opportunity model—force level, initiator sexual desirability, and the level of initiator romantic relationship—have predictable effects on men's anticipated reactions to female sexual coercion. One recommendation for future research is to investigate the fourth factor, "violation of sexual standards." When we first developed the model, we speculated that a coercive sexual advance by a woman would not violate most men's sexual standards because they value variable and casual sexual interactions. After collecting personal opinions from our past two studies, we now know that a substantial portion of men believe that sex should be reserved for an appropriate time, place, and partner. If men could be categorized as either "sexual opportunists" versus "sexual gatekeepers," we believe that the gatekeepers would exhibit strong negative reactions to hypothetical female sexual coercion.

The major limitation of the present study is that it assessed men's anticipated reactions to an imaginary situation. We do not know yet if these results can be extended to real-life situations in which men encounter sexually coercive women. However, the vignette research has helped explain the results of our studies of actual male victims (Struckman-Johnson, 1988; Struckman-Johnson & Struckman-Johnson, 1994a). Originally, we were mystified by the finding that most men reported few negative effects from encounters with female sexual coercion. Based upon the results of the present vignette study, we now understand that because many men were pressured into sex by girlfriends who used low levels of coercion, they most likely viewed the advances as expressions of romantic interest and sexual desire. As would be predicted by our vignette research on coercion level, we found that actual male victims reported high levels of negative impact for incidents involving physical force or restraint by the woman. Finally, the beauty bias effect found in our previous vignette study may explain why some men reported strong negative effects from low force encounters with women whom they described as unattractive.

In addition to offering insight, we believe that the results of vignette research can be usefully applied to future research on male victims. For example, one might have men rate their real life experiences for qualities for coercion level, initiator sexual desirability, and relationship. One could then determine which factors, if any, are predictive of the level of psychological harm resulting from actual incidents of female sexual coercion.

REFERENCES

Anderson, P. B., & Aymami, R. (1993). Reports of female initiation of sexual contact: Male and female differences. *Archives of Sexual Behavior, 22,* 335-343.

Christopher, F. S. (1988). An initial investigation into a continuum of premarital sexual pressure. *The Journal of Sex Research, 25,* 255-266.

Long, P. J., & Muehlenhard, C. L. (April, 1987). *Why some men don't say no: A comparison of men who did versus did not resist pressure to have unwanted sexual intercourse.* Paper presented at the Midcontinent Meeting of the Society for the Scientific Study of Sex, Bloomington, IN.

Lottes, I. I. (1991). The relationship between nontraditional gender roles and sexual coercion. *Journal of Psychology and Human Sexuality, 4,* 89-109.

Murphy, J. E. (1988). Date abuse and forced intercourse among college students. In G. P. Hotaling, D. Finkelhor, J. T. Kirkpatrick, & M. A. Straus (Eds.), *Family abuse and its consequences: New directions in research* (pp. 285-296). Beverly Hills, CA: Sage.

Poppen, P. J., & Segal, N. J. (1988). The influence of sex and sex role orientation on sexual coercion. *Sex Roles, 19,* 689-701.

Sandberg, G., Jackson, T. L., & Petretic-Jackson, P. (1987). College dating attitudes regarding sexual coercion and sexual aggression: Developing education and prevention strategies. *Journal of College Student Personnel, 28,* 302-310.

Siegel, J. M., Golding, J. M., Burnam, M. A., & Sorenson, S. B. (1990). Reactions to sexual assault: A community study. *Journal of Interpersonal Violence, 5,* 229-246.

Simon, W., & Gagnon, J. H. (1986). Sexual scripts: Permanence and change. *Archives of Sexual Behavior, 15,* 97-120.

Smith, R. E., Pine, C. J., & Hawley, M. E. (1988). Social cognition about adult male victims of female sexual assault. *The Journal of Sex Research, 24,* 101-112.

Struckman-Johnson, C. J. (1988). Forced sex on dates: It happens to men, too. *The Journal of Sex Research, 24,* 234-240.

Struckman-Johnson, D. L., & Struckman-Johnson, C. J. (1991). Men and women's acceptance of coercive sexual strategies varied by initiator gender and couple intimacy. *Sex Roles, 25,* 661-676.

Struckman-Johnson, C. J., & Struckman-Johnson, D. L. (1993). College men's and women's reactions to hypothetical sexual touch varied by initiator gender and coercion level. *Sex Roles, 29,* 371-385.

Struckman-Johnson, C. J., & Struckman-Johnson, D. L. (1994a). Men pressured and forced into sexual experiences. *Archives of Sexual Behavior,* 93-114.

Struckman-Johnson, C. J., & Struckman-Johnson, D. L. (1994b). Men's reactions to hypothetical sexual advances: A beauty bias in response to sexual coercion. *Sex Roles, 31,* 387-405.

Sexism, Erotophobia, and the Illusory "No": Implications for Acquaintance Rape Awareness

Mary Krueger, PhD

SUMMARY. I examined erotophobic, sex-negative attitudes toward female sexuality as they relate to acquaintance rape. Evidence suggests that sexist assumptions about female eroticism are intrinsically related to sexual violence against women. The argument is made that society's willingness to acknowledge women as sexual *victims* while simultaneously failing to validate women as sexual *agents* creates an ideal breeding ground for acquaintance rape. Accordingly, an analysis will be offered: in a culture that denies women freedom to say "yes" to sex without negative stigma, "no" does *not* always mean "no." In this article, I will assert that those who care about stopping sexual aggression in dating relationships have an obligation to work to eradicate sexist assumptions that neuter women's erotic selves. *[Article copies available from The Haworth Document Delivery Service: 1-800-342-9678.]*

> We are violated by those
> Who would contain our greatest spirits and
> Confine our largest passions

Mary Krueger is Director of Health Education and Adjunct Professor of Psychology, Emory University.

[Haworth co-indexing entry note]: "Sexism, Erotophobia, and the Illusory "No": Implications for Acquaintance Rape Awareness." Krueger, Mary. Co-published simultaneously in *Journal of Psychology & Human Sexuality* (The Haworth Press, Inc.) Vol. 8, No. 1/2, 1996, pp. 107-115; and: *Sexual Coercion in Dating Relationships* (ed: E. Sandra Byers, and Lucia F. O'Sullivan) The Haworth Press, Inc., 1996, pp. 107-115. Single or multiple copies of this article are available from The Haworth Document Delivery Service [1-800-342-9678, 9:00 a.m. - 5:00 p.m. (EST)].

> Into the small image of chastity.
> We are raped by those who
> Would have us believe that
> Nice girls don't like sex.
> They harm us more, and harm more of us, than
> All of the violence
> of meat shot on split beaver.

>   –*Radical Femme*, Scarlet Woman
>   (Steinberg, 1992, p. 211)

Among the greatest challenges to therapists and educators in the field of sexology has been affirming the essential positivity of human eroticism while simultaneously working to prevent sexual violence. Unfortunately (and perhaps tellingly), a paradoxical dissonance can result from doing both *pro-sex* and *anti-rape* work. However, dedication to both perspectives are presented in this treatise, in which I analyze a crucial, underrecognized point of intersection between sexism and sexual violence (specifically, acquaintance rape), and the overarching influence of erotophobia. That sexual violence operates in alliance with sexism is scarcely novel ideology. Most commonly, that connection is understood to reflect one or more of the following factors:

1. Males are socialized to be aggressive/females are socialized to be passive (Sanday, 1986; Lottes, 1988; among many others).
2. Males suffer from "testosterone poisoning" and are inherently aggressive animals (for example, Moyer, 1987).

And, particularly with regard to acquaintance rape:

3. Females are socialized to need a boyfriend/husband to feel valid and therefore fear refusing sex out of fear of losing the man in question (in other words, they acquiesce to "put out or get out" threats) (for example, Lewin, 1985).

I am suggesting that a new item be added to that list:

4. Females are socialized to believe they must be overcome by the moment, swept away–by romance, not desire–before they have sex. Any female who deviates from that norm is not a "good girl."

Arguably, such an analysis is not new. Indeed, a full decade has passed since the publication of Cassell's uniquely detailed exploration of female sexuality, "*Swept Away: Why Women Fear Their Own Sexuality.*" However, I offer for consideration not only that the erotophobic, sexist constraints of "swept away" are still being passed on to new generations of girls and women, but also that they relate specifically and directly to acquaintance rape.

Female sexual restraint is at the core of what Cassell (1984, p. 72) called "the amorphous and insidious credo of the Good Girl." To operate within this credo, a woman must be a fundamentally non-erotic person who, under the influence of love, alcohol, or skillful seduction at the hands of another (always a male), lapses temporarily into eroticism. Only under such circumstances may she be released from the burden of Good Girlism long enough to be lustful. Within this rubric, sex happens *to* her because she loses control (and because under such circumstances she makes no willful or calculated decision, she is not responsible for breaking the Good Girl rules). *She* isn't horny—*he* is.

The molding of good girls begins in childhood, and females learn early to deny or reinterpret any interest in things erotic. In few, if any instances, are girls given the message that their eroticism is normal, natural, or in any way positive. For example, according to Jessie Potter (cited in *Clitoris: Still a forbidden word,* 1989), the majority of sex education curricula, parents, nurses, and physicians do not identify or even name the clitoris (and certainly do not describe its function) when discussing female sexuality with girls and young women. As Potter noted,

> I believe the problem is caused by the awareness that the only answer we have if we call a girl's attention to her clitoris and she asks, "What's it for?" is, "It just hangs there and feels good," and that just strikes us mute. (1989, p. 3)

Once girls reach adolescence, the messages not to allow themselves to become sexually aroused, or to acknowledge or act in response to arousal, are ubiquitous and powerful. Deborah Tolman, a member of the Harvard Project on the Psychology of Women and the Development of Girls, found that adolescent girls internalize erotophobic scripts to such a degree they are unable to "admit" even to physiological indices of sexual arousal, much less the psychological experience of sexual desire. Tolman noted that

> Coming of age in a culture in which their embodied sexual desire is silenced, obscured, and denigrated poses a problem for girls. If girls know about their sexual desire from their experience of their own bodies, but encounter a disembodied way of speaking, hearing, and

knowing about their sexuality, then a central dilemma is posed . . .:
In what relationship can an adolescent girl be with her sexual desire,
with her own body, with her own experience? (1991, p. 59)

In service of the culture's deep commitment to suppressing women's
erotic expression, females are taught that sex is their enemy, a beast–a
male beast (Steinberg, 1992). Sexuality therefore carries with it the risk of
losing one's membership in the community of "good girls." Women have
license to sexual pleasure only *if* it is a coincidental by-product of the
expression of romantic love for their male partners, but sexual pleasure for
its own sake–lust, passion, desire–are unfeminine, Bad Girl things, "inter-
ruptions of the condoned version of what happens in girls' bodies" (Tolman, 1991, p. 67). According to Fine (1988), this silence regarding girls'
sexual desire, combined with an ever-present but ill-defined emphasis on
sexual victimization, may well inhibit their ability to develop sexual sub-
jectivity.

Good Girl rules are by no means a thing of the past, as evidenced by the
following letter to the editor of a university newspaper, written by a
21-year-old female student:

There is a continuous struggle between being a lady and being a
woman. We all get so infuriated at the double standard that rules our
social sphere of 'if guys fool around, they're cool; if girls fool
around, they're sluts.' . . . we all buy into [that myth], whether we
admit it or not. How many times have you heard women refer to
other women as sluts or stood by quietly as others referred to them as
such? (Froelich, 1994, p. 7)

Today's adolescent girls and young adult women, straddling the fence
in the immediate post-feminist generation, are seemingly trapped in a
conundrum: Yes, women have rights, including sexual rights. It's just not
okay to act on them.

Young women, especially those in high school or college, *are,* however,
regularly warned about sexual harassment, assault, and abuse–all the ways
in which men hurt women. They are encouraged to speak of, and receive
compassion and support regarding, their experiences of sexual victimization. On university campuses across the country, including the one at
which I work, "date" rape is the most frequently requested topic for
presentations in residence halls and greek letter organizations. In such
classes and programs, female sexuality is rarely construed in terms other
than those reflecting "prevention" [of medical problems such as sexually
transmitted diseases or unwanted pregnancy, but frequently of sex itself],

reactivity (responding to sexual overtures by others–always male), and victimization (rape, "date" rape, harassment).

Such programming reinforces the notion that males' exploitation of their very real social and physical power is inevitable, and renders women hopelessly disempowered before they begin. Yet, the opportunity for young women to examine the other side of their sexual experiences–passion, pleasure, lust–is markedly absent. Little permission exists for young women to explore and acknowledge the positive ways in which consensual erotic expression braids into the whole of their lives, and virtually *no* permission exists for them to explore eroticism as "[a] well of replenishing and provocative force; [a] lifeforce of women" (Lorde, 1984, p. 54). Hollibaugh (1984) described the dilemma in the following way:

> . . . in all our [women's] talking about sex, we have continuously focused on that part of sexuality where we [are] victims. Our horror at what [has] happened to us [makes] it impossible to acknowledge any response other than fury. . . . But looking at the danger and damage done us is only a part of coming to terms with sex. (pp. 401-402)

Society's willingness to recognize women as sexual victims, and simultaneous failure to recognize women as sexual agents, creates an ideal breeding ground for acquaintance rape. The horrific prevalence of sexualized crime inflicted upon women, in tandem with the imbalances of social, economic, and physical power between the genders, demands no less than society's full recognition and attention. However, disavowing women's erotic needs and/or denigrating their sources of erotic pleasure neither empowers nor creates safety for women. It merely "cuts [them] off from the source of their strength and energy" (Vance, 1984, p. 7).

Because sexual initiation within heterosexual relationships is still viewed as the male prerogative, exceedingly negative stigma attend women who take the sexual initiative with men, and the woman who unhesitatingly acts on her sexual desire is "subject to vilification unique to her gender" (Steinberg, 1992, p. xvii). Repeatedly evidenced in contemporary research, this stigma was expressed succinctly by the male subjects in Rubin's 1989 survey of college students, over half of whom said they would not want a woman who "had been around the block too many times," or one who "[slept] around"–that a woman who did so was "a slut" (Rubin, 1989, p. 41). Perhaps understandably, the young women in Rubin's survey reported feeling compelled to understate the breadth of their sexual histories to avoid being branded "slut."

The snare of such a double standard renders women, especially young women, acutely vulnerable to being shamed about sex. As a result, girls and women–in the absence of any sociocultural permission to be erotic or lustful–*have no choice but to say "no" when they mean "yes."* They do the "sexual side-step" (I want sex but I can't say I want sex, so I must make him persuade me) in what Cassell (1984) described as an aligning action, to resolve the conflict between society's prohibitions and their own sexual desires.

What becomes self-evident, therefore, is that the facile phrase "no means no"–the de facto motto of most rape-prevention efforts–is an ironic misnomer. In a society that denies women freedom to say "yes" to sex with men without disdain and negative stigma, "no" does not always mean "no." Indeed, it may well mean what many men, acquaintance rapists and not, have long said they assumed it meant: "talk me into it."

Such an analysis is painful to make, and dangerous to speak aloud for those who care about rape victims. One fears the misogynists who may well leap at it to challenge the legitimacy of rape crisis services, or the cynics who would exploit it as "proof" that women are not to be trusted in their allegations of sexual violence because they cannot discern between "bad sex" and rape. Yet, when the full panorama is taken into account–the inordinate power of cultural proscription against female eroticism as melded with the reality of acquaintance rape–such a conclusion appears inevitable.

In an ideal culture, heterosexual eroticism would be the basis for a celebration of the genders, a prism through which women and men could better understand each other (and themselves) as full human beings. What often results instead is more a "war between the sexes"–that destructively polarizing construct of gender relations from which we are yet unable to extricate ourselves. Boys try to *get* sex from girls; girls complain about boys' "one track minds"; men resent that women won't *give* them sex; women are wary that, via sex, men are trying to "use" them. Much pain, little trust–and hovering over all the reverberating insecurity, confusion, and taboos, the spectre of rape. In the face of the latter, as noted by Vance (1984, p. 4), "passion often doesn't have a chance."

Much needs to be done to give girls and women permission to "trust their lust," proudly and fearlessly to assert their desires. Societal efforts, both toward ending rape and honoring female sensuality and eroticism are, as yet, not forthcoming. Consequently, pleasure and safety remain "either/or" choices for girls and women, creating for them a predicament wherein they lose either way. Vance (1984) described women's dilemma in this way:

The tension between sexual danger and sexual pleasure is a powerful one in women's lives. To focus only on pleasure and gratification ignores the patriarchal structure in which women act, yet to speak only of sexual violence and oppression ignores women's experience with sexual agency and choice, and unwittingly increases the sexual terror and despair in which women live. (p. 1)

Hollibaugh (1984) expanded on this analysis:

We [women] live terrified of harassment or attack on the street and in our homes, and we live terrified that other people will discover our secret sexual desires. By recognizing the dangers of our circumstances, we have said, "There is no way to be a woman in this culture and be sexual too. I will live first with the anger and then hope we can change enough about the world that the women after me may be safe enough to fuck. For now, it will have to be enough." But this isn't enough, and we know it. (pp. 404, 407)

Our culture has yet to confront what Fine (1988) called "the missing discourse of desire." Nor have we validated as real the hesitation that heterosexual women feel when pleasure is within their reach, or their fear of saying "yes" to sex with men. Women's normal and healthy sexual cravings, their times of urgent, breathless lust, are viewed as perversions or reduced to fodder for dirty jokes. Because few if any models of "respectable" women or "good" girls who want and safely get sexual pleasure are available, and because women's needs for both safety and pleasure have been constructed as mutually exclusive options, women may well be as afraid of the prospect of erotic autonomy as they now are of rape.

In undertaking the redesign of cultural attitudes, we must realize that deconstructing such a time-honored myth requires little less than a revolution, because the pathology involved is cultural, not personal or individual (in either women or men). Educators, therapists, and sexologists must "counter the triple-whammy that love, ignorance, and guilt already exercise over girls' [and women's] ability to accept themselves as sexual beings" (Thompson, 1990, p. 358), and speak explicitly about the sexual constraints placed on women—not only the *oppression* of sexualized violence, but the *repression* of female eroticism. Professionals in these fields should also encourage women to resist ignorance, deprivation, and suppression *as well as* coercion and victimization (Vance, 1984). Concomitantly, feminists must cultivate a polemic that not only fights the misogynist realities of sexual violence, but resists stigma and censorship, refuses to glorify sensual denial, and advocates for erotic pleasure as one of women's inherent rights. In doing so, however, the words of Vance (1984, p. 24), sound the caution: "It is not safe to be a woman, and it never has been. [And] female attempts to claim pleasure are especially dangerous." Yet, in the words of an early 1970s feminist conscience-raising group (as quoted by Morgan, 1975, p. 22), "Maybe freedom is learning to fuck back."

In a society highly suspicious (if not wholly condemnatory) of female eroticism, those who care about stopping sexual violence against women have an obligation to work to eradicate sexist assumptions that neuter women's erotic selves, and not to place pleasure and safety in opposition. Unless women *en masse* have cultural permission to say they want erotic relationships on their terms and to say "yes" to, and even initiate, sexual intimacy, the legitimacy of an *individual* woman's "no" will remain subject to question—because cultural change does not happen one-on-one. Until then, we can be assured that acquaintance rape will prevail as an ugly, damaging experience in the lives of too many girls and women; "no means no" will continue to be a glib catch phrase that disregards and trivializes the ultimate sociopolitical context of women's erotic relationship to men; and another generation of "good girls" will condemn themselves for their sexual hungers, blame themselves when they are raped, and be convinced that their only sexual power is in the hoarding of sex away from men.

In service of decreasing sexual violence to women, we must not merely move *away* from the danger of sexual violence; we must move *toward* sensual pleasure, self-determination, and the celebration of sexual passion. The task is to create a culture in which people care as much about increasing women's access to erotic joy as they do about decreasing their risk of rape—because, particularly in the case of acquaintance rape, the former will directly facilitate the latter. Indeed, one will not happen without the other.

The task is also to challenge the ubiquitous gender imbalances that color all arenas in which females and males live with and among each other. The reward of such an attitudinal realignment will not only be a reduction in acquaintance rape, but a society of women no longer "in their place"– and thus able to offer their bodies honorably, with respect and trust (and to receive the same in return from their chosen partners). If eroticism is to be "[an] open and fearless underlining of [our] capacity for joy" (Lorde, 1984, p. 56), and if women are to be liberated from the ever-present threat of male sexual aggression, there can be no other path.

REFERENCES

Cassell, C. (1984). *Swept away: Why women fear their own sexuality.* New York: Simon & Schuster, Inc.

Clitoris: Still a forbidden word. (1989). *Contemporary Sexuality, 21*(2), 3.

Fine, M. (1988). Sexuality, schooling, and adolescent females: The missing discourse of desire. *Harvard Educational Review, 58,* 29-53.

Froelich, P. (1994, March 18). Do-me feminism does it right. *The Emory Wheel* (p. 7).

Hollibaugh, A. (1984). Desire for the future: Radical hope in passion and pleasure. In C. Vance (Ed.), *Pleasure and danger: Exploring female sexuality* (pp. 401-409). Boston: Routledge & Kegan Paul.

Lewin, M. (1985). Unwanted intercourse: The difficulty of saying no. *Psychology of Women Quarterly, 9,* 184-192.

Lorde, A. (1984). Uses of the erotic: The erotic as power. In A. Lorde (Ed.), *Sister outsider: Essays and speeches by Audre Lorde* (pp. 53-59). Freedom, CA: Crossings Press.

Lottes, I. (1988). Sexual socialization and attitudes toward rape. In A. Burgess (Ed.), *Rape and sexual assault II* (pp. 193-220). New York: Garland Publishers.

Morgan, E. (1975). *The erotization of male dominance/female submission.* Ann Arbor, MI: University of Michigan Papers in Women's Studies.

Moyer, K. E. (1987). *Violence and aggression: A physiological perspective.* New York: Paragon House Publishers.

Rubin, L. (1989, May). How we played the game. *Ms.,* 40-42.

Sanday, P. R. (1986). Rape and the silencing of the feminine. In S. Tomasalli & R. Porter (Eds.), *Rape: An historical and social inquiry* (pp. 84-101). New York: Basil Blackwell, Inc.

Scarlet Woman (1992). *Radical femme.* In D. Steinberg (Ed.), *The erotic impulse: Honoring the sexual self* (p. 211). New York: Jeremy P. Tarcher/Perigee Books.

Steinberg, D. (Ed.). (1992). *The erotic impulse: Honoring the sensual self.* New York: Jeremy P. Tarcher/Perigee Books.

Thompson, S. (1990). Putting a big thing into a little hole: Teenage girls' accounts of sexual initiation. *The Journal of Sex Research, 27,* 341-361.

Tolman, D. L. (1991). Adolescent girls, women, and sexuality: Discerning dilemmas of desire. In C. Gilligan, A. Rogers, & D. Tolman (Eds.), *Women, girls, and psychotherapy: Reframing resistance* (pp. 55-69). New York: The Haworth Press, Inc.

Vance, C. (Ed.). (1984). *Pleasure and danger: Exploring female sexuality.* Boston: Routledge & Kegan Paul.

Webster, P. (1984). The forbidden: Eroticism and taboo. In C. Vance (Ed.), *Pleasure and danger: Exploring female sexuality* (pp. 385-398). Boston: Routledge & Kegan Paul.

A Cognitive Ecological Model
of Women's Response
to Male Sexual Coercion in Dating

Paula S. Nurius, PhD
Jeanette Norris, PhD

SUMMARY. We offer a theoretical model that consolidates background, environmental, and intrapersonal variables related to women's experience of sexual coercion in dating into a coherent ecological framework and present for the first time a cognitive analysis of the processes women use to formulate responses to sexual coercion. An underlying premise for this model is that a woman's coping response to sexual coercion by an acquaintance is mediated through cognitive processing of background and situational influences. Because women encounter this form of sexual coercion in the context of relationships and situations that they presume will follow normative expectations (e.g., about making friends, socializing and dating), it is essential to consider normative processes of learning, cognitive mediation, and coping guiding their efforts to interpret and respond to this form of personal threat. Although acts of coercion unquestionably remain the responsibility of the perpetrator, a more complete understanding of the multilevel factors shaping women's perception of and response to threats can strengthen future inquiry and prevention efforts. *[Article copies available from The Haworth Document Delivery Service: 1-800-342-9678.]*

Paula S. Nurius and Jeanette Norris are both affiliated with the University of Washington.

The authors thank Irene Hanson Frieze and Thomas Graham for their helpful input on earlier versions of this article.

[Haworth co-indexing entry note]: "A Cognitive Ecological Model of Women's Response to Male Sexual Coercion in Dating." Nurius, Paula S., and Jeanette Norris. Co-published simultaneously in *Journal of Psychology & Human Sexuality* (The Haworth Press, Inc.) Vol. 8, No. 1/2, 1996, pp. 117-139; and: *Sexual Coercion in Dating Relationships* (ed: E. Sandra Byers, and Lucia F. O'Sullivan) The Haworth Press, Inc., 1996, pp. 117-139. Single or multiple copies of this article are available from The Haworth Document Delivery Service [1-800-342-9678, 9:00 a.m. - 5:00 p.m. (EST)].

117

Research over the last decade has demonstrated the high prevalence of sexual violence in dating. Up to 80% of women experience some form of sexual coercion, perpetrated primarily by someone they know (Koss, 1988; Muehlenhard & Linton, 1987; Rapaport & Burkhart, 1984). Approximately 25% of women have been found to be victims of rape or attempted rape (Finkelhor & Yllo, 1985; Koss, Gidycz, & Wisniewski, 1987; Koss & Oros, 1982; Russell, 1984). Because of the high prevalence of sexual coercion perpetrated by acquaintances, preventing coercion by dating partners is receiving increased attention. Although acts of sexual coercion remain the responsibility of the perpetrator, effective individual resistance can be key to preventing victimization. Because women encounter this form of sexual coercion in the context of relationships and situations that they presume will follow normative expectations (e.g., about making friends, socializing and dating), it is essential to consider normative processes of learning, cognitive mediation, and coping that will be guiding their efforts to interpret and respond to this form of personal threat.

Many researchers have demonstrated that a woman's active resistance dramatically decreases the likelihood of a completed rape without increasing the probability of physical injury. Although many of these researchers have focused on attacks by strangers (Griffin & Griffin, 1981, Marchbanks, Lui, & Mercy, 1990; Ullman & Knight, 1991, 1992), evidence suggests that the same physical strategies are as effective in warding off acquaintance rape as stranger rape (Levine-MacCombie & Koss, 1986; Murnen, Perot, & Byrne, 1989). However, little attention has been paid to the way that women develop responses to sexual coercion. More generally, previous researchers have not attempted to unify disparate findings from many different types of influences into a coherent theoretical structure.

The purpose of this article is twofold: (a) to offer a theoretical model that consolidates background, environmental, and intrapersonal variables related to women's experience of sexual coercion in dating into a coherent framework and (b) to present for the first time a cognitive analysis of the process by which women formulate responses to sexual coercion. The underlying premise for this model is that a woman's coping response to sexual coercion by an acquaintance is mediated through cognitive processing of background and situational influences. This model incorporates findings related to normative developmental learning, cognitive mediation, and coping processes in general, in addition to findings specifically related to sexual victimization by acquaintances and dating partners. In this article, we focus on women's responses to men's sexual coercion within heterosexual relationships. Although some of the specific variables may differ in situations of same-sex relationships or of a woman's sexual coercion against a man, the model that we present here should generalize as an organizing framework.

The term *dating* refers to the continuum of courtship and relationship development from first social encounter to premarital intimate relationship. Although there is difficulty achieving consensus in defining sexual coercion, most researchers agree that sexually coercive behavior, including use of physical coercion to obtain unwanted sexual contact, rape, or attempted rape constitutes victimization (Muehlenhard, Powch, Phelps, & Giusti, 1992). However, because sexual coercion during dating often escalates, beginning with behaviors that are ambiguous as to their inappropriateness or threat, and because we are concerned here with women's perceptions and responses in the face of unfolding degrees and forms of threat, we include a broader definition of sexual coercion as "any unwanted sexual contact–from fondling to sexual intercourse–through the use of verbal or physical pressure" (Struckman-Johnson, 1991).

It is important to note that the preponderance of research to date–and thus the work that we are drawing upon in this conceptual formulation–is largely based on samples of White, middle-class, young women. Therefore, it is as yet unclear whether or in what ways factors such as age, socioeconomic status, race, and culture may be significant factors in terms of women's experiences, interpretations, and inclinations toward responding to sexual coercion in dating. This relative lack of attention to women's heritage and social contexts is part of what indicates the need for a more ecological approach to study and intervention development. The cognitive appraisal processes that are posited here as serving important mediating roles would not be expected to differ as a function of factors such as race or socioeconomic status. However, the content or qualitative nature of cognitive factors such as knowledge, beliefs, and expectations and of social variables such as peer norms and patterns of socializing may well be shaped by these differences. Within an ecological framework, diversity variables are seen not only as individual status variables, but also as indicators of formal and informal social variables that need to be more vigorously investigated regarding their potential influence on women's risk of and response to the threat of sexual coercion by a dating partner.

AN ECOLOGICAL FRAMEWORK

An approach that incorporates both background and situational variables and also provides a coherent, organizing framework that further distinguishes the multilevel influences of intrapersonal, interpersonal, and sociocultural factors is an ecological or nested ecological framework

(Belsky, 1980; Bronfenbrenner, 1979). The ecological model serves as a metaphor for human interaction and human behavior (Germain & Gitterman, 1980). The principle of ecology is predicated on a view of reciprocal deterministic relations between persons and their environments and of interdependence among multiple systems in which smaller units are embedded within and influenced by larger ones. Use of the term *cognitive ecological* emphasizes the role of cognitive processes in governing perception and interpretation as individuals strive to establish meaning and predictability in their experiences and transactions (Brower & Nurius, 1993).

Ecological models have been previously applied to the study of violence against women (Dutton, 1988; Malamuth, Sockloskie, Koss, & Tanaka, 1991). Different levels of influence have been operationalized in terms of: (1) the macrosystem, which includes broader cultural values and belief systems, such as the messages pairing male sexual coercion with success and acceptance and the "normality" of sexual coercion (Check & Malamuth, 1985); (2) the ontogeny, or individual development factors, such as dating socialization, assertiveness, and prior experience with sexual victimization; (3) the exosystem, which includes both social units, such as peer influences and relationship variables, and interpersonal goals and expectations; and (4) the microsystem, is defined both in terms of the immediate setting within which a man and a woman interact, as well as the woman's prevailing cognitive appraisal of that context. Although macrosystem variables may have some indirect influence on women's recognition of and resistance to sexual coercion, their influences should be sufficiently captured through more proximal variables; thus, they will not be discussed further. While variables in Levels 1-3 "set the stage" as antecedents, variables in Level 4 are seen as those that most directly influence how risk is individually perceived and how emotional and behavioral responses are "released" in a particular situation.

Part of the utility in operationalizing an ecological framework is that it distinguishes multiple levels and forms of influence. This specification, in turn, provides theoretical guides for hypothesizing the relative effects of a potentially large set of predictor variables as well as indicating multiple levels and opportunities for prevention interventions (see Figure 1). In the remainder of this article we "walk through the model," reviewing the identified variables that have emerged from work to date and explaining the undergirding mechanisms of influence of each system, specifically, developmental learning, cognitive mediation, and coping processes.

Our greatest focus is on the microsystem variables and the processes of cognitive mediation and subsequent coping responses. We have adopted

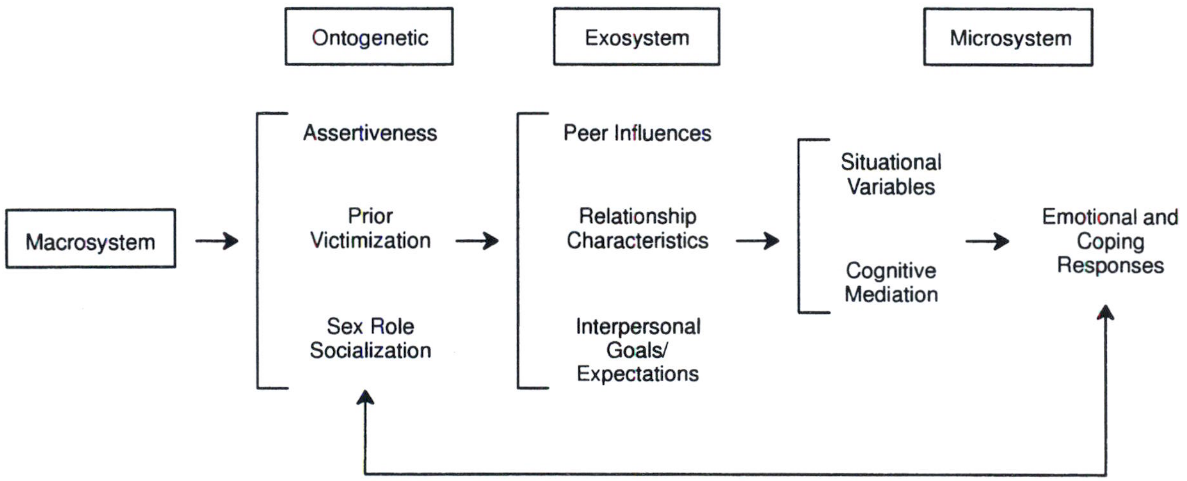

FIGURE 1. Conceptual Model of Women's Responses to Male Sexual Coercion in Dating

this focus because of the dearth of prior integration of these processes in the literature on sexual coercion during dating and because of their crucial role in shaping individual women's perception and response in individual situations. The specific variables that we present are not an exhaustive list, but rather those with the greatest supportive evidence to date and ones expected to come into play with respect to cognitive appraisal processes. We recognize that there may be other relationships among the various levels of variables that are not specified. Rather, we present a conceptual model that will serve as an organizing framework for meaningfully clustering sets of variables. Likewise, we recognize that the particular responses women perform when coerced can feed back on and influence other levels of variables. Our figures do not reflect all of these potential relationships because of our reliance on published findings. To date, longitudinal studies required for specification about possible feedback loops have not yet appeared. We have, however, indicated in a general way that this sort of feedback is possible and expected.

ONTOGENETIC VARIABLES

Ontogenetic variables are the carriers of historical influences in individuals' lives and are one conduit through which macrosystem forces exert an effect. That is, through our interactions with our environment, we receive information and develop theories about what is normative and what to expect, as well as develop personal attitudes, skills, and propensities. Although ontogenetic influences are relatively distal in relation to situation-specific responses, examination of ontogenetic variables should nevertheless provide insight into ways that this system has an impact on the formation of a woman's detection of and resistance to sexual coercion.

Personality variables have by and large not been useful in directly predicting effective resistance to sexual coercion (Amick & Calhoun, 1987; Murnen et al., 1989). However, there is evidence that at least three background factors may have an indirect effect by being mediated through microsystem variables. The first of these is assertiveness. Although assertiveness as a global trait has not been found to contribute directly to effective resistance (Amick & Calhoun, 1987), assertive behavior at the time of the incident has been found to decrease the likelihood of a completed rape (Amick & Calhoun, 1987; Bart & O'Brien, 1985; Murnen et al., 1989). Thus, the extent to which a woman is prepared to see assertive behavior as a reasonable resistance stance and is assisted to gain assertiveness skills and habits may have an indirect effect mediated through a woman's cognitive structures operating at the time of the coercion.

A parallel line of thought is applicable to prior victimization. Several researchers have found that a substantial number of rape victims have also been victimized earlier in life (see Browne & Finkelhor, 1986, for a review). However, a history of victimization has not always directly predicted victimization as an adult (Atkeson, Calhoun, & Morris, 1989; Mandoki & Burkhart, 1989). Mandoki and Burkhart (1989), however, did find that early victimization was related to an increased number of sexual partners later in life. This factor in turn was found to be a significant predictor of degree of adult sexual victimization. Prior victimization may have indirect effects, too, on the response to sexual coercion. Prior victimization may hamper a woman's ability to mount an effective response, rather than allow her to draw on her previous experiences in a beneficial way.

Intuitively, one might think that a history of victimization would result in increased vigilance on a woman's part when interacting with men. However, recent work on responses to threatening life events suggests that such events typically evoke strong short-term coping mobilization and long-term minimization responses (Taylor, 1991). In terms of victimization, this means that a woman, even when quite young, would respond to a threatening situation using all of her available coping resources. However, over time she would minimize the importance of the event. There are a variety of reasons posited for this pattern, including normative inclinations to resist negative information about self and to reestablish a sense of security to dampen the effects of past negative events. Such a pattern of minimization efforts by victims could impair their chances to translate their prior victimization experiences into effective abuse prevention and resistance that constructively builds upon this experience. Even though prior victimization is embedded in past history, i.e., it is not a characteristic of the immediate situation in which she finds herself; it can nevertheless affect the type of response she can mobilize. What is unclear at present are the specific ways in which prior victimization may influence future coping.

Female sex role socialization has also been mentioned as a factor in women's vulnerability to sexual coercion (see Muehlenhard & Hollabaugh, 1988, and Muehlenhard & McCoy, 1991, for recent discussions). Once again, any effect of a woman's sex role orientation on her ability to resist sexual coercion is likely to be indirect. Murnen et al. (1989) found that the trait known as hyperfemininity, a measure of sex role orientation specifically designed to assess the importance of relationships and the use of sexuality to maintain them, was not related to resistance to sexual coercion. However, a high degree of hyperfemininity was related to self-blame for being attacked. If a woman feels responsible for being coerced at the time it occurs, it follows that she would not mount as effective a resistance response than if she believed she was truly being violated. Thus, this aspect of a woman's socialization specifically associated with dating, in conjunction with other background characteristics, could form part of a larger pattern of determinants of a woman's resistance to sexual coercion.

Another aspect of traditional sex role socialization that could affect a woman's response to sexual coercion is her motivation to maintain the relationship. Byers, Giles, and Price (1987) found in a role-play situation that women were less verbally definite about their refusals when they were romantically interested in their dates. Thus, if this aspect of her socialization is especially salient, a woman may not be as resistant as someone who does not value maintaining a relationship as highly.

Within the ecological framework, at least three ontogenetic variables may have some indirect influence on how a woman responds to sexual coercion. The focus here has been on factors related to a woman's individual development. Discussion of these factors should not be interpreted as placing the onus for victimization on particular "types" of women. Rather, the intent is to give some examples of the way in which a woman's developmental history may play some role in responding to a man's aggressive advances. The following section emphasizes a woman's interaction with peers and partner in determining her reactions to a sexually coercive experience.

EXOSYSTEM VARIABLES

Exosystem variables, although still considered part of one's "background," are more proximal influences than ontogenetic variables on the way a woman cognitively processes cues in a coercion situation and responds to them. They consist of key person and environmental factors that set the stage for this cognitive mediation. Peers and romantic partners (or potential partners) are particularly strong sources of social influence in learning appropriate social roles associated with dating. These immediate peer and partner influences (as opposed to the more dating socialization pattern discussed in the previous section) can exert a major impact on the development of one's interpersonal goals and expectations surrounding dating. Given that these peer influences occur during the time when the risk of sexual coercion is highest, the type of norms transmitted about the content of appropriate dating roles and rituals can play a major role in a woman's response to them. Thus, consideration of peer influences, relationship characteristics, and interpersonal goals and expectations is an important component of the larger model.

Although peer influences have not been previously considered in attempting to understand how women respond to sexual coercion, there is reason to expect that, as in so many other areas of social behavior, peers exert a major impact. A woman's perceptions of what constitutes appropriate male sexual behavior, how to respond to men's advances in general, and unwanted advances in particular, are likely to be affected to some extent by the types and degree of interaction a woman has had about these topics with friends. Norris (1989, 1991) has shown that both men's and women's sexual and affective responses to both violent and nonviolent sexual material are influenced to a great extent by information regarding peers' responses. It is also likely that knowledge of friends' experiences with and reactions to sexual victimization have an impact on a woman's responses. Knowing someone who has been raped by an acquaintance or a dating partner might make a woman more aware of this possibility and thus heighten her defensiveness in social interactions (Mandoki & Burkhart, 1989).

Recent conceptualizations indicate that, rather than a one-time or an all-or-nothing phenomenon, different causes and patterns of coercion may be evident for different types of relationships. Thus, the type of relationship in which a woman is involved can affect her perception of sexually coercive cues and her responses to them. A woman might be at least somewhat wary of a man she has just met, but her level of trust increases the more deeply involved she becomes with him. Findings even indicate this sense of security may not be warranted (Lane & Gwartney-Gibbs, 1985). White (1992) found that length of time in a relationship, especially beyond five dates, is an important predictor of sexual coercion. Thus, although sexual coercion might have a high likelihood of occurring in longer-term relationships, a woman would tend to be less prepared to respond to a sexual coercion the longer she was involved. In fact, Shotland and Goodstein (1992) have shown that having had sex with someone a number of times leads individuals to believe that sex is obligated in the future. Thus, the longer a woman is in a relationship, not only is she less likely to resist unwanted sexual advances successfully (Amick & Calhoun, 1987), but evidence suggests that she actually blames herself more for the coercion than with someone she knows less well (Murnen et al., 1989). Furthermore, she is most likely to voluntarily have future contact with an assailant if she had been in an intimate relationship with him (Murnen et al., 1989).

Shotland (1992) contended that there may be as many as five varieties of dating or courtship rape. Each type arises at a different stage of a romantic relationship, these stages measured in terms of both the length of the relationship and previous sexual activity between the couple (i.e., early date rape, beginning date rape, relationship date rape, and rape within sexually active couples that does and does not include battery). Thus, it is apparent that a situational perspective that takes into account historical factors associated with the relationship holds great promise for elucidating further a woman's cognitive appraisal of a man's actions toward her.

A final form of exosystem variables that we address here is the interpersonal goals and expectations that the woman holds upon entering social situations and relationships. With respect to the risk of dating sexual coercion, dating-related constructs and the relationship of these constructs to women's perception of coercion signals and perceived response options are particularly important. Dating-related constructs are influenced, although distantly, by macrosystem variables such as cultural and media messages (Linz, Wilson, & Donnerstein, 1992), personal experiences (ontogenetic variables), and personally significant social units (peers and partners). These dating-related constructs, in turn, form the basis of women's social perceptual processes relative to dating and to dating coercion (Cantor & Zirkel, 1990; Markus & Cross, 1990; Nurius, 1991; and Showers & Cantor, 1985, provide general summaries about the cognitive mechanisms through which goals and expectations are formed and exert influence).

Both as social products and social forces, cognitive constructs such as these can be thought of both as exosystem and microsystem variables. At the exosystem level are women's developmentally predominant goals, assumptions, and expectancies about prototypical person and situation characteristics that define dates, dating, friendship, and intimacy. At the microsystem level is the more delimited and situationally biased (e.g., by setting cues, emotional state, effects of alcohol) subset of cognitive constructs likely to be active in information processing in the encounter of coercion. Attention to women's interpersonal goals and expectations involves recognition of developmental influences, framed in Eriksonian terms as the current life stage or, more recently, in terms of current concerns or life tasks (Cantor & Kihlstrom, 1987; Klinger, 1989). Within the context of developing friendships and romantic relationships, goals and expectations related to affiliation and intimacy are likely to be most prominent and, thus, substantial to influence the woman's "cognitive starting point" for her transactions within social situations that serve as the forums for pursuit of these interpersonal goals.

Exosystem variables are an important part of setting the stage for subsequent microsystem variables. How peer influences, relationship factors, and individual goals and expectations merge can significantly contribute to a woman's operating assumptions and "perceptual set" as she enters a situation she believes to be normative and affiliative but that turns out to be threatening. In the next section, we discuss how the two types of background variables—ontogenetic and exosystem—are transformed at the immediate cognitive level into a particular type of behavioral response.

MICROSYSTEM VARIABLES

Microsystem variables include both immediate situational influences on a woman's response and the cognitive appraisal processes that she undertakes in evaluating the situation. These are considered to have the strongest impact on her behavioral and emotional responses. In this section, we discuss in detail the cognitive appraisal processes involved in determining: first, the meaningfulness of a situation and the degree of risk present, and second, the factors that affect a woman's ability to respond. In addition, we address how particular factors, such as physical setting and alcohol consumption, can affect a woman's responses.

Situational Factors

Several aspects of a social situation can add to the ambiguity of cues present and thus, the appraisal process that a woman undertakes in interpreting and responding to a man's actions. Examples of such situational factors include the type of relationship between the man and the woman (Amick & Calhoun, 1987; Atkeson et al., 1989; Murnen et al., 1989); how much alcohol they have consumed (Abbey & Ross, 1992; Hawks & Welch, 1991; Muehlenhard & Linton, 1987), and the physical setting in which they socialize (Muehlenhard & Linton, 1987; Murnen, Perot, & Byrne, 1989). These situational factors have all been shown to affect the occurrence of and a woman's response to sexual coercion. The issue of base rate needs to be taken into account in interpreting the "typicality" of factors associated with high risk of coercion; to distinguish what is typical of dates in general, versus dates on which coercion occurs. For the purposes of this paper, the focus is less on incidence and more on understanding how situational factors alone or in combination with other variables would be expected to affect a woman's cognitive appraisal of and response to a situation—questions that have not yet been well addressed.

Amick and Calhoun (1987) found that unsuccessful resisters were more likely to be assaulted in an isolated site than successful resisters. Murnen et al. (1989) also indicated the importance of physical setting, noting that most reported incidents in their study occurred at the residence of either the assailant or the victim. Certain aspects of a setting may affect a woman's cognitive interpretation of a man's actions (i.e., the cues that a situation may be dangerous, and thus make her more or less likely to engage in a particular resistance response). For example, she might feel "safer" with other people around, assuming that a man would be less likely to "try something" in those circumstances. Thus, in this situation she might be less inclined to interpret the man's behavior as coercion and to take any action to ward him off.

Major studies have demonstrated a link between alcohol consumption and the occurrence of sexual coercion by acquaintances in college populations (Koss et al., 1987; Muehlenhard & Linton, 1987). Abbey and Ross (1992) found that alcohol consumption by a woman was much more likely to be associated with completed rape than with attempted rape. Furthermore, Hawks and Welch (1991) found that women who had been drinking at the time of a rape reported less resistance on their part and less clarity of nonconsent than women who were not consuming alcohol when raped. Consistent with these findings, Norris, Nurius, Dimeff, and White (1993) found that approximately one-third of sorority women surveyed reported that alcohol consumption would be a significant barrier to making an effective response to sexual coercion. By themselves, these studies leave open the question of whether a woman is simply less able to resist coercion when drinking because of physical impairment or whether more complex cognitive processes also come into play.

Research by Norris and her colleagues has demonstrated two ways in which alcohol can affect cognitions associated with sexual coercion. First, the mere presence of alcohol can act as a cue to construct an atmosphere of sexual permissiveness, while simultaneously diminishing the gravity of sexual coercion (Norris & Cubbins, 1992; Norris & Kerr, 1993). Second, even when consuming a moderate amount, that is, not enough to debilitate one physically, alcohol appears to increase women's acceptance of male sexual coercion. Intoxicated women have even reported a greater likelihood of enjoying victimization than did sober ones (Norris & Kerr, 1993). Thus, it is clear that alcohol is an important factor to be considered in understanding the cognitive appraisal of a sexually coercive situation.

A third set of variables that affects the cognitive formation of a resistance response concerns the characteristics of the sexual coercion itself. As defined earlier, sexual coercion can encompass a wide variety of verbal and physical behaviors, ranging from comments such as "Oh, come on, you know you like it" to outright physical force and rape. It appears from the research that the exact form of the coercion will have an impact on a woman's response to it. For instance, Atkeson et al. (1989) found that the presence of a weapon was less likely to result in physical resistance than when no weapon was used, whereas Murnen et al. (1989) found that women resisted more strongly as the assailant's means of attack escalated.

Although helpful in demonstrating the link between specific coercion characteristics and resistance, these researches did not address how a woman's interpretation of particular actions by the man develops and results in a resistance response. The role of interpretation is particularly important to acquaintance sexual coercion because this form of coercion often does not involve the use of an unmistakable cue such as a deadly weapon. For instance, if, after a couple has engaged in some amount of mutually consensual sexual behavior, the man slowly escalates his verbal or physical demands for further sexual interaction, then whether the man is engaging in sexual coercion can be ambiguous. It might take repeated refusals on the part of the woman before she decides that the man's behavior is inappropriate, especially if her cognitive processes are further affected by alcohol consumption. At the other extreme, if a man almost immediately attacks a woman physically, the cognitive processing of her defensive response would probably be quite rapid and strong.

Cognitive Appraisal Factors

A major difference affecting the ability to resist coercion by strangers versus acquaintances lies in the cognitive appraisal processes that a woman must undertake before she engages in a behavioral response. Recognizing danger cues in a social context requires much more complex psychological processing than does recognition of such cues in a stranger attack (Amick & Calhoun, 1987). To identify how cognitive appraisal variables affect women's perception of danger cues and responses to them, the recent social cognitive literature related to threatening life events is particularly informative. A considerable amount of work in this area has focused on adaptation and coping in the aftermath of negative events. However, recent analyses of appraisal processes as situations turn from neutral or positive to threatening provide important advances in our understanding of the cognitive challenges and tasks that a woman must undertake and ways by which her situational appraisals influence emotional and behavioral responding.

In this work, appraisals are defined as evaluations of what one's relationship to the environment implies for personal well-being. The first set, referred to as primary appraisals, has to do with searching for meaning in the event. This takes an initial form in appraisal of whether a phenomenon or event is self-relevant and whether it is neutral, poses benefit, or poses threat (Lazarus & Folkman, 1984). With respect to sexual coercion in dating, this involves the woman appraising that some aspect of the setting or the man's behavior is incongruent with her affiliation and safety goals, as well as an accurate assessment of whether the situation is potentially dangerous to her. Because recognizing danger cues is the first step in mounting an effective defense (Rozée, Bateman, & Gilmore, 1991), understanding the elements that lead a woman to interpret a social situation as threatening is crucial.

When the threat takes form suddenly and severely, primary appraisals are relatively straightforward. These appraisals can be complicated, however, by several aspects of the situation and social interaction, some of which were discussed previously. An additional element influencing women's cognitive mediation of cues related to sexual coercion by acquaintances involves influences of "working knowledge." At any one point in time, only a limited amount of our total repertoire of knowledge, beliefs, and capabilities can be active in awareness or working memory (Anderson, 1983). Those cognitive structures that are currently active will have their greatest influence on information processing in the moment. Factors that influence what gets activated include the goals and expectations that were prominent upon entering the situation, as well as the individual's mood and the setting cues (Browne & Taylor, 1986; Fiske & Taylor, 1991). Thus, one cognitive challenge for women arises at this early stage of detecting threat—a safety-related search and appraisal task that is likely to be discrepant with the social scenario of fun and friendship and with her affiliation-oriented goals, expectancies, mood, and situational interpretations.

The second type of cognitive appraisal, referred to as secondary appraisals, centers more around determinations of coping resources, options, and outcomes. The amount and type of coping or mastery potential a woman believes herself to have in the moment will in part determine the specific response she actually draws on from the total repertoire possible. If the event is judged to pose a personal threat, a number of subsequent interpretations are needed: (a) what is the nature of this threat? (b) who is at fault or accountable? (c) what are my coping options or resources? (d) how well can I draw upon these options or resources? (e) what barriers do I face in enacting these options? and (f) what are the possibilities of change in the situation that could make it more or less threatening? (Smith & Lazarus, 1990, 1993; Smith, Haynes, Lazarus, & Pope, 1993). Figure 2 dis-

FIGURE 2. Primary and Secondary Appraisal Processes Mediating Emotional and Coping Responses to Sexual Coercion

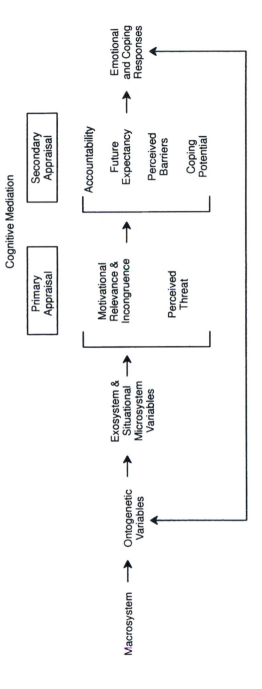

plays the function of these primary and secondary appraisal processes in cognitively mediating the effects of background and contextual variables.

Again, these appraisals are more straightforward when the situation is more clear-cut. In sexual coercion during dating, there are different types of threat or loss that the woman may have to simultaneously weigh, constituting a kind of multivariate cost-benefit analysis involving potentially conflicting goals and concerns: personal safety related to sexual victimization (e.g., "If I give in, maybe he won't hurt me"), personal safety related to resistance efforts (e.g., "He might just get angrier if I resist"), social costs associated with drawing the attention of others to what she may see as a stigmatizing event (e.g., "Maybe they'll think I led him on"), and concerns related to damaging her relationship with the male (e.g., "What if I'm wrong about his intentions and he is insulted?"). Thus, women encounter another form of cognitive challenge in needing to undertake secondary appraisals under conditions of the potentially disruptive effects of confusion, competing concerns, and high emotionality. Findings from a recent study of sorority women's expectations about the feelings and concerns they would have in encountering sexual coercion during dating, and how these thoughts and feelings would influence their behavioral responses reflected this kind of cognitive challenge (Nurius, Norris, & Dimeff, 1995). The psychological barriers to responding effectively to sexual coercion most strongly endorsed by these women concerned being viewed as "loose," getting a reputation as a "tease," and fear of embarrassment (Norris et al., 1993).

The importance of emotional responses is their role in mobilizing the person to cope and in biasing the directions of this coping effort. Emotion has a powerful influence in information processing–what gets searched for, noticed, recalled, and decided tends to be mood-congruent–at times interfering with cognitive activity and coping (e.g., Schwarzer, 1984). Recent analysis also indicates that emotions are cognitively represented in memory and that different emotions tend to be associated with information about different modes of responding. Thus, different emotions predispose individuals to certain forms of action readiness (Frijda, 1987; Frijda, Kuipers, & ter Schure, 1989). Specific cognitions, such as evaluations about circumstances, have been found to be strongly related to specific emotions. Anger has been associated with blaming someone for an unwanted situation, guilt with blaming oneself, fear with thinking that one is endangered, and hurt or sadness with perceived betrayal or loss (see Folkman & Lazarus, 1988; Lazarus & Smith, 1988; Smith et al., 1993; and Smith & Lazarus, 1993, for reviews).

Thus, women's emotional responses experienced at the time of a sexual coercive experience are closely intertwined with her behavioral responses. For example, experiencing anger and its concomitant appraisal that the assailant is indeed responsible for the situation is likely to result in assertive and situationally-focused coping responses (Folkman, Lazarus, Dunkel-Schetter, DeLongis, & Gruen, 1986). On the other hand, a woman whose predominant cognitive and emotional set involves guilt (e.g., "This is awful. I must have given him the wrong impression; otherwise, he would not be acting this way.") is more likely to try to appease her date while also trying to set limits, resulting in mixed messages and less physically assertive resistance responses. Although it is by no means impossible to access cognitive structures associated with perpetrator accountability and skills associated with physical resistance under the latter conditions, their incongruence with the prevailing feelings of guilt will be an impediment to such interpretations and behavioral responses.

One factor that complicates the appraisals that women make about a situation is a set of cognitive biases manifested by unrealistic optimism, exaggerated perceptions of mastery, and overly positive self-evaluations. Typically, this normative "illusory glow" is associated with positive mental health and social functioning, as well as with successful coping and reestablishing psychological well-being in the aftermath of threat (Friedland, Keinan, & Regev, 1992; Greenwald, 1980; Scheier & Carver, 1985; Taylor, 1989; Taylor & Brown, 1988). However, these cognitive predispositions may serve to exacerbate women's risk with respect to sexual coercion in dating. For example, although traditional sexual scripts may incline women to expect sexual pressure from men and adversarial interactions related to refusal of men's advances, positivity bias would incline women on an individual basis to believe that this would remain in manageable limits, that the men they know would be unlikely to "cross the line," and that they could handle the situation. In short, the double-edged sword here is biasing effect on women of underestimating their own likelihood of encountering sexual coercion in spite of having knowledge of the risks for women in general (Norris et al., 1993); of overlooking or misinterpreting coercion cues (Rozée et al., 1991); and of overestimating their efficacy in effectively resisting sexual coercion (Murnen et al., 1989).

Because of its widespread and generally health-promoting effects, this positivity bias is a particularly difficult phenomenon to address. Its presence suggests that education about risk is insufficient for effective sexual coercion resistance and prevention intervention and that greater understanding of the dynamics to women's appraisal processes related to risk and protection is needed. Findings about the cognitive appraisal variables reviewed here suggest the need to build upon prior educational efforts to include attention to such factors as: difficulties in making the step from intellectual recognition of the social problem of sexual coercion in dating to recognition of the personal relevance of this problem and risk; impediments to early detection of threat (e.g., to searching for and interpreting threat cues from dating partners); the conflicts and cost-benefit dilemmas that may serve as impediments to rapid and decisive response; ways in which resistance actions may be affected by microsystem, exosystem, and ontogenetic variables; and the need for anticipatory coping, for cognitive and behavioral rehearsal and for involvement of supportive others such as peers.

At the microsystem level, at least three categories of immediate context variables—the physical setting, alcohol consumption, and the characteristics of the coercion—could all influence a woman's cognitive interpretation of a man's actions and her behavioral response to him. The ways that these variables affect her behavior are mediated through the cognitive processes discussed previously. These cognitive processes are the mechanisms by which women appraise dating events for their risk to her. It is apparent that cognitive appraisals serve the important mediational role of linking prior goals and beliefs with situational cognitive interpretations and subsequent behavioral and emotional responses (cf. Nurius, Furrey, & Berliner, 1993, in relation to abusive partners.) These contextual variables and cognitive appraisal processes, because of their situational immediacy, are believed to have the strongest impact on a resistance response. However, there is reason to believe that more distal variables—macrosystem, ontogenetic, exosystem—also affect, at least indirectly, a woman's ability to resist sexual coercion.

CONCLUSIONS AND IMPLICATIONS

Although different researchers have identified factors associated with women's resistance to sexual coercion, no one has previously presented a model integrating several levels of variables that can determine such a response. We have shown here that an analysis of women's cognitive appraisals at the time of a sexual coercion may be a useful approach to understanding how women appraise the risk of being sexually coerced and formulate a response based on that risk. Furthermore, we have identified a number of background variables in the form of the individual's ontogeny, or individual development and history, and the exosystem, or social influences and individual goals and expectations related to the specific situation, that can affect a woman's resistance, albeit indirectly. We have presented evidence to support the various components of the model. However, it remains for future researchers to test this model in part or entirety and determine the strength of its causal links.

The importance of assessing these categories of variables is their bearing on understanding the corresponding contextual and interpretive frameworks within which women appraise and respond to threat by a partner. This model will guide future researchers who extend beyond college populations and who, ultimately, guide development of prevention strategies tailored to the needs of women with differing backgrounds exposed to differing forms and severity of coercion. As noted earlier, inquiry into acquaintance sexual coercion has not yet done full justice to the diversity of women, their life experiences, or their environments. Given that age, socioeconomic status, and race have been found to be significant distinguishing factors in patterns of dating and marital aggression (Day, 1992; Hotaling & Sugarman, 1986; Sugarman & Hotaling, 1989), these factors constitute important deficits in research to date. Future researches should make a special effort to include greater diversity with respect to these characteristics.

It is important to emphasize that teaching women to detect and respond to sexual coercion does not place the onus for its occurrence on them. The act is still the responsibility of the perpetrator. But it is necessary to acknowledge that, for the foreseeable future, there will be sexually coercive men in this society and that women can empower themselves by preparing to recognize and cope with high-risk situations.

REFERENCES

Abbey, A., & Ross, L. T. (1992). *The role of alcohol in understanding misperception and sexual assault.* Paper presented at the 100th annual meeting of the American Psychological Association, August.

Amick, E. A., & Calhoun, K. S. (1987). Resistance to sexual aggression: Personality, attitudinal, and situational factors. *Archives of Sexual Behavior, 16,* 153-163.

Anderson, J. R. (1983). *The architecture of cognition.* Cambridge, MA: Harvard University Press.

Atkeson, B. M., Calhoun, K. S., & Morris, K. T. (1989). Victim resistance to rape: The relationship of previous victimization, demographics, and situational factors. *Archives of Sexual Behavior, 18,* 497-507.

Bart, P. B., & O'Brien, P. H. (1985). *Stopping rape: Successful survival strategies.* Elmsford: Pergamon.

Belsky, J. (1980). Child maltreatment: An ecological integration. *American Psychologist, 35,* 320-335.

Bronfenbrenner, U. (1979). *The ecology of human development.* Cambridge, MA: Harvard University Press.

Brower, A., & Nurius, P. S. (1993). *Social cognition and individual change: Current theory and counseling guidelines.* New York: Sage.

Browne, J. D., & Taylor, S. E. (1986). Affect and processing of personal information: Evidence for mood-activated self-schemata. *Journal of Experimental Social Psychology, 22,* 436-452.

Browne, A. & Finkelhor, D. (1986). Impact of child sexual abuse: A review of the research. *Psychological Bulletin, 99,* 66-77.

Byers, E. S., Giles, B. L., & Price, D. L. (1987). Definiteness and effectiveness of women's responses to unwanted sexual advances: A laboratory investigation. *Basic and Applied Social Psychology, 8,* 321-338.

Cantor, N., & Kihlstrom, J. F. (1987). *Personality and social intelligence.* Englewood Cliffs, NJ: Prentice-Hall.

Cantor, N., & Zirkel, S. (1990). Personality, cognition, and purposive behavior. In L. A. Pervin (Ed.), *Handbook of personality theory and research* (pp. 135-164). New York: Guilford.

Check, J. V. P., & Malamuth, N. (1985). An empirical assessment of some feminist hypotheses about rape. *International Journal of Women's Studies, 8,* 414-423.

Day, R. D. (1992). The transition to first intercourse among racially and culturally diverse youth. *Journal of Marriage and the Family, 54,* 749-762.

Dutton, D. G. (1988). *The domestic assault of women: Psychological and criminal justice perspectives.* Boston: Allyn & Bacon.

Finkelhor, D., & Yllo, K. (1985). *License to rape.* New York: Holt, Rinehart, & Winston.

Fiske, S. T., & Taylor, S. E. (1991). *Social cognition* (2nd ed.). New York: McGraw Hill.

Folkman, S., & Lazarus, R. S. (1988). Coping as mediator of emotion. *Journal of Personality and Social Psychology, 54,* 466-475.

Folkman, S., Lazarus, R. S., Dunkel-Schetter, C., DeLongis, A., & Gruen, R. (1986). The dynamics of a stressful encounter: Cognitive appraisal, coping, and encounter outcomes. *Journal of Personality and Social Psychology, 50,* 992-1003.

Friedland, N., Keinan, G., & Regev, Y. (1992). Controlling the uncontrollable: Effects of stress on illusory perceptions of controllability. *Journal of Personality and Social Psychology, 63,* 923-931.

Frijda, N. H. (1987). Emotion, cognitive structure, and action tendency. *Cognition and Emotion, 1,* 115-143.

Frijda, N. H., Kuipers, P., & ter Schure, E. (1989). Relations among emotion, appraisal, and emotional action readiness. *Journal of Personality and Social Psychology, 57,* 212-228.

Germain, C. B., & Gitterman, A. (Eds.). (1980). *The life model of social work practice.* New York: Columbia University Press.

Greenwald, A. G. (1980). The totalitarian ego: Fabrication and revision of personal history. *American Psychologist, 35,* 603-618.

Griffin, B. S., & Griffin, C. T. (1981). *Victims in rape confrontation. Victimology: An International Journal, 6,* 59-75.

Hawks, B. K., & Welch, C. D. (1991). *Alcohol and the experience of rape.* Paper presented at the annual meetings of the American Psychological Association, August, San Francisco.

Hotaling, G. T., & Sugarman, D. B. (1986). An analysis of risk markers in husband to wife violence: The current state of knowledge. *Violence & Victims, 1,* 101-124.

Klinger, E. (1989). Goal orientation as psychological linchpin: A commentary on Cantor and Kihlstrom's "Social intelligence and cognitive assessments of personality." In R. S. Wyer & T. K. Srull (Eds.), *Advances in social cognition* (Vol. 2, pp. 123-130). Hillsdale, NJ: Erlbaum.

Koss, M. P. (1988). Hidden rape: Sexual aggression and victimization in a national sample of students in higher education. In A. W. Burgess (Ed.), *Sexual assault* (Vol. II, pp. 3-25). New York: Garland.

Koss, M. P., Gidycz, C. J., & Wisniewski, N. (1987). The scope of rape: Incidence and prevalence of sexual aggression and victimization. *Journal of Consulting and Clinical Psychology, 55,* 162-170.

Koss, M. P., & Oros, C. J. (1982). The sexual experiences survey: A research instrument investigating sexual aggression and victimization. *Journal of Consulting and Clinical Psychology, 50,* 455-457.

Lane, K. A., & Gwartney-Gibbs, P. A. (1985). Violence in the context of dating and sex. *Journal of Family Issues, 6,* 45-59.

Lazarus, R., & Folkman, S. (1984). *Stress, appraisal, and coping.* New York: Springer.

Lazarus, R., & Smith, C. A. (1988). Knowledge and appraisal in the cognition-emotion relationship. *Cognition and Emotion, 2,* 281-300.

Levine-MacCombie, J., & Koss, M. P. (1986). Acquaintance rape: Effective avoidance strategies. *Psychology of Women Quarterly, 10,* 311-320.

Linz, D., Wilson, B. J., & Donnerstein, E. (1992). Sexual violence in the mass media: Legal solutions, warnings, and mitigation through education. *Journal of Social Issues, 48,* 145-171.

Malamuth, N. M., Sockloskie, R. J., Koss, M. P., & Tanaka, J. S. (1991). Characteristics of aggressors against women: Testing a model using a national sample of college students. *Journal of Consulting and Clinical Psychology, 59,* 670-681.

Mandoki, C. A., & Burkhart, B. R. (1989). Sexual victimization: Is there a vicious cycle? *Violence and Victims, 3,* 179-190.

Marchbanks, P. A., Lui, K-J, & Mercy, J. A. (1990). *American Journal of Epidemiology, 132,* 540-549.

Markus, H., & Cross, S. (1990). The interpersonal self. In L. A. Pervin (Ed.), *Handbook of personality theory and research* (pp. 576-598). New York: Guilford.

Muehlenhard, C. L., & Hollabaugh, L. C. (1988). *Journal of Personality and Social Psychology, 54,* 872-879.

Muehlenhard, C. L., & Linton, M. A. (1987). Date rape and sexual aggression in dating situations: Incidence and risk factors. *Journal of Counseling Psychology, 34,* 186-196.

Muehlenhard, C. L., & McCoy, M. L. (1991). Double standard/double bind: The sexual double standard and women's communication about sex. *Psychology of Women Quarterly, 15,* 447-461.

Muehlenhard, C. L., Powch, I. G., Phelps, J. L., & Giusti, L. M. (1992). Definitions of rape: Scientific and political implications. *Journal of Social Issues, 48,* 23-44.

Murnen, S. K., Perot, A., & Byrne, D. (1989). Coping with unwanted sexual activity: Normative responses, situational determinants, and individual differences. *The Journal of Sex Research, 26,* 85-106.

Norris, J. (1991). Social influence effects on responses to sexually explicit material containing violence. *The Journal of Sex Research, 28,* 67-76.

Norris, J. (1989). Normative influence effects on sexual arousal to nonviolent sexually explicit material. *Journal of Applied Social Psychology, 19,* 341-352.

Norris, J., & Cubbins, L. A. (1992). Dating, drinking, and rape: Effects of victim's and assailant's alcohol consumption on judgments of their behavior and traits. *Psychology of Women Quarterly, 16,* 179-191.

Norris, J., & Kerr, K. L. (1993). Alcohol and violent pornography: Responses to permissive and nonpermissive cues. *Journal of Studies on Alcohol.*

Norris, J., Nurius, P. S., Dimeff, L. A., & White, R. (1993, April 16). *Gender comparisons and the experience of rape.* Paper presented at a meeting of the Society for the Scientific Study of Sex, Western Region, Seattle WA.

Nurius, P. S. (1991). Possible selves and social support: Social cognitive resources for coping and striving. In J. Howard & P. Callero (Eds.), *The self-society dynamic.* Cambridge, MA: Cambridge Press.

Nurius, P. S., Furrey, J., & Berliner, L. (1993). Coping capacity among women with abusive partners. *Violence and Victims, 7*(3).

Nurius, P. S., Norris, J., & Dimeff, L. A. (1995). *Through her eyes: Cognitive challenges for women in perceiving acquaintance rape threat.* Manuscript under review.

Rapaport, K., & Burkhart, B. R. (1984). Personality and attitudinal characteristics of sexually coercive college males. *Journal of Abnormal Psychology, 93,* 216-221.

Royce, P. D., Bateman, P., & Gilmore, T. (1991). The personal perspective of acquaintance rape prevention: A three-tier approach. In A. Parrot & L. Beckhofer (Eds.), *Acquaintance rape: The hidden crime* (pp. 9-25). New York: John Wiley & Sons.

Rozée, P. D., Bateman, P., & Gilmore, T. (1991). The personal perspective of acquaintance rape prevention: A three-tier approach. In A. Parrot and L. Beckhofer (Eds.), *Acquaintance rape: The hidden crime* (pp. 337-354). New York: John Wiley & Sons.

Russell, D. E. H. (1984). *Sexual exploitation: Rape, child sexual abuse, and workplace harassment.* Beverly Hills, CA: Sage.

Scheier, M. F., & Carver, C. S. (1985). Optimism, coping and health: Assessment and implications of generalized outcome expectancies. *Health Psychology, 4,* 219-247.

Schwarzer, R. (Ed.). (1984). *The self in anxiety, stress, and depression.* Amsterdam: Elsevier.

Shotland, R. L. (1992). A theory of the causes of courtship rape: Part 2. *Journal of Social Issues, 48,* 127-143.

Shotland, R. L., & Goodstein, L. (1992). Sexual precedence reduces the perceived legitimacy of sexual refusal: An examination of attributions concerning date rape and consensual sex. *Personality and Social Psychology Bulletin, 18,* 756-764.

Showers, C., & Cantor, N. (1985). Social Cognitives: A look at motivated strategies. *Annual Review of Psychology, 36,* 275-305.

Smith, C. A., & Lazarus, R. S. (1993). Appraisal components, core relational themes, and the emotions. *Cognition and Emotion, 7,* 233-269.

Smith, C. A., & Lazarus, R. S. (1990). Emotion and adaptation. In L. A. Pervin (Ed.), *Handbook of personality: Theory and research.* New York: Guilford Press.

Smith, C. A., Haynes, K. N., Lazarus, R. S., & Pope, L. K. (1993). In search of the "hot" cognitions: Attributions, appraisals, and their relation to emotion. *Journal of Personality and Social Psychology, 65,* 916-929.

Struckman-Johnson, C. (1991). Male victims of acquaintance rape. In A. Parrot and L. Bechhofer (Eds.), *Acquaintance rape: The hidden crime* (pp. 192-214). New York: John Wiley & Sons, Inc.

Sugarman, D. B., & Hotaling, G. T. (1989). Dating violence: Prevalence, context and risk markers. In M. A. Pirog-Good & J. E. Stets (Eds.), *Violence in dating relationships: Emerging social issues.* New York: Praeger.

Taylor, S. E., & Brown, J. D. (1988). Illusion and well-being: A social psychological perspective on mental health. *Psychological Bulletin, 103,* 193-210.

Taylor, S. E. (1991). Asymmetrical effects of positive and negative events: The mobilization-minimization hypothesis. *Psychological Bulletin, 110,* 67-85.

Taylor, S. E. (1989). *Positive illusions: Creative self-deception and the healthy mind.* New York: Basic Books.

Ullman, S. E., & Knight, R. A. (1991). A multivariate model for predicting rape and physical injury outcomes during sexual assaults. *Journal of Consulting and Clinical Psychology, 59,* 724-731.

Ullman, S. E., & Knight, R. A. (1992). Fighting back: Women's resistance to rape. *Journal of Interpersonal Violence, 7,* 31-43.

White, J. Personal communication, November 1992.

Beyond "Just Saying No": Dealing with Men's Unwanted Sexual Advances in Heterosexual Dating Contexts

Charlene L. Muehlenhard, PhD
Sandra L. Andrews, PhD
Ginna K. Beal, MSW, BCSW

SUMMARY. How can women deal with unwanted sexual advances from male dating partners in ways that are effective and that, at least initially, take the men's feelings into account? In Study 1, 354 undergraduate men watched videotapes in which a woman either did or did not openly communicate early during a date that she did not want to do more than kiss. Open communication decreased men's ratings of how much she wanted petting and intercourse, how likely they would be to attempt these behaviors with her, and how "led on" they would feel if they attempted these behaviors and she refused. In Study 2, 424 undergraduate men were presented with 28 responses women could make to a man's sexual advances. They rated each on

Charlene L. Muehlenhard is affiliated with the University of Kansas. Sandra L. Andrews is affiliated with the Austin-Travis County Mental Health Mental Retardation Center. Ginna K. Beal is affiliated with the Louisiana State University Department of Medicine.

Address correspondence to Charlene Muehlenhard, Department of Psychology, 426 Fraser Hall, University of Kansas, Lawrence, KS 66045.

The authors thank all the undergraduate research assistants who helped with these studies. Study 2 was conducted as the third author's senior honors thesis.

[Haworth co-indexing entry note]: "Beyond 'Just Saying No': Dealing with Men's Unwanted Sexual Advances in Heterosexual Dating Contexts." Muehlenhard, Charlene L., Sandra L. Andrews, and Ginna K. Beal. Co-published simultaneously in *Journal of Psychology & Human Sexuality* (The Haworth Press, Inc.) Vol. 8, No. 1/2, 1996, pp. 141-168; and: *Sexual Coercion in Dating Relationships* (ed: E. Sandra Byers, and Lucia F. O'Sullivan) The Haworth Press, Inc., 1996, pp. 141-168. Single or multiple copies of this article are available from The Haworth Document Delivery Service [1-800-342-9678, 9:00 a.m. - 5:00 p.m. (EST)].

141

its effectiveness in getting them to stop their advances and its effect on the relationship. Women can use this information when responding to unwanted sexual advances, taking into account the relative importance of stopping the advance and maintaining the relationship. *[Article copies available from The Haworth Document Delivery Service: 1-800-342-9678.]*

Dating frequently involves unwanted sexual advances. Many women have been pressured into unwanted sexual activity with men, sometimes because of physical force, but more often because of verbal pressure or the man's simply proceeding without asking for consent (Byers & Lewis, 1988; Koss, Gidycz, & Wisniewski, 1987; Mosher & Anderson, 1986; Muehlenhard & Linton, 1987; Rapaport & Burkhart, 1984). In one study, 16.7% of the women and 17.0% of an independent sample of men reported that during their most recent date the man had made sexual advances unwanted by the woman (Muehlenhard & Linton, 1987). Byers and Lewis (1988) found that, in four weeks of dating, almost half the women sampled reported a disagreement in which the man wanted sexual activity that the woman did not. These findings highlight the importance of women's being able to deal effectively with men's unwanted sexual advances.

Dealing with a man's unwanted sexual advances may seem simple: just say no! This situation, however, is complicated by several considerations: the woman may be concerned about protecting the man's feelings and maintaining the relationship; the man may not believe her refusal; and the man may ignore her refusal, even if he believes her.

WOMEN'S CONCERNS ABOUT THE MAN'S FEELINGS AND THE RELATIONSHIP

Women's responses to unwanted sexual advances are affected by their concerns about the man and the relationship. In role plays of unwanted sexual advances from men, women who were the most romantically interested in the man gave the least verbally definite refusals; men, in turn, rated these indefinite refusals as least effective in getting themselves and other men to stop their sexual advances (Byers, Giles, & Price, 1987). The majority of the women sampled–58%–indicated that their feelings about the man were the most important determinant influencing their response to his unwanted sexual advances (Byers et al., 1987). In a study of dating situations in which the man wanted a higher level of sexual activity than did the woman, more than half the women reported being very or extremely romantically interested in their partners, and the more romantically interested women were, the less the men complied with the women's refusals (Byers & Lewis, 1988).

MEN'S DISBELIEF OF WOMEN'S REFUSALS

Men do not always believe women's refusals. In role-play situations, only about a third of the men interpreted the woman's refusal to mean that she wanted him to stop; about half interpreted her refusal to mean that they should try again later; the others interpreted her refusal to mean that they should try again right away or continue (Byers & Wilson, 1985). In a study in which men evaluated a written description of a date, men's mean rating of how much the woman wanted to have sexual intercourse was 4.5 on a 1-9 scale (Muehlenhard, Linton, Felts, & Andrews, 1985). This occurred even though the woman was depicted as engaging in behavior generally regarded as not indicative of sexual interest (she wore a pleated woolen skirt and penny loafers, she drank no alcohol, etc.), and even though she responded to the man's sexual advances by saying no three times and trying to move away. Why might men disbelieve women's refusals?

Men interpret many dating behaviors as signaling interest in sexual intercourse: when the woman asks a man for a date; goes to his apartment or house; allows him to pay the dating expenses rather than splitting the expenses; dresses "provocatively"; drinks alcohol; or engages in some other sexual behavior, such as kissing (Abbey, 1991; Goodchilds & Zellman, 1984; Kanin, 1967; Muehlenhard, 1988; Muehlenhard et al., 1985). Men tend to regard these dating behaviors as more flirtatious, sexy, or seductive than do women (Abbey, 1982, 1991; Goodchilds & Zellman, 1984; Johnson, Stockdale, & Saal, 1991; Kowalski, 1993; Muehlenhard, 1988).

Once a man has misinterpreted a woman's behavior and has concluded that she wants to have sex, he may remain unconvinced by her refusal. He may assume that she is following the sexual script dictating that women should not directly and openly acknowledge their interest in sexual activity, and that instead, women should offer "token" refusals, which men should ignore (Abbey, 1991; Check & Malamuth, 1983; Muehlenhard, Giusti, & Rodgers, 1993; Muehlenhard & Hollabaugh, 1988; Muehlenhard & McCoy, 1991). He may, thus, interpret her refusals to be insincere (Bart & O'Brien, 1985, p. 10; Warshaw, 1988, p. 91).

MEN'S IGNORING WOMEN'S REFUSALS

Even if a woman eventually convinces a man that she does not want to engage in sexual activity, he may disregard her wishes and proceed without her consent. If he previously had misinterpreted her behavior as indicative of willingness to engage in sex, he might feel that she had "led him on" by feigning sexual interest. Many boys and men regard rape and other forms of sexual coercion as justifiable if a girl or woman "leads them on" (Goodchilds & Zellman, 1984; Kanin, 1967; Muehlenhard et al., 1985).

Even if a man did not feel "led on," he might proceed with sex and ignore the woman's refusals for numerous reasons, such as: peer pressure and a desire for male bonding; sexual arousal; anger or hostility toward that woman or toward women in general; or simply a desire to have sex whenever he wants, regardless of the woman's feelings (Barbaree & Marshall, 1991; Groth, Burgess, & Holmstrom, 1977; Sanday, 1990).

Thus, it would be useful to identify ways in which women can deal effectively with men's unwanted sexual advances in dating situations. Because a woman in a dating situation is likely to be concerned about the relationship, it would be useful to identify ways that women can deal with men's advances while still taking the relationship into account. Because men sometimes ignore women's refusals and continue their advances, however, it would also be useful to identify the best ways to stop men's unwanted advances, regardless of the impact on the relationship. The two studies presented here provide information women can use in such situations.

STUDY 1

Study 1 was an investigation of one way in which a woman might deal preemptively with a man's sexual advances: openly communicating her sexual limits early in the date. Encouraging open communication about sex is a theme of many rape-prevention programs and pamphlets (e.g., American College Health Association, 1992; also see Parrot, 1991).

Our first concern was assessing the effect of using versus not using open communication. If a woman communicates her sexual limits prior to any sexual activity, the man may never make unwanted sexual advances. If he does make a sexual advance that she refuses, he may be less likely to regard her refusal as merely token or to feel "led on" if she had communicated her sexual limits early in the date.

Our second concern involved timing: When during the date should the woman communicate her limits? Perhaps this is best done early during the date, such as when the couple first decides to go to a location where petting or sexual intercourse is possible (e.g., to one of their apartments). Perhaps the earlier the woman communicates her limits, the less "led on" the man is likely to feel. Alternatively, perhaps it would seem presumptuous or inappropriate for the woman to communicate her sexual limits before the man has expressed any interest in sex, or perhaps if she express-es her limits too early, he is likely to forget what she said or to assume that she has subsequently changed her mind.

Our third concern was whether the effectiveness of open communica-tion would vary as a function of men's attitudes related to sexual coercion. We conceptualized three patterns of attitudes likely to affect men's re-sponses. Some men believe that if a woman "leads a man on," then the man is justified in using force to engage in the sexual behavior (we labeled men who endorse this belief the *leading-on group*). Other men do not believe that force is justified if they feel "led on," but they do believe that women's refusals are often merely token (the *token-refusal group*). Still other men do not believe either of these myths (the *low-myth group*).

To investigate these concerns, we showed men one of five videotapes of a woman and man who go on a date. In Tapes 1 through 4, the woman openly communicated her sexual limits to the man at some point during the date by saying that she did not want to "do anything more than kiss." In Tape 5, the control tape, she did not say this. We conducted three sets of analyses:

1. We assessed the effects of using versus not using open communica-tion by comparing Tapes 1 through 4 with Tape 5, the control tape. We predicted that open communication would decrease men's rat-ings of how much the woman wanted to engage in petting and inter-course, how likely they would be to attempt these behaviors, how "led on" they would feel if they attempted these behaviors and she refused, and how justified it would be to engage in these behaviors after she refused.
2. We assessed the effects of the timing of the open communication by comparing all five tapes with each other. No predictions were made about which timing would be most effective.
3. We assessed the effectiveness of open communication as a function of men's attitudes related to sexual coercion. We expected main ef-fects for attitude group, such that the leading-on group would be most accepting and the low-myth group would be least accepting of the man's attempts at unwanted petting and intercourse. We ex-pected Group × Timing interactions. For the leading-on group, a woman's open communication was expected to be more effective early rather than later during the date because it might preclude them from feeling "led on." For the token-refusal and the low-myth groups, however, the timing of the woman's open communication was expected to be less important.

Method

Participants

Participants were 382 male introductory psychology students. We neglected to ask about their age and ethnicity; based on other studies done with the same population, however, we estimated that the men's mean age was about 19, and they were approximately 85% to 90% European American/White and 5% to 10% Hispanic American/Latino. They signed up without knowing the topic of the study. Participation counted toward a course research requirement. Anyone who failed the manipulation check or who had excessive missing data was dropped from the study ($n = 28$), yielding a final sample of 354. (The ns vary somewhat in the following analyses because subjects with occasional missing data were retained in the data set.)

Videotapes

Five videotapes depicting a couple on a date were filmed. All the videos depicted the same general scenario: A woman asked a male classmate for a date. They went to a restaurant and then to his apartment, where they listened to music, drank wine, and kissed.

These videos included many dating characteristics that previous studies have shown to increase men's ratings of how much a woman wants to have sex or how justified rape is. For example, the woman initiated the date; she was dressed rather "suggestively" in a tight spaghetti-strap top, tight pants, and high-heeled shoes; the man paid for both meals at the restaurant; they went to the man's apartment after dinner; they drank wine at dinner and at his apartment; and they kissed as they listened to music at his apartment.

In four tapes, the woman communicated her sexual intentions to the man at some point during the date, saying, "I hope you don't misinterpret my going to your apartment on the first date, but seriously, I don't want to do anything more than kiss tonight." She made this statement at the restaurant when they decided to go to his apartment (Tape 1), when they got to his apartment (Tape 2), immediately after they started kissing (Tape 3), or after he attempted above-the-waist petting the first time (Tape 4). In Tape 5, the control tape, she never said this.

At the end of each tape, the man attempted above-the-waist petting. Three times, the man began to put his hand under her top; each time, the woman stopped him by moving his hand away with her hand. After the third time, the woman said, "No! I mean it! I really don't want to!"

Questionnaires

Midvideo Ratings. After the couple got to the apartment and began to drink wine and kiss, but before the final exchange in which the woman three times halted the man's attempts at above-the-waist petting, research assistants stopped the video, and participants completed a short questionnaire. The purpose of these *midvideo ratings* was to assess whether open communication affected the likelihood that men would attempt sexual activities beyond the woman's limits. Participants were asked how much they thought the woman wanted to engage in each of four sexual behaviors–kissing, petting above the waist, petting below the waist, and sexual intercourse–and how likely they would be to try these four sexual behaviors if they were the man in the video. They were also asked how attractive they found the woman's personality and how appropriate they found her behavior. They made their ratings by putting *X*s on 127 mm lines; at the ends of each line were anchors beginning with *not at all* and *very* (e.g., *not at all appropriate* and *very appropriate*).

Postvideo Ratings. After watching the rest of the video, participants completed another questionnaire. The purpose of these *postvideo ratings* was to assess whether prior open communication had any effects over and above refusing at the time of the man's sexual advances. They were again asked how attractive they found the woman's personality and how appropriate they found her behavior. For each of the four sexual behaviors, they were asked how much they thought the woman wanted to engage in the behavior, how "led on" the man would have felt if he had tried the behavior but the woman did not want to, how justified the man would have been in going ahead and engaging in the behavior if the woman had said no, and how justified this would have been if the man had been absolutely sure that the woman did not want to engage in the sexual behavior; as before, all these questions had anchors with a *not at all/very* format. Participants were next asked, if they had been in the same situation as the man in the video, how likely they would have been to go ahead and engage in each of the four sexual behaviors if the woman said no, and how likely this would have been if they had been absolutely sure that she did not want to do so; both ranging from *0% probability–you definitely would not go ahead* to *100% probability–you definitely would go ahead*. They again made their ratings by putting *X*s on 127 mm lines with anchors at each end.

As a manipulation check, the men were asked if they could remember whether the woman in the video had said anything about "how far she wanted to go sexually," and, if so, what she had said. Anyone who had seen Tapes 1 through 4 and who did not recall the content of this line was dropped from the final sample, as was anyone who had seen Tape 5, the control tape, and who incorrectly recalled that the woman had communicated her limits (other than refusing the three petting attempts at the end).

On the next page of the questionnaire, the men were told what the woman had said: "I hope you don't misinterpret my going to your apartment on the first date, but seriously, I don't want to do anything more than kiss tonight." They were asked, given that a woman did not want to do anything more than kiss, how appropriate they regarded this statement, when during a date such a statement would be most appropriate, how many times a woman should say this, and how they would feel about a woman who said this on a date.

Sexual Beliefs Scale. Finally, the men were asked to complete the Sexual Beliefs Scale-Long Form (SBS; Muehlenhard & Felts, 1992). This is a 40-item scale consisting of five 8-item subscales, each measuring a belief related to sexual coercion. Each item is rated on a 4-point scale, ranging from *disagree strongly* (0) to *agree strongly* (3). Items on each subscale are summed, yielding subscale scores ranging from 0 to 24. The two subscales used in the present analyses were the Token Refusal subscale, which measures respondents' belief that women frequently offer token refusals to sex, saying no but meaning yes (e.g., "When girls say 'No,' they often mean 'Yes'"), and the Leading on Justifies Force subscale, which measures respondents' belief that if women "lead men on," implying that they want to have sex when they do not, men are justified in obtaining sex forcefully (e.g., "Girls who lead guys on deserve what they get"). These subscales have Cronbach alphas of .840 and .925 and test-retest reliabilities of .758 and .758, respectively (Muehlenhard & Felts, 1992). Also administered were the Men Should Dominate, Women Like Force, and No Means Stop subscales. Several studies have demonstrated the validity of the SBS (Jones & Muehlenhard, 1990; Muehlenhard & Cook, 1988; Muehlenhard & Hollabaugh, 1988; Muehlenhard & MacNaughton, 1988).

Procedure

The men met in small groups of about 6 to 12. Each group saw one of the five tapes. Assignment to tapes was done randomly with the constraint that more men be assigned to Tape 5 (the control tape) than to any one of Tapes 1 through 4, to facilitate analyzing the presence or absence of open communication, in which Tapes 1 through 4 were combined and compared with Tape 5. The numbers of men assigned to Tapes 1 through 5, respectively, were 52, 51, 51, 55, and 145.

After the men signed the consent form, research assistants played the videotape, pausing midway for participants to make midvideo ratings.

Afterwards, participants completed the postvideo ratings and the SBS. Finally, they were debriefed about the purpose of the study and were given the researchers' phone numbers in case they had any questions or concerns about the study.

Results

Creation of Three Attitudinal Groups

Means, standard deviations, and ranges for the relevant Sexual Beliefs Scale subscales were as follows ($n = 350$): Leading on Justifies Force, $M = 7.78$, $sd = 5.78$, range = 0 to 24; Token Refusal, $M = 10.97$, $sd = 4.61$, range = 0 to 23. Each subscale could range from 0 to 24; men's scores spanned the entire range–or almost the entire range–for both subscales.

Men were divided into three groups. The *leading-on group* consisted of men whose Leading on Justifies Force subscale scores were greater than 12, the midpoint of the scale ($n = 67$). The *token-refusal group* consisted of men whose Leading on Justifies Force subscale scores were less than or equal to 12 and whose Token Refusal subscale scores were greater than 12 ($n = 117$). The *low-myth group* consisted of the remaining men, whose Leading on Justifies Force scores were less than or equal to 12 and whose Token Refusal scores were less than 12 ($n = 161$).

The Effects of Open Communication and Men's Attitudes

A series of thirty-six 2 × 3 analyses of variance (ANOVAs) was conducted to assess the effects of whether the woman had openly communicated her sexual limits (yes, Tapes 1 through 4, or no, Tape 5) and the men's beliefs related to sexual coercion (leading-on, token-refusal, or low-myth group). Dependent variables were participants' questionnaire responses; participants' marks on the 127 mm lines were measured and then linearly transformed so that their answers could range from 0 to 100. Because of the large number of statistical analyses, alpha was set at .01. There were no significant interactions for any of these ANOVAs. Therefore, the main effects for using open communication and for men's attitudes will be discussed separately.

The Effect of Using Open Communication

Midvideo Ratings. These ratings had been made after the couple had begun kissing but before the woman three times stopped the man's attempts at above-the-waist petting. Whether the woman openly communicated her intentions had no significant effect on how attractive the men rated her personality or how appropriate they rated her behavior. The experimental condition also had no effect on participants' ratings related to kissing (see Table 1); this was as expected because both the experimental and the control videos depicted the woman willingly engaging in kissing.

The experimental condition did influence participants' ratings of the other sexual behaviors, however (see Table 1). When the woman had communicated that she did not want to do anything more than kiss, participants rated her as less likely to want to engage in petting above and below the waist and sexual intercourse, and they indicated that if they were in this situation, they would be less likely to attempt petting below the waist and sexual intercourse.

Postvideo Ratings. These ratings had been made after the final exchange in which the woman three times stopped the man from engaging in above-the-waist petting and said, "No! I mean it! I really don't want to!" in all the tapes. Thus, any significant differences would reflect the impact of her earlier open communication over and above her negative reaction to his attempts at petting.

Participants rated the woman's behavior as more appropriate when she openly stated her sexual intentions than when she did not (see Table 1).

In the experimental tapes, the woman's statement about her sexual limits did not exclude kissing. Not surprisingly, open communication had no effect on any ratings involving kissing.

The woman's previous open communication had no impact—over and above her negative reaction to his attempts at petting—on men's ratings of how much she wanted to engage in petting above or below the waist or sexual intercourse, how justifiable any of these sexual behaviors would be if she refused, or how likely they would be to try to engage in these sexual activities with her. For all three of these sexual behaviors, however, participants rated the man as feeling significantly less "led on" when the woman had previously communicated her sexual limits, compared with when she had not (see Table 1).

Toward the end of the questionnaire, the men in all experimental conditions were told the woman's statement and asked how they would feel about a woman who said this on a date. Their responses were as follows: positive, 50.4%; neutral, 37.2%; or negative, 12.4%. They rated the appropriateness of such a statement as $M = 74.7$ on a 100-unit scale.

Men's Attitudes Related to Sexual Coercion

Midvideo Ratings. As shown in Table 1, the three groups did not differ significantly in their attractiveness or appropriateness ratings. The three

TABLE 1. Men's Mean Responses as a Function of the Woman's Open Communication and the Men's Attitudes Related to Rape

Question	Open communication		Attitude group		
	No[a]	Yes[b]	Leading on[c]	Token refusal[d]	Low myth[e]
Midvideo questionnaire					
Attractive personality	40.74	45.37	42.73	44.02	43.34
Appropriate behavior	47.26	52.03	48.37	49.37	51.26
How much does she want					
kissing	89.70	89.59	89.92	91.30	88.30
petting above waist	79.68	62.51***	75.60	71.51	65.71
petting below waist	57.44	38.31***	54.11	45.16	43.70
sexual intercourse	50.46	23.50***	45.74_a	36.43_b	28.68_c***
Would you try					
kissing	87.99	89.37	87.75	91.11	87.56
petting above waist	78.98	71.42	80.52_a	80.36_a	67.85_b***
petting below waist	64.96	51.04***	65.52_a	61.79_a	49.57_b***
sexual intercourse	53.54	31.45***	52.94_a	47.71_a	30.30_b***
Postvideo questionnaire					
Attractive personality	41.95	47.72	44.93	45.54	45.36
Appropriate behavior	45.86	57.03*	49.12	51.43	54.51
How much does she want					
kissing	87.28	88.40	89.04	89.40	86.40
petting above waist	32.34	32.13	35.79	34.69	28.92
petting below waist	18.10	19.54	23.03	18.88	17.29
sexual intercourse	14.55	10.23	15.48	13.17	9.73
How "led on" would he feel if she did not want					
kissing	54.04	60.53	62.53	56.95	56.55
petting above waist	50.93	39.53*	53.27_a	45.92_{ab}	39.26_b*
petting below waist	40.76	27.23***	40.82	31.54	30.44
sexual intercourse	34.18	17.97***	31.56	26.33	20.57

TABLE 1 (continued)

Question	Open communication		Attitude group		
	No[a]	Yes[b]	Leading on[c]	Token refusal[d]	Low myth[e]
If she said no, how justifiable is					
kissing	24.05	22.64	41.42_a	21.41_b	17.02_b***
petting above waist	18.55	14.69	28.65_a	16.60_b	10.93_c***
petting below waist	14.49	11.38	21.78_a	13.22_b	8.48_c***
sexual intercourse	10.07	7.98	17.00_a	8.94_b	5.42_b***
If he is sure she does not want to, how justifiable is					
kissing	11.66	10.92	19.40_a	10.67_b	8.27_b***
petting above waist	10.02	8.31	14.53_a	8.86_b	6.86_b***
petting below waist	9.51	7.49	13.06_a	8.94_b	5.92_b***
sexual intercourse	7.13	6.54	9.60_a	7.15_{ab}	5.36_b*
If she said no, would you engage in[f]					
kissing	23.53	22.06	33.76_a	23.62_b	17.42_b***
petting above waist	13.57	12.78	22.49_a	14.43_b	8.29_c***
petting below waist	10.13	8.13	15.41_a	9.50_b	5.90_c***
sexual intercourse	6.09	4.92	8.35_a	5.94_b	3.79_c**
If you were sure she did not want to, would you engage in[f]					
kissing	11.33	11.75	20.20_a	12.33_b	7.46_c***
petting above waist	9.23	8.07	15.96_a	9.18_b	5.02_c***
petting below waist	7.70	6.04	12.41_a	6.82_b	4.30_b***
sexual intercourse	5.18	4.11	7.04_a	4.74_b	3.37_b**

Note: Each scale ranged from 0 (*not at all*) to 100 (*very*). In these analyses, *n*s ranged from 344 to 347 due to missing data. Means in each row with different subscripts differ significantly at $p < .05$ (Duncan).

[a]Control group—Tape 5. The woman did not openly state her sexual intentions. [b]Experimental groups—Tapes 1 through 4. The woman openly stated her sexual intentions. [c]Group high on the Leading on Justifies Force subscale. [d]Group high on the Token Refusal subscale but not on the Leading on Justifies Force subscale. [e]Group low on both of these subscales. [f]For these questions, table entries represent self-reported probabilities of engaging in the behavior.
*$p < .01$. **$p < .001$. ***$p < .0001$.

groups of men did differ significantly in how much they thought the woman wanted to engage in sexual intercourse and in how likely they would be to try the three behaviors other than kissing. Post hoc tests revealed that, for all these analyses, the leading-on group was significantly higher than the low-myth group. The token-refusal group was always intermediate, sometimes differing significantly from the leading-on group and sometimes not.

Postvideo Ratings. The three groups did not differ significantly in their ratings of the attractiveness of the woman's personality, the appropriateness of her behavior, or how much she wanted to engage in any of the sexual behaviors. The leading-on group was significantly higher than the low-myth group in their ratings of how "led on" the man would feel if the woman did not want to engage in petting above the waist. For all four sexual behaviors, the leading-on group was significantly higher than the low-myth group in their ratings of how justifiable it would be for the man to engage in the behavior if the woman said no, how justifiable this would be even if the man was sure that she meant no, how likely they would be to engage in the behavior if the woman said no, and how likely they would be to engage in the behavior even if they were sure that she meant no. Ratings of the token-refusal group were intermediate between the other two groups, sometimes differing significantly for the other two and sometimes not.

Timing of the Women's Open Communication

Toward the end of the questionnaire, the men were told what the woman had said and were asked to indicate the most appropriate time for a woman to make such a statement. Their responses were as follows: never, 4.6%; when they first decide to go out, 3.7%; when they first decide to go to one of their apartments or dorm rooms, 37.6%; when they first get to the apartment or dorm room, 9.4%; after they first start kissing but before the man tries to "go further," 25.1%; after the man tries to "go further," 15.1%; and other, 4.6%. When asked how many times a woman should say this, their responses were as follows: never, 7.5%; once, 62.7%; twice, 13.6%; and repeatedly, 16.2%.

Additionally, we investigated whether the men's ratings varied as a function when the woman in the videotape openly stated her intentions. Thirty-six 5 (tapes) × 3 (attitude groups) ANOVAs were conducted, this time analyzing the five videotapes separately rather than combining the four tapes in the experimental condition. There were no significant interactions, and the main effects for attitude group were the same as discussed previously, except that group differences were no longer significant for how justifiable participants rated petting above and below the waist and sexual intercourse if the man could be sure that it was unwanted by the woman.

Regarding timing, post hoc analyses revealed significant differences among the four experimental conditions for only 5 of the 10 midvideo ratings and for none of the 26 postvideo ratings. This suggests that the timing of the woman's stating her intentions had some impact prior to her stopping the man's attempts at above-the-waist petting. In contrast, after she had stopped his attempts at petting, the timing of when she had previously stated her intentions was unimportant.

The means that differed significantly among the four experimental videos are shown in Table 2. They show a recency effect: the earlier she stated her intentions, the more similar the means were to the control condition in which she did not state her intentions; the more recently she stated her intentions, the more discrepant the means were from the control condition.

Discussion

The Effects of Using Open Communication

A woman's open communication about her sexual limits seems to be moderately effective for dealing with unwanted sexual advances. Based on

TABLE 2. Timing of Women's Open Communication: Means Differing Significantly Among the Four Experimental Videos

Question	Control[a]	Tape 1[b]	Tape 2[c]	Tape 3[d]	Tape 4[e]
			Tape		
			Midvideo questionnaire		
How much does she want					
petting above waist	79.68_a	67.61_b	65.44_b	65.31_b	52.21_c**
petting below waist	57.44_a	46.85_b	43.36_b	33.63_c	29.58_c**
sexual intercourse	50.46_a	33.21_b	27.95_b	18.87_c	14.14_c**
Would you try					
petting below waist	64.96_a	59.66_{ab}	50.07_{bc}	47.92_c	46.53_c*
sexual intercourse	53.54_a	44.09_a	30.90_b	29.74_b	21.35_b**

Note: Each scale ranged from 0 (not at all) to 100 (very). In these analyses, ns ranged from 344 to 347 due to missing data. Means in each row with different subscripts differ significantly at $p < .05$ (Duncan).

[a]Control group—Tape 5. The woman did not openly state her sexual intentions. [b]Tape 1—She stated her intentions when they decided to go to his apartment. [c]Tape 2—She stated her intentions when they got to his apartment. [d]Tape 3—She stated her intentions after they first started kissing. [e]Tape 4—She stated her intentions after the man attempted above-the-waist petting the first time.

*$p < .001$. **$p < .0001$.

the midvideo ratings, men who had heard the woman state her sexual limits rated her as less likely to want petting above and below the waist and sexual intercourse–and they rated themselves as less likely to attempt petting below the waist and sexual intercourse–than did men who had not heard her state her sexual limits. The men did not totally believe the woman's open communication, however. Even when the woman stated that she did not want to do anything more than kiss, men's mean rating of how much the woman wanted to have sexual intercourse was 23.50 on a 100-unit scale, and their mean rating of how likely they would be to attempt sexual intercourse was 31.45. These results are consistent with those of Byers and Wilson (1985), who found that in role-play situations in which the man made sexual advances that the woman refused, approximately 14% of the men interpreted her refusal to mean, "Try again right away" or "Continue"; about one-third continued their advances, complied with displays of anger or upset, or complied only after continued attempts at persuasion.

The postvideo ratings showed that after the men had seen the final exchange in which the woman responded negatively to the man's attempts at petting, they rated her behavior as more appropriate when she had previously communicated her sexual limits than when she had not. Thus, if a woman does not want to do anything other than kiss, men seem to appreciate being told this ahead of time.

The postvideo ratings revealed that the woman's having previously communicated her sexual limits had little effect over and above her resisting his attempts at petting, except for one set of dependent variables: how "led on" the man would feel. When the woman had previously communicated her sexual limits, participants rated the man as feeling less "led on" if she did not want to engage in all three sexual behaviors other than kissing. These results suggest that open communication early in the date may decrease the likelihood that men will think sexual coercion is justifiable because the woman "led him on," a belief that has been linked to rape and other forms of sexual coercion (Goodchilds & Zellman, 1984; Kanin, 1967; Muehlenhard et al., 1985). Even here, however, open communication was not totally effective. Even when the woman clearly stated that she did not want to do anything more than kiss, participants' mean rating of how "led on" the man would feel if the woman did not want to engage in other sexual activities was 39.53 for petting above the waist and 17.97 for sexual intercourse on a 100-unit scale.

Other than having some impact on how "led on" men might feel, open communication early in the date had no effect over and above saying no at the time of the man's sexual advances. For these other variables, setting limits early in the date was no better or worse than resisting, once a sexual advance had been made.

Timing of Women's Open Communication

Men's modal preference was that a woman state her sexual limits once, when they first decide to go to one of their apartments or dorm rooms. This describes what occurred in Tape 1. Interestingly, Tape 1 showed the weakest effect on the midvideo ratings, suggesting that the impact of stating her intentions decreased over time (see Table 2). Men often interpret women's refusals to mean, "Try again" (Byers & Wilson, 1985). Perhaps after a couple engages in prolonged kissing, men will assume that women have changed their minds.

Men's Attitudes Related to Sexual Coercion

Men's attitudes related to sexual coercion, as measured by the Sexual Beliefs Scale, were related to their ratings of the video. As expected, the most potentially aggressive group seemed to be the group that believed that a woman's "leading a man on" justifies his use of force to obtain sexual behaviors. Compared with the other two groups, they rated all four sexual behaviors after the woman said no as more justified, and they rated themselves as more likely to engage in all four sexual behaviors after she said no, even if they were sure that she meant no.

The token-refusal group—men who did not accept the idea that "leading a man on" justifies force, but who did accept the idea that women frequently say no when they mean yes—was less likely than the leading-on group to rate sexual behavior after the woman said no as justified or to predict that they themselves would engage in sexual behavior even if she said no. Nevertheless, they were more likely than the low-myth group to rate petting after she said no as justifiable and to report that they would engage in petting or intercourse even if the woman refused. However, when they were asked to imagine that they were sure that the woman did not want to engage in the behavior—that is, when they were instructed to take the woman's refusal seriously—the ratings of the token-refusal group did not differ significantly from those of the low-myth group for the justifiability of any of the four sexual behaviors or for the likelihood that they would engage in petting below the waist or sexual intercourse.

It is possible that there could have been some carry-over effects from viewing the video to responses to the SBS. In future studies, the order in which participants view the video and complete the SBS could be counterbalanced, or SBS data could be collected at a separate session.

STUDY 2

Based on Study 1, open communication appears to be only moderately effective in convincing men that certain sexual behaviors are unwanted or in guaranteeing that men will not attempt these sexual behaviors.

In a dating context, a woman would probably want her response to a man's initial sexual advance to be fairly effective in getting him to stop his sexual advances, while still maintaining the relationship. If he persisted with his sexual advances after the woman refused, however, she would probably want to use the response most likely to get the man to stop his advances, regardless of the effect on the relationship. Thus, in Study 2, we presented men with several ways that a woman could respond to a man's unwanted sexual advances. For each response, we asked men how positively or negatively the response would affect the relationship and how likely they would be to continue their sexual advances. Women can use this information when responding to unwanted sexual advances, taking into account the relative importance of stopping the advance and maintaining the relationship.

Method

Pilot Study

An open-ended pilot questionnaire was completed anonymously by 60 female and 60 male introductory psychology students. The questionnaire asked respondents to describe ways in which men had made sexual advances toward women and in which women had resisted unwanted sexual advances from men. Respondents were asked to describe their experiences, if any, or hypothetical experiences, if they had no such experience. This protected participants' anonymity by preventing anyone from knowing who had had such experiences based on who was writing. To develop the questionnaire for the next phase of the study, the researchers and undergraduate research assistants read women's and men's reports of their experiences (hypothetical responses were not used). We compiled a list of responses women had made to men's unwanted sexual advances. Similar responses were collapsed. For the final questionnaire, we chose 26 responses that seemed to span the range from ambiguous to extremely negative. To this list we added two hypothetical positive responses, one of which we put first on the list, because we wanted a variety of responses to encourage participants to evaluate each response individually rather than regarding all responses as signals of disinterest in sex.

Participants

Participants were 488 male introductory psychology students, who signed up without knowing the topic of the study. Participants whose questionnaires were incomplete or filled out incorrectly were eliminated from the study, yielding a final sample of 424 men. They were predominantly White. Their ages ranged from 17 to 29, with a mean of 19.4. Participation counted toward a course research requirement.

Questionnaire

The men were given four brief situations in which they were asked to imagine making a sexual advance toward a woman. In these four situations, type of sexual advance (verbal or physical) was crossed with the level of the man's persistence (an initial advance or persistent advances). Thus, they were asked to imagine that they had made an *initial verbal sexual advance, persistent verbal advances* after the woman had already said no, an *initial physical sexual advance,* and *persistent physical advances* after the woman had already said no. To control for order effects, some participants received the two verbal situations before the two physical situations; others received the physical before the verbal. For logical reasons, however, initial advances always preceded persistent advances. Half the respondents received situations about a woman they did not know well; the other half received situations about a woman they had been dating awhile.

Initial Verbal/Physical Sexual Advances. Each questionnaire began by asking, "Imagine that you are alone with a girl *you don't know well/you've been dating for awhile.* You really want to have sex with her. *You verbally suggest this to her* [initial verbal advance]/*As you are making out, you start to unzip her jeans* [initial physical advance]." We used the term *girl* rather than *woman* because that is the term generally used by both male and female college students to refer to college-age females.

Respondents were asked whether they thought they could ever be in this situation. Those who answered *no* were asked to go to the next question set. Those who answered *yes* were given a list of 28 responses a woman could make to a man's advance, derived from the pilot study (see Table 3). Some responses were positive (e.g., "She smiles and kisses you"), some were ambiguous (e.g., "She tells you she's on her period"), and some were negative (e.g., "She slaps you").

For each of the 28 responses, the men were asked two questions: (a) "How would this response affect your relationship?", with response options ranging from *definitely help the relationship* (0) to *definitely hurt the relationship* (4) (we chose a 5-point scale, which has a midpoint, because

TABLE 3. Twenty-Eight Responses Women Could Make to a Man's Sexual Advances

---

A. She smiles and kisses you.
B. She says, "I really care about you, but I'm not ready. Let's wait until the relationship is stronger."
C. She says, "I'm scared to."
D. She says, "No!"
E. She yells, "No!"
F. She tells you she's on her period.
G. She asks you to take her home.
H. She gets up to leave.
I. She tells you it's against her beliefs and she wants to wait until marriage.
J. She says she has herpes.
K. She slaps your hands playfully, smiles, and says no.
L. She responds with physical violence, such as kneeing you, biting you, slugging you, kicking you, or clawing you.
M. She threatens you with physical violence, such as threatening to knee, bite, slug, kick, or claw you.
N. She presses her body to your's and caresses your neck.
O. She slaps you.
P. She cries.
Q. She says, "I'm tired and I have to get up early."
R. She calls you names such as jerk, creep, or sex-crazed maniac.
S. She screams.
T. She says, "I can't."
U. She says, "I'm not sure we should."
V. She tells you, "This is rape, and I'm calling the cops."
W. She pushes you away.
X. She breaks the mood, such as by beginning a conversation or suggesting going to get something to eat.
Y. She says she's afraid of getting pregnant.
Z. She tells you she doesn't want to do anything beyond kissing and making out.
1. She says, "You hurt my feelings by trying to take advantage of me."
2. She cries, pleads, and asks God to help her.

---

it seemed likely that some responses would have neither a positive nor a negative effect on the relationship); (b) "What would you do?", with response options ranging from *I would definitely continue with my sexual advances* (0) to *I would definitely stop my sexual advances* (3) (here we chose a 4-point scale, which does not have a midpoint, so that the men would have to indicate whether they would be more likely to stop or continue their advances).

Persistent Verbal/Physical Advances. Next, participants were asked to "imagine that you are alone with a girl *you don't know well/you've been dating for awhile.* You really want to have sex with her. *You have approached her about a sexual relationship and she has said no. You try to verbally persuade her several more times that evening* [persistent verbal advances]/*You have tried to unzip her jeans and she has said no. You continue to try to undress her* [persistent physical advances]." Again, respondents were asked whether they thought they could be in such a situation. Those who answered *no* were asked to go to the next question set. Those who answered *yes* were again given the list of 28 responses the woman could make, and they were again asked to indicate how they thought each response would affect the relationship and whether they would continue making advances.

Modified Sexual Experiences Survey. This 19-item survey was administered to assess men's experiences with being sexually coercive. It was derived from the Sexual Experiences Survey (SES), developed by Koss and her colleagues (Koss et al., 1987; Koss & Oros, 1982). The reliability and validity of the SES have been demonstrated (Koss & Gidycz, 1985; Koss et al., 1987).

Respondents were first asked how often they had engaged in (a) necking and petting and (b) sexual intercourse with a woman when they both wanted to. They were then asked how often they had engaged in these sexual behaviors with a woman who did not want to by threatening to end the relationship, pressuring her with continual arguments, saying things they did not mean, getting her intoxicated, threatening to use physical force (twisting her arm, holding her down) if she did not cooperate, or using physical force. They were also asked if they had attempted to engage in these sexual behaviors by threatening or actually using physical force, but the sexual behaviors did not occur. Finally, they were asked if they had engaged in anal or oral intercourse with a woman who did not want to by using threats or physical force.

Procedure

Respondents were tested in groups. After signing consent forms, they completed the questionnaires anonymously. They were then debriefed about the purpose of the study and given the researchers' phone numbers in case they had any questions or concerns about the study.

Results

Men's Identification with the Four Situations

Respondents had been asked if they thought they could ever be in each of the four situations. Most men indicated that they could be in a situation in which they made initial verbal (87.9%) and physical (93.1%) sexual advances toward a woman. Fewer men, although still a majority, indicated that they could be in a situation in which they made persistent verbal (52.7%) and physical (53.4%) sexual advances toward a woman after she had already said no.

Men's Reactions to the Twenty-Eight Responses Women Could Make

We conducted a series of MANOVAs assessing whether men's ratings were affected by level of acquaintance (situations involving a woman they did not know well or a woman they had been dating for awhile), type of advance (verbal or physical), or persistence of advance (initial or persistent). As in Study 1, because of the large number of statistical analyses, alpha was set at .01. There were few significant effects, and even significant differences were small, all less than 0.25 (more detailed information is available from the authors). Thus, we collapsed the men's ratings across level of acquaintance and type and persistence of advance to yield the data plotted in Figure 1. Plotted along the abscissa are men's reports of whether they would continue or stop their advances following each of the 28 responses; plotted along the ordinate are men's reports of the effect that each response would have on the relationship. In general, the more likely a response was to stop a man's sexual advances, the more negative effect it would have on the relationship, $r = .865$, $p < .0001$. Some responses, however, such as the woman's saying that she cared about the man but wanted to wait until the relationship was stronger (i.e., Response B), seemed to be fairly effective both in getting the man to stop his advances and in having a positive effect on the relationship.

Men's History of Sexual Coercion

Based on their responses to the Modified Sexual Experiences Scale, 12 men (2.9%) reported never having been involved in necking, petting, or sexual intercourse with a woman. We divided the remaining, heterosexually-experienced men into three groups: the *noncoercive group,* men who reported consensual sexual behavior with a woman but no coercive experiences ($n = 155$, 37.5%); the *nonviolent coercive group,* men who reported obtaining sexual behavior with an unwilling woman using coercion other than physical force, including threatening to end the relationship, pressuring her with continual arguments, saying things they did not mean, or getting her intoxicated ($n = 228$, 55.2%); and the *violent coercive group,* men who reported obtaining or attempting to obtain sexual behavior with a

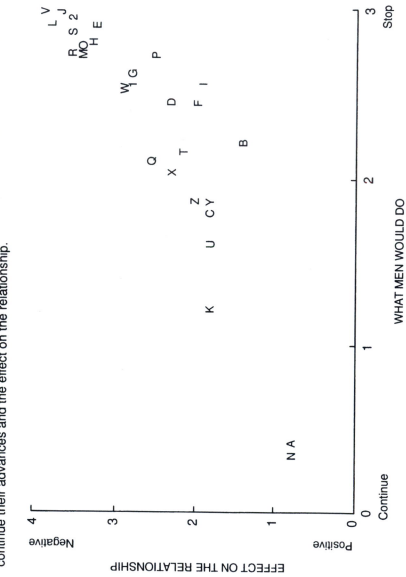

FIGURE 1. For each of the 28 responses women could make, men's mean ratings of whether they would continue their advances and the effect on the relationship.

woman by threatening or using physical force ($n = 18$, 4.4%). (Eleven men were omitted because of missing data.)

We then conducted eight MANOVAs: one for each of the 2 types of sexual advances (verbal or physical) × 2 levels of persistence of the sexual advances (initial or persistent) × 2 types of dependent variables (whether the men would continue their advances or the effect of the relationship). For each analysis, the independent variable was men's level of sexual coercion: consensual, nonviolent coercive, and violent coercive; dependent variables were the men's reactions to the 28 responses women could make. Three of the eight MANOVAs were significant; they were followed by subsequent ANOVAs.

Rather than discussing the results of these ANOVAs in detail, we will summarize them by saying that for virtually all significant differences pertaining to whether men would stop or continue their advances (for 13 of the 15 significant ANOVAs), the violent coercive men reported being significantly more likely than the noncoercive men to continue their sexual advances; the nonviolent coercive men were generally intermediate between the other two groups. Furthermore, for three of the five significant ANOVAs pertaining to the effect on the relationship, the violent coercive men reported that the woman's response would have a significantly more negative effect on the relationship than did the noncoercive men.

A final question of interest was what responses would get the most sexually aggressive men to stop their advances. To answer this question, we assessed the responses of men in the violent coercive group who had indicated that they could imagine themselves continuing to make physical sexual advances even after the woman had said no ($n = 9$). Based on these men's reports, the most effective responses a woman could make was saying, "This is rape, and I'm calling the cops!" ($M = 3.0$) or crying, pleading, and asking God to help her ($M = 3.0$). All of these men reported that they would definitely stop their advances faced with these responses. The next most effective responses, in order, were: saying that she had herpes ($M = 2.63$); screaming ($M = 2.57$); yelling no ($M = 2.56$); and responding with physical violence, such as kneeing, biting, or kicking him ($M = 2.50$).

Discussion

Most men indicated that they could be in a situation in which they made persistent verbal (52.7%) and physical (53.4%) sexual advances toward a woman even after she had already said no. This finding is consistent with the results of Study 1 and previous research (Byers, 1988; Byers & Wilson, 1985; Muehlenhard et al., 1985), suggesting that men frequently do not stop their advances the first time that a woman says no.

Saying "I really care about you, but I want to wait until the relationship is stronger" stood out as being fairly likely to get the man to stop his advances, while still having a positive effect on the relationship. If a man makes an initial advance that a woman wants to refuse while still maintaining a good relationship with him, this type of response seems promising. Consistent with this finding, Byers and Lewis (1988) found that in disagreements about the level of sexual activity, almost one-third of the women responded by saying that the disputed activity might be acceptable in the future, a response which seemed to be effective.

Other responses are even more likely to get a man to stop his advances, such as telling him that this is rape and threatening to call the police. Such responses tend to have a more negative effect on the relationship, but if a man will not take no for an answer, maintaining the relationship should not, we think, be a major concern.

We were especially interested in responses rated as effective by the most violent men—those who reported obtaining or attempting to obtain sexual behavior by threatening or using physical force and who reported that they could imagine themselves making physical advances after the woman had refused. Based on their reports, the most effective responses are to label the situation as rape and threaten to call the police; to cry, plead, and ask God to help her; to claim she has herpes; to scream; to yell no; and to use physical violence such as kneeing, biting, or kicking. Several of these strategies have previously been found to be effective. Active strategies such as physically fighting (e.g., pushing, punching, kicking, biting, or using self-defense techniques or a weapon), yelling, screaming, and fleeing or trying to flee have generally been associated with rape avoidance or lower levels of sexual abuse (Bart & O'Brien, 1985; Levine-MacCombie & Koss, 1986; Ullman & Knight, 1992, 1993; Zoucha-Jensen & Coyne, 1993). In contrast, in these studies, researchers have generally found begging, pleading, crying, and reasoning to be ineffective, especially in studies of rapes reported to police, which involved primarily stranger rape. An exception to this pattern involves a study specifically of acquaintance rape, in which Levine-MacCombie and Koss (1986) found that crying or reasoning were associated with avoiding rape, although not as strongly as screaming or running away. Levine-MacCombie and Koss speculated that perhaps the relationship between the victim and offender may make offenders more responsive to these strategies, compared with stranger rape situations.

The results of this study were based on men's self-reports, which may not reflect their behavior in actual situations, especially if they are sexually aroused, intoxicated, angry, or facing peer pressure (e.g., Byers, 1988; Sanday, 1990). In previous studies, however, researchers have found links between men's self-reported attitudes and more objective data related to sexual coercion; for example, attitudinal data have been linked to self-reports of past coercive behavior (Malamuth, 1986; Muehlenhard & Falcon, 1990) and to being incarcerated for rape (Feild, 1978).

Taken together, these studies suggest that open communication about sexual limits may be somewhat effective in preventing men from making unwanted sexual advances and in reducing the likelihood that men will feel "led on" if the woman subsequently refuses. If the man does make a sexual advance, telling him she cares about him but wants to wait until the relationship is stronger may be a way to get him to stop his advance while still maintaining a positive relationship. If he does not stop, increasingly forceful responses such as yelling, screaming, fighting, and threatening to call the police may be effective. No strategy is totally effective, however, and if rape occurs, the fault lies with the perpetrator, not the victim.

In future studies, researchers could address these issues using other methodologies. Descriptions of women's experiences dealing with men's unwanted sexual advances could be obtained via women's retrospective reports or contemporaneously recorded diaries (e.g., Byers & Lewis, 1988; O'Sullivan & Byers, 1992). A convergence of results from laboratory and naturalistic studies would strengthen confidence in the present results. In addition, unwanted sexual advances are also made by women toward men in heterosexual relationships (O'Sullivan & Byers, 1993) and by both women and men in lesbian and gay relationships (Waterman, Dawson, & Bologna, 1989). Researchers could also address the effectiveness of dealing with unwanted sexual advances in these relationships.

REFERENCES

Abbey, A. (1982). Sex differences in attributions for friendly behavior: Do males misperceive females' friendliness? *Journal of Personality and Social Psychology, 42,* 830-838.

Abbey, A. (1991). Misperception as an antecedent of acquaintance rape: A consequence of ambiguity in communication between women and men. In A. Parrot & L. Bechhofer (Eds.), *Acquaintance rape: The hidden crime* (pp. 96-111). New York: John Wiley and Sons.

American College Health Association. (1992). *Acquaintance rape* [pamphlet]. Baltimore, MD: Author.

Barbaree, H. E., & Marshall, W. L. (1991). The role of male sexual arousal in rape: Six models. *Journal of Consulting and Clinical Psychology, 59,* 621-630.

Bart, P. B., & O'Brien, P. H. (1985). *Stopping rape: Successful survival strategies.* New York: Pergamon.

Byers, E. S. (1988). Effects of sexual arousal on men's and women's behavior in sexual disagreement situations. *The Journal of Sex Research, 25,* 235-254.

Byers, E. S., Giles, B. L., & Price, D. L. (1987). Definiteness and effectiveness of women's responses to unwanted sexual advances: A laboratory investigation. *Basic and Applied Social Psychology, 8,* 321-338.

Byers, E. S., & Lewis, K. (1988). Dating couples' disagreements over the desired level of sexual intimacy. *The Journal of Sex Research, 24,* 15-29.

Byers, E. S., & Wilson, P. (1985). Accuracy of women's expectations regarding men's responses to refusals of sexual advances in dating situations. *International Journal of Women's Studies, 8,* 376-387.

Check, J. V. P., & Malamuth, N. M. (1983). Sex role stereotyping and reactions to depictions of stranger versus acquaintance rape. *Journal of Personality and Social Psychology, 45,* 344-356.

Feild, H. S. (1978). Attitudes toward rape: A comparative analysis of police, rapists, crisis counselors, and citizens. *Journal of Personality and Social Psychology, 36,* 156-179.

Goodchilds, J. D., & Zellman, G. L. (1984). Sexual signaling and sexual aggression in adolescent relationships. In N. M. Malamuth & E. Donnerstein (Eds.), *Pornography and sexual aggression* (pp. 234-243). Orlando, FL: Academic Press.

Groth, A. N., Burgess, A. W., & Holmstrom, L. L. (1977). Rape: Power, anger, and sexuality. *American Journal of Psychiatry, 134,* 1239-1243.

Johnson, C. B., Stockdale, M. S., & Saal, F. E. (1991). Persistence of men's misperceptions of friendly cues across a variety of interpersonal encounters. *Psychology of Women Quarterly, 15,* 463-475.

Jones, J. M., & Muehlenhard, C. L. (1990, November). *Using education to prevent rape on college campuses.* Paper presented at the annual meeting of the Society for the Scientific Study of Sex, Minneapolis, MN.

Kanin, E. J. (1967). Reference groups and sex conduct norm violations. *Sociological Quarterly, 8,* 495-504.

Koss, M. P., & Gidycz, C. A. (1985). Sexual Experiences Survey: Reliability and validity. *Journal of Consulting and Clinical Psychology, 53,* 422-423.

Koss, M. P., Gidycz, C. A., & Wisniewski, N. (1987). The scope of rape: Incidence and prevalence of sexual aggression and victimization in a national sample of higher education students. *Journal of Consulting and Clinical Psychology, 55,* 162-170.

Koss, M. P., & Oros, C. J. (1982). Sexual Experiences Survey: A research instrument investigating sexual aggression and victimization. *Journal of Consulting and Clinical Psychology, 50,* 455-457.

Kowalski, R. M. (1993). Inferring sexual interest from behavioral cues: Effects of gender and sexually relevant attitudes. *Sex Roles, 29,* 13-36.

Levine-MacCombie, J., & Koss, M. P. (1986). Acquaintance rape: Effective avoidance strategies. *Psychology of Women Quarterly, 10,* 311-320.

Malamuth, N. M. (1986). Predictors of naturalistic sexual aggression. *Journal of Personality and Social Psychology, 50,* 953-962.

Mosher, D. L., & Anderson, R. D. (1986). Macho personality, sexual aggression, and reactions to guided imagery of realistic rape. *Journal of Research in Personality, 20,* 77-94.

Muehlenhard, C. L. (1988). Misinterpreted dating behaviors and the risk of date rape. *Journal of Social and Clinical Psychology, 6,* 20-37.

Muehlenhard, C. L., & Cook, S. W. (1988). Men's self-reports of unwanted sexual activity. *The Journal of Sex Research, 24,* 58-72.

Muehlenhard, C. L., & Falcon, P. L. (1990). Men's heterosocial skill and attitudes toward women as predictors of verbal sexual coercion and forceful rape. *Sex Roles, 23,* 241-259.

Muehlenhard, C. L., & Felts, A. S. (1992). *Sexual Beliefs Scale.* Unpublished manuscript.

Muehlenhard, C. L., Giusti, L. M., & Rodgers, C. S. (1993, November). The social construction of "token resistance to sex": The nature and function of the myth. In G. Smeaton (Chair), *Token resistance, ambivalent refusal, and sexual aggression: Myths and reality.* Symposium conducted at the annual meeting of the Society for the Scientific Study of Sex, Chicago.

Muehlenhard, C. L., & Hollabaugh, L. C. (1988). Do women sometimes say no when they mean yes? The prevalence and correlates of women's token resistance to sex. *Journal of Personality and Social Psychology, 54,* 872-879.

Muehlenhard, C. L., & Linton, M. A. (1987). Date rape and sexual aggression in dating situations: Incidence and risk factors. *Journal of Counseling Psychology, 34,* 186-196.

Muehlenhard, C. L., Linton, M. A., Felts, A. S., & Andrews, S. L. (1985, June). Men's attitudes toward the justifiability of date rape: Intervening variables and possible solutions. In E. R. Allgeier (Chair), *Sexual coercion: Political issues and empirical findings.* Symposium conducted at the Midcontinent meeting of the Society for the Scientific Study of Sex, Chicago.

Muehlenhard, C. L., & MacNaughton, J. S. (1988). Women's beliefs about women who "lead men on." *Journal of Social and Clinical Psychology, 7,* 65-79.

Muehlenhard, C. L., & McCoy, M. L. (1991). Double standard/Double bind: The sexual double standard and women's communication about sex. *Psychology of Women Quarterly, 15,* 447-461.

O'Sullivan, L. F., & Byers, E. S. (1992). College students' incorporation of initiator and restrictor roles in sexual dating interactions. *The Journal of Sex Research, 29,* 435-446.

O'Sullivan, L. F., & Byers, E. S. (1993). Eroding stereotypes: College women's attempts to influence reluctant male sexual partners. *The Journal of Sex Research, 30,* 270-282.

Parrot, A. (1991). Institutional response: How can acquaintance rape be prevented? In A. Parrot & L. Bechhofer (Eds.), *Acquaintance rape: The hidden crime* (pp. 355-367). New York: John Wiley and Sons.

Rapaport, K., & Burkhart, B. R. (1984). Personality and attitudinal characteristics of sexually coercive college males. *Journal of Abnormal Psychology, 93,* 216-221.

Sanday, P. R. (1990). *Fraternity gang rape: Sex, brotherhood, and privilege on campus.* New York: New York University Press.

Ullman, S. E., & Knight, R. A. (1992). Fighting back: Women's resistance to rape. *Journal of Interpersonal Violence, 7,* 31-43.

Ullman, S. E., & Knight, R. A. (1993). The efficacy of women's resistance strategies in rape situations. *Psychology of Women Quarterly, 17,* 23-38.

Warshaw, R. (1988). *I never called it rape.* New York: Harper & Row.

Waterman, C. K., Dawson, L. J., & Bologna, M. J. (1989). Sexual coercion in gay male and lesbian relationships: Predictors and implications for support services. *The Journal of Sex Research, 26,* 118-124.

Zoucha-Jensen, J. M., & Coyne, A. (1993). The effects of resistance strategies on rape. *American Journal of Public Health, 83,* 1633-1634.

Index

Haworth
DOCUMENT DELIVERY
SERVICE

This valuable service provides a single-article order form for any article from a Haworth journal.

- *Time Saving:* No running around from library to library to find a specific article.
- *Cost Effective:* All costs are kept down to a minimum.
- *Fast Delivery:* Choose from several options, including same-day FAX.
- *No Copyright Hassles:* You will be supplied by the original publisher.
- *Easy Payment:* Choose from several easy payment methods.

Open Accounts Welcome for . . .
- Library Interlibrary Loan Departments
- Library Network/Consortia Wishing to Provide Single-Article Services
- Indexing/Abstracting Services with Single Article Provision Services
- Document Provision Brokers and Freelance Information Service Providers

---

MAIL or *FAX* THIS ENTIRE ORDER FORM TO:

Haworth Document Delivery Service
The Haworth Press, Inc.
10 Alice Street
Binghamton, NY 13904-1580

or **FAX:** 1-800-895-0582
or **CALL:** 1-800-342-9678
9am-5pm EST

PLEASE SEND ME PHOTOCOPIES OF THE FOLLOWING SINGLE ARTICLES:

1) Journal Title: _____

   Vol/Issue/Year:_____Starting & Ending Pages:_____

Article Title:_____

_____

2) Journal Title: _____

   Vol/Issue/Year:_____Starting & Ending Pages:_____

Article Title:_____

_____

3) Journal Title: _____

   Vol/Issue/Year:_____Starting & Ending Pages:_____

Article Title:_____

_____

4) Journal Title: _____

   Vol/Issue/Year:_____Starting & Ending Pages:_____

Article Title:_____

(See other side for Costs and Payment Information)

COSTS: Please figure your cost to order quality copies of an article.

1. Set-up charge per article: $8.00

     ($8.00 × number of separate articles) _____

2. Photocopying charge for each article:

     1-10 pages: $1.00 _____

     11-19 pages: $3.00 _____

     20-29 pages: $5.00 _____

     30+ pages: $2.00/10 pages _____

3. Flexicover (optional): $2.00/article _____

4. Postage & Handling: US: $1.00 for the first article/

     $.50 each additional article _____

     Federal Express: $25.00 _____

     Outside US: $2.00 for first article/

     $.50 each additional article _____

5. Same-day FAX service: $.35 per page _____

GRAND TOTAL: _____

METHOD OF PAYMENT: (please check one)

❑ Check enclosed   ❑ Please ship and bill. PO # _____

     (sorry we can ship and bill to bookstores only! All others must pre-pay)

❑ Charge to my credit card: ❑ Visa; ❑ MasterCard; ❑ Discover;

     ❑ American Express;

Account Number: _____ Expiration date: _____

Signature: ✗ _____

Name: _____ Institution: _____

Address: _____

_____

City: _____ State: _____ Zip: _____

Phone Number: _____ FAX Number: _____

MAIL or *FAX* THIS ENTIRE ORDER FORM TO:

Haworth Document Delivery Service	**or FAX: 1-800-895-0582**
The Haworth Press, Inc.	**or CALL: 1-800-342-9678**
10 Alice Street	9am-5pm EST)
Binghamton, NY 13904-1580	